Collins

BOOK OF
English
VERSE

Chosen by Edwin Moore and
Fiona Mackenzie Moore

GW00468282

HarperCollins*Publishers*

HarperCollinsPublishers
Westerhill Road, Glasgow G64 2QT

The HarperCollins website address is **www.fireandwater.com**

First published 2001

Reprint 10 9 8 7 6 5 4 3 2 1 0

This selection © HarperCollins Publishers 2001

Designed and typeset by Clare Crawford

ISBN 0 00 712183 0

A catalogue record for this book is available from the British Library

All rights reserved. No part of this publication may be reproduced, stored in a retrieval system or transmitted, in any form or by any means, without the prior permission of the publisher.

This book is sold subject to the conditions that it shall not, by way of trade or otherwise, be lent, re-sold, hired out or otherwise circulated without the publisher's prior consent in any form of binding or cover other than that in which it is published and without a similar condition including this condition being imposed on the subsequent publisher.

Printed and bound in Great Britain by Omnia Books Ltd, Glasgow G64.

CONTENTS

For our daughters,
Helen and Rowan

INTRODUCTION

Compilers of anthologies of verse generally begin their introductions by defining their terms, dates and other parameters, and indeed it is always useful to explain what is and is not on your stall before the customer starts complaining that this or that item is not present.

But one person's deeply moving lyric is another person's doggerel, and most arguments about poetry, song and verse end in mutual incomprehension. For a great critic like Christopher Ricks (and for many others) Bob Dylan is not just a great songwriter, he is also a great poet, the equal of Keats. For others, Dylan is a great songwriter but not really a great poet. If Dylan is a great poet, what praise is appropriate for Cole Porter's lyrics? (Which is our cue to sneak in a bit of 'Anything Goes': 'If old hymns you like,/If bare limbs you like,/If Mae West you like,/Or me undressed you like,/Why, nobody will oppose.')

The Dylan debate is not dissimilar to previous debates about the worth of long-forgotten verse dramatists: it is now difficult, for example, to understand why the verse plays of Stephen Phillips gathered such phenomenal critical praise at the beginning of the 20th century: one can only assume that the stage performances resulted in a suspension of critical faculties, perhaps similar to listening to 'Blonde on Blonde' while stoned, or like being part of an 18th-century audience watching John Home's verse play *Douglas*, which seemed to many of Home's contemporaries to be a masterpiece of verse drama but is now chiefly remembered for the excited Scottish patriot who shouted 'Whaur's yer Wullie Shakespeare noo' during its Edinburgh premiere. Well, Wullie Shakespeare can be found here, but we have managed to resist any verse, dramatic or otherwise, by the extinct Mr Home.

Some compilers also feel compelled to explain the difference between poetry and verse, but the distinction escapes most of us. The following lines from W. E. Bowman's mountaineering classic, *The Ascent of Rum Doodle*, are certainly verse:

> Organ grinders, kings and queens
> Call for Binder's butter beans.
> Three times daily, knave and noodle
> Eat them gaily, on Rum Doodle.

But why are they not also poetry? Poetry is supposed to be capable of moving one in a way that verse cannot, yet a great many hillwalkers will testify that Bowman's lines can – by the end of a long day on the hill – acquire an almost supernatural depth of meaning. And what about Kipling? Since 'If—' first appeared in 1910, the poem has been seen by many otherwise rational people as an essentially bombastic and terribly unpoetic piece of versifying: yet, as Dr Sheila Cassidy testifies in her remarkable memoir, *Audacity to Believe*, the poem – precious scraps of which were handed back and forth between political prisoners in Chile – brought comfort and strength to men and women suffering the most terrible tortures and privations.

Great verse such as Kipling's 'If—' is not simply a matter of arranging a platitude into doggerel: the truth is we don't know how great verse is created, all we know is that it can affect our lives deeply, and occasionally the effect is temporal – and again we don't know why. No aesthetic progression or cycle will ever bring back the verse of John Home, but it is certainly the case that some poets have periods in which they seem, in the beautiful Quaker phrase, to speak to one's condition, and periods in which their importance recedes. George Orwell, in one of his essays, pointed out that Housman's poem 'The Sigh That Heaves the Grasses' was once deeply moving but now merely 'tinkled'; he further conjectured that there would come a time when the lines would cease from tinkling but would become moving again. The poem (see inside and judge for yourself) is just possibly even more tinkly than it was in Orwell's day, but we suspect that Orwell was right in guessing that the poem's day will come again, so we have included it. Another poem that is generally thought to 'tinkle' is Wordsworth's 'The Daffodils', which is possibly the most maligned poem ever written. A 1960s' poet used to court popularity among schoolchildren by telling them 'Daffodils' was a dreadful poem: we think 'Daffodils' is a great poem and have included it.

Our guiding principle, indeed, has been to steer the anthology down the centre of the great broad current of English verse, a principle our A–Z arrangement is intended to reinforce: the siting (indeed sighting) of Don Marquis between Marlowe and Marvell, the juxtaposition of U. A. Fanthorpe with Edward Fitzgerald, demonstrate the power of great verse from all periods. And 'power' is what the best verse is about: there are many traditions contributing to the history of English verse, but what all the memorable poems have is the ability to impact on the reader. William Dunbar wrote in Scots and saw himself as part of a Scottish tradition, but he also saw English Chaucer as the master. William Soutar also wrote (largely) in Scots, but that didn't stop *The Spectator* in 1932 from being the first to publish (for thirty shillings) 'The Tryst', that most magical of all night-visitor lyrics, a poem that speaks as clearly to Buffy fans as to 1930s' intellectuals.

What else do we have? We have the whole texts of several poems that are usually cut for anthologies of this size, namely Goldsmith's 'The Deserted Village', the 'Rubaiyat' (in the first, 1859 edition). 'The Ballad of Reading Gaol' (in the latest version, from the Collins Centenary edition), Blake's 'Auguries of Innocence', Wordsworth's 'Intimations of Immortality', and 'The Old Vicarage, Grantchester'. Among the shorter poems are the Leo Marks' poem Violette Szabo took with her into Occupied France, and the greatest sports poem ever written, Francis Thompson's 'At Lord's'.

The time scale of the anthology extends from anonymous medieval lyrics to the great Benjamin Zephaniah (born 1958). As for annotations, these have been kept to to a minimum. We have explained 'mon waxe wod' in 'Fowls in the Frith' but are content for 'Duggie' and his reliable payments in Orwell's 'A Happy Vicar I Might Have Been' to remain mysterious: explanations, like introductions, can go on too long. It is certainly possible to quarrel with our choices (we were not always in perfect agreement ourselves, to say the least), but the poems we have ended up choosing can all speak for themselves.

Edwin Moore and Fiona Mackenzie Moore

ENGLISH VERSE

S<small>IR</small> K<small>INGSLEY</small> A<small>MIS</small> (1922–1995)

A Bookshop Idyll

Between the GARDENING and the COOKERY
  Comes the brief POETRY shelf;
By the Nonesuch Donne, a thin anthology
  Offers itself.

Critical, and with nothing else to do,
  I scan the Contents page,
Relieved to find the names are mostly new;
  No one my age.

Like all strangers, they divide by sex:
  Landscape near Parma
Interests a man, so does *The Double Vortex*,
  So does *Rilke and Buddha*.

'I travel, you see', 'I think' and 'I can read'
  These titles seem to say;
But *I Remember You, Love is my Creed*,
  Poem for J.,

The ladies' choice, discountenance my patter
  For several seconds;
From somewhere in this (as in any) matter
  A moral beckons.

Should poets bicycle-pump the human heart
  Or squash it flat?
Man's love is of man's life a thing apart;
  Girls aren't like that.

We men have got love well weighed up; our stuff
  Can get by without it.
Women don't seem to think that's good enough;
  They write about it,

And the awful way their poems lay them open
    Just doesn't strike them.
Women are really much nicer than men:
    No wonder we like them.

Deciding this, we can forget those times
    We sat up half the night
Chockfull of love, crammed with bright thoughts, names, rhymes,
    And couldn't write.

L'Invitation au Voyage

—Welcome aboard the Nautilus, monsieur!
I vow you shall confess yourself amazed
Ten thousand times before our cruise is done.
What spectacles are mustered in the deep!
Beauty mere words are useless to depict,
Marvels unknown to science, dangers too,
Which we expunge with electricity.
Salute your comrades now: Ned Land, Conseil,
Brave fellows, and Professor Aronnax,
The eminent pelagiologist,
Whose fund of knowledge is at your desire,
As is my library, well-stocked and calm,
Matchless for the conducting of research.
Should you set store by music, you will find
That organ a trustworthy instrument,
While, for comestibles, we pride ourselves
On our sea-urchin loaf and shark ragout.
Till dinner, then . . .

—Thanks, Captain Nemo, this is always what
I think I want. But after weeks of Ned
On whaling, good Conseil just being good,
And Aronnax as Aronnax, I might
Start to browse round that matchless library,
Thrum at the organ, savour the thick film
Choking my tongue; and if, one afternoon,
A mermaid swam from the dead coral-groves
And looked in, sea-eyed, at the fat window,

Her olive hair writhing about her head,
Her turquoise nipples pried at by small fish,
Someone like me would say: 'Remarkable!
Behold, my friends, a rare phenomenon!
Doubtless, the lungs have been replaced by gills,
The hide, withstanding eighty atmospheres,
Moreover toughened—the Creator's hand
Lavish as always with new wonderment!'
    The long-boat, please. . .

The Shrimp in the Rubbish-Bin

I lived in my own world of sea
    Till someone came and caught me,
Boiled me and sent me to a shop
    Where someone came and bought me.
I ask you, human beings all,
    Was that the way to treat me,
To do to me what you have done
    And then not even eat me?

ANONYMOUS

'Fowls in the frith'

Fowls in the frith,[1]
The fishes in the flood,
And I mon waxe wod;[2]
Much sorrow I walke with
For beast of bone and blood.

The Maidens Came

The maidens came when I was in my mother's bower;
I had all that I would.
The bailey beareth the bell away;
The lily, the rose, the rose I lay.

---

[1] frith = forest. [2] mon waxe wod = must go mad.

The silver is white, red is the gold;
The robes they lay in fold.
The bailey beareth the bell away;
The lily, the rose, the rose I lay.

And through the glass window shines the sun.
How should I love and I so young?
The bailey beareth the bell away;
The lily, the rose, the rose I lay.

'Lully, lully'

Lully, lully, lully, lulley,
The falcon hath borne my mate away.

He bare him up, he bare him down,
He bare him into an orchard brown.

In that orchard there was an halle
That hangèd was with purple and pall.

And in that hall there was a bed;
It was hangèd with gold so red.

And in that bed there lieth a knight,
His wounds bleeding day and night.

By that bed side kneeleth a may,[1]
And she weepeth both night and day.

Mother and Maiden

I sing of a maiden
   That is matchless.
King of all kings
   For her son she chose.

He came all so still
   Where his mother was,
As dew in April
   That falleth on the grass.

[1] may = maiden.

He came all so still
  To his mother's bower,
As dew in Aprll
  That falleth on the flower.

He came all so still—
  There his mother lay,
As dew in April
  That falleth on the spray.

Mother and maiden
  Was never none but she;
Well may such a lady
  God's mother be.

Sir Patrick Spens

The king sits in Dumfermline town
  Drinking the blood-red wine:
'O where will I get a skilful skipper
  To sail this ship of mine?'

Up and spake an elder knight,
  Sat at the king's right knee:
'Sir Patrick Spens is the best sailor
  That ever sailed the sea.'

The king has written a broad letter
  And sealed it with his hand,
And sent it to Sir Patrick Spens
  Was walking on the strand.

'To Noroway, to Noroway,
  To Noroway o'er the foam;
The King's own daughter of Noroway,
  'Tis thou must bring her home!'

The first line that Sir Patrick read
  A loud, loud laugh laughed he:

The next line that Sir Patrick read,
    The tear blinded his ee.[1]

'O who is this has done this deed,
    This ill deed unto me;
To send me out this time o' the year,
    To sail upon the sea?

'Make haste, make haste, my merry men all,
    Our good ship sails the morn:'
'O say not so, my master dear,
    For I fear a deadly storm.

'I saw the new moon late yestreen,
    With the old moon in her arm;
And if we go to sea, master,
    I fear we'll come to harm.'

They had not sailed a league, a league,
    A league, but barely three,
When the sky grew dark, the wind blew loud,
    And angry grew the sea.

The anchor broke, the topmast split,
    'Twas such a deadly storm.
The waves came over the broken ship
    Till all her sides were torn.

O long, long may the ladies sit
    With their fans into their hand,
Or ere they see Sir Patrick Spens
    Come sailing to the strand.

O long, long may the maidens sit,
    With their gold combs in their hair,
Before they'll see their own dear loves
    Come home to greet them there.

Half-o'er, half-o'er to Aberdour,
    'Tis fifty fathoms deep;
And there lies good Sir Patrick Spens
    With the Scots lords at his feet.

[1] ee = eye

The Twa Corbies

As I was walking all alane,
I heard twa corbies making a mane;[1]
The tane unto the t'other say,[2]
'Where sall we gang and dine today?'

'In behint yon auld fail dyke,[3]
I wot there lies a new-slain knight;
And naebody kens that he lies there,
But his hawk, his hound, and lady fair.

'His hound is to the hunting gane,
His hawk to fetch the wild-fowl hame;
His lady's ta'en another mate,
So we may make our dinner sweet.

'Ye'll sit on his white hause-bane,[4]
And I'll pick out his bonny blue een:
Wi' ae lock o' his gowden hair[5]
We'll theek our nest when it grows bare.[6]

'Mony a one for him makes mane,
But nane sall ken where he is gane;
O'er his white banes, when they are bare,
The wind sall blaw for evermair.'

'Westron wind'

Westron wind, when wilt thou blow,
    The small rain down doth rain.
Christ, that my love were in my arms,
    And I in my bed again.

---

[1] twa corbies = two crows; mane = moan. [2] tane = the one.
[3] yon auld fail dyke = that old turf wall. [4] hause-bane = neckbone.
[5] ae = one; gowden = golden. [6] theek = thatch.

Ballad of Otterburn

It fell about the Lammas tide,[1]
    When the muir-men win their hay,[2]
The doughty Douglas bound him to ride
    Into England, to drive a prey.

He chose the Gordons and the Graemes,
    With them the Lindsays, light and gay;
But the Jardines would not with him ride,
    And they rue it to this day.

And he has burned the dales of Tyne,
    And part of Bambrough shire:
And three good towers on Reidswire fells,
    He left them all on fire.

And he marched up to Newcastle,
    And rode it round about:
'O wha's the lord of this castle?
    Or wha's the lady o't?'

But up spake proud Lord Percy then,
    And O but he spake hie!
'I am the lord of this castle,
    My wife's the lady gay.'

'If thou'rt the lord of this castle,
    Sae weel it pleases me!
For, ere I cross the Border fells,
    The tane of us sall die.'

He took a lang spear in his hand,
    Shod with the metal free,
And for to meet the Douglas there,
    He rode right furiously.

[1] Lammas = 1 August, a Scottish quarter day.
[2] muir-men = raiding Borderers.

But O how pale his lady looked,
  Frae aff the castle wa',
When down, before the Scottish spear,
  She saw proud Percy fa'.

'Had we twa been upon the green,
  And never an eye to see,
I wad hae had you, flesh and fell;
  But your sword sall gae wi' me.'

'But gae ye up to Otterburn,
  And wait there dayis three;
And, if I come not ere three day is end,
  A false knight ca' ye me.'

'The Otterborn's a bonnie burn;
  'Tis pleasant there to be;
But there is nought at Otterburn,
  To feed my men and me.

'The deer rins wild on hill and dale,
  The birds fly wild from tree to tree;
But there is neither bread nor kale,
  To feed my men and me.

'Yet I will stay at Otterburn,
  Where you shall welcome be;
And, if ye come not at three dayis end,
  A false lord I'll ca' thee.'

'Thither will I come,' proud Percy said,
  'By the might of Our Lady!'—
'There will I bide thee,' said the Douglas,
  'My troth I plight to thee.'

They lighted high on Otterburn,
  Upon the bent sae brown;[1]
They lighted high on Otterburn,
  And threw their pallions down.

---

[1] bent = hillock covered with coarse grass.

And he that had a bonnie boy,
    Sent out his horse to grass,
And he that had not a bonnie boy,
    His ain servant he was.

But up then spake a little page,
    Before the peep of dawn:
'O waken ye, waken ye, my good lord,
    For Percy's hard at hand.'

'Ye lie, ye lie, ye liar loud!
    Sae loud I hear ye lie;
For Percy had not men yestreen,
    To fight my men and me.

'But I have dreamed a dreary dream,
    Beyond the Isle of Skye;
I saw a dead man win a fight,
    And I think that man was I.'

He belted on his guid braid sword,
    And to the field he ran;
But he forgot the helmet good,
    That should have kept his brain.

When Percy wi the Douglas met,
    I wat he was fu' fain!
They swakked their swords, till sair they swat,[1]
    And the blood ran down like rain.

But Percy with his good broad sword,
    That could so sharply wound,
Has wounded Douglas on the brow,
    Till he fell to the ground.

Then he called on his little foot-page,
    And said—'Run speedily,
And fetch my ain dear sister's son,
    Sir Hugh Montgomery.

[1] swakked = swung; sair = greatly; swat = sweated.

'My nephew good,' the Douglas said,
    'What recks the death of ane!
Last night I dreamed a dreary dream,
    And I ken the day's thy ain.

'My wound is deep; I fain would sleep;
    Take thou the vanguard of the three,
And hide me by the bracken bush,
    That grows on yonder lily lee.

'O bury me by the bracken bush,
    Beneath the blooming briar;
Let never living mortal ken
    That ere a kindly Scot lies here.'

He lifted up that noble lord,
    Wi the salt tear in his e'e;
He hid him in the bracken bush,
    That his merry men might not see.

The moon was clear, the day drew near,
    The spears in flinders flew,
But mony a gallant Englishman
    Ere day the Scotsmen slew.

The Gordons good, in English blood,
    They steeped their hose and shoon;
The Lindsays flew like fire about,
    Till all the fray was done.

The Percy and Montgomery met,
    That either of other were fain;
They swapped swords, and they twa swat,
    And aye the blood ran down between.

'Yield thee, now yield thee, Percy,' he said,
    'Or else I vow I'll lay thee low!'
'To whom must I yield,' quoth Earl Percy,
    'Now that I see it must be so?'

'Thou shalt not yield to lord nor loon,
    Nor yet shalt thou yield to me;

But yield thee to the bracken bush,
    That grows upon yon lily lee!'

'I will not yield to a bracken bush,
    Nor yet will I yield to a briar;
But I would yield to Earl Douglas,
    Or Sir Hugh the Montgomery, if he were here.'

As soon as he knew it was Montgomery,
    He stuck his sword's point in the ground;
The Montgomery was a courteous knight,
    And quickly took him by the hand.

This deed was done at Otterburn,
    About the breaking of the day;
Earl Douglas was buried at the bracken bush,
    And the Percy led captive away.

Thomas the Rhymer

True Thomas lay on Huntlie bank;
    A marvel he did see;
And there he saw a lady bright
    Come riding down by the Eildon tree.[1]

Her skirt was of the grass-green silk,
    Her mantle of the velvet fine;
On every lock of her horse's mane,
    Hung fifty silver bells and nine.

True Thomas he pulled off his cap,
    And bowed low down on his knee:
'All hail, thou mighty Queen of Heaven!
    For thy peer on earth could never be.'

'O no, O no, Thomas,' she said,
    'That name does not belong to me;
I'm but the Queen of fair Elfland,
    That hither am come to visit thee.

[1] The Eildon tree was the tree of magic under which the Rhymer delivered his prophecies.

'Harp and carp, Thomas,' she said;
　　'Harp and carp along with me;
And if ye dare to kiss my lips,
　　Sure of your body I will be.'

'Betide me weal, betide me woe,
　　That weird shall never daunten me!'
Then he has kissed her on the lips,
　　All underneath the Eildon tree.

'Now ye must go with me,' she said,
　　'True Thomas, ye must go with me;
And ye must serve me seven years,
　　Through weal or woe as may chance to be.'

She's mounted on her milk-white steed,
　　She's taken True Thomas up behind;
And aye, whene'er her bridle rang,
　　The steed flew swifter than the wind.

O they rode on, and farther on,
　　The steed flew swifter than the wind;
Until they reached a desert wide,
　　And living land was left behind.

'Light down, light down now, Thomas,' she said,
　　'And lean your head upon my knee;
Light down, and rest a little space,
　　And I will show you marvels three.

'O see ye not yon narrow road,
　　So thick beset with thorns and briars?
That is the path of righteousness,
　　Though after it but few enquires.

'And see ye not yon broad, broad road,
　　That stretches o'er the lily leven?
That is the path of wickedness,
　　Though some call it the road to heaven.

'And see ye not yon bonny road
    That winds about the green hillside?
That is the way to fair Elfland,
    Where you and I this night must bide.

'But, Thomas, ye shall hold your tongue,
    Whatever ye may hear or see;
For if ye speak word in Elfin land,
    Ye'll ne'er win back to your own countree!'

O they rode on, and farther on;
    And they waded through rivers above the knee;
And they saw neither sun nor moon,
    But they heard the roaring of a sea.

It was mirk, mirk night; there was no starlight;
    They waded through red blood to the knee;
For all the blood that's shed on earth
    Runs through the springs o' that countree.

At last they came to a garden green,
    And she pulled an apple from on high—
'Take this for thy wages, True Thomas;
    It will give thee the tongue that can never lie!'

'My tongue is my own,' True Thomas he said,
    'A goodly gift ye would give to me!
I neither could to buy or sell
    At fair or tryst where I might be.

'I could neither speak to prince or peer,
    Nor ask of grace from fair ladye!'
'Now hold thy peace!' the lady said,
    'For as I say, so must it be.'

He has gotten a coat of the even cloth,
    And a pair of shoes of the velvet green;
And till seven years were gone and past,
    True Thomas on earth was never seen.

Mad Song

or *Tom O' Bedlam's Song*

From the hag and hungry goblin
That into rags would rend ye,
    All the spirits that stand
    By the naked man
In the book of moons, defend ye,

That of your five sound senses
You never be forsaken,
    Nor wander from
    Yourselves with Tom
Abroad to beg your bacon.

With a thought I took for Maudlin,
And a cruse of cockle pottage,
    With a thing thus tall,
    Sky bless you all,
I befell into this dotage.

I slept not since the Conquest,
Till then I never wakèd,
    Till the roguish boy
    Of love where I lay
Me found and stript me naked.

The moon's my constant mistress,
And the lonely owl my marrow;[1]
    The flaming drake
    And the night-crow make
Me music to my sorrow.

I know more than Apollo,
For oft, where he lies sleeping,
    I see the stars
    At mortal wars
In the wounded welkin weeping,[2]

[1] marrow = mate. [2] welkin = sky.

The moon embrace her shepherd,
And the queen of love her warrior,
　　While the first doth horn
　　The star of morn,
And the next the heavenly farrier.

With an host of furious fancies,
Whereof I am commander,
　　With a burning spear
　　And a horse of air
To the wilderness I wander;

By a knight of ghosts and shadows
I summoned am to tourney
　　Ten leagues beyond
　　The wide world's end—
Methinks it is no journey.

MATTHEW ARNOLD (1822–1888)

Philomela

Hark, ah, the nightingale—
The tawny-throated!
Hark, from that moonlit cedar what a burst!
What triumph! hark!—what pain!

O wanderer from a Grecian shore,
Still, after many years, in distant lands,
Still nourishing in thy bewildered brain
That wild, unquenched, deep-sunken, old-world pain—
Say, will it never heal?
And can this fragrant lawn
With its cool trees, and night,
And the sweet, tranquil Thames,
And moonshine, and the dew,
To thy racked heart and brain
Afford no balm?

Dost thou tonight behold,
Here, through the moonlight on this English grass,

The unfriendly palace in the Thracian wild?
Dost thou again peruse
With hot cheeks and seared eyes
The too clear web, and thy dumb sister's shame?
Dost thou once more assay
Thy flight, and feel come over thee,
Poor fugitive, the feathery change
Once more, and once more seem to make resound
With love and hate, triumph and agony,
Lone Daulis, and the high Cephissian vale?
Listen, Eugenia—
How thick the bursts come crowding through the leaves!
Again—thou hearest?
Eternal passion!
Eternal pain!

Shakespeare

Others abide our question. Thou art free.
We ask and ask. Thou smilest and art still,
Out-topping knowledge. For the loftiest hill,
Who to the stars uncrowns his majesty,
Planting his steadfast footsteps in the sea,
Making the heaven of heavens his dwelling-place,
Spares but the cloudy border of his base
To the foiled searching of mortality;
And thou, who didst the stars and sunbeams know,
Self-schooled, self-scanned, self-honoured, self-secure,
Didst tread on earth unguessed at.—Better so!
All pains the immortal spirit must endure,
All weakness which impairs, all griefs which bow,
Find their sole speech in that victorious brow.

To Marguerite—Continued

Yes! in the sea of life enisled,
With echoing straits between us thrown,
Dotting the shoreless watery wild,
We mortal millions live alone.
The islands feel the enclasping flow,
And then their endless bounds they know.

But when the moon their hollows lights,
And they are swept by balms of spring,
And in their glens, on starry nights,
The nightingales divinely sing;
And lovely notes, from shore to shore,
Across the sounds and channels pour—

Oh! then a longing like despair
Is to their farthest caverns sent;
For surely once, they feel, we were
Parts of a single continent!
Now round us spreads the watery plain—
Oh might our marges meet again!

Who ordered, that their longing's fire
Should be, as soon as kindled, cooled?
Who renders vain their deep desire?—
A God, a God their severance ruled!
And bade betwixt their shores to be
The unplumbed, salt, estranging sea.

Dover Beach

The sea is calm tonight.
The tide is full, the moon lies fair
Upon the Straits—on the French coast, the light
Gleams, and is gone; the cliffs of England stand,
Glimmering and vast, out in the tranquil bay.

Come to the window, sweet is the night air!
Only, from the long line of spray
Where the sea meets the moon-blanched sand,
Listen! you hear the grating roar
Of pebbles which the waves suck back, and fling,
At their return, up the high strand,
Begin, and cease, and then again begin,
With tremulous cadence slow, and bring
The eternal note of sadness in.

Sophocles long ago
Heard it on the Aegean, and it brought

Into his mind the turbid ebb and flow
Of human misery; we
Find also in the sound a thought,
Hearing it by this distant northern sea.

The sea of faith
Was once, too, at the full, and round earth's shore
Lay like the folds of a bright girdle furled;
But now I only hear
Its melancholy, long, withdrawing roar,
Retreating to the breath
Of the night-wind, down the vast edges drear
And naked shingles of the world.

Ah, love, let us be true
To one another! for the world, which seems
To lie before us like a land of dreams,
So various, so beautiful, so new,
Hath really neither joy, nor love, nor light,
Nor certitude, nor peace, nor help for pain;
And we are here as on a darkling plain
Swept with confused alarms of struggle and flight,
Where ignorant armies clash by night.

W. H. Auden (1907–1973)

On This Island

Look, stranger, on this island now
The leaping light for your delight discovers,
Stand stable here
And silent be,
That through the channels of the ear
May wander like a river
The swaying sound of the sea.

Here at the small field's ending pause
Where the chalk wall falls to the foam and its tall ledges
Oppose the pluck
And knock of the tide,

And the shingle scrambles after the suck-
ing surf,
And the gull lodges
A moment on its sheer side.

Far-off like floating seeds the ships
Diverge on urgent voluntary errands,
And the full view
Indeed may enter
And move in memory as now these clouds do,
That pass the harbour mirror
And all the summer through the water saunter.

'Stop all the clocks'
(from 'Twelve Songs')

Stop all the clocks, cut off the telephone,
Prevent the dog from barking with a juicy bone,
Silence the pianos and with muffled drum
Bring out the coffin, let the mourners come.

Let aeroplanes circle moaning overhead
Scribbling on the sky the message He Is Dead,
Put crêpe bows round the white necks of the public doves,
Let the traffic policemen wear black cotton gloves.

He was my North, my South, my East and West,
My working week and my Sunday rest,
My noon, my midnight, my talk, my song:
I thought that love would last for ever: I was wrong.

The stars are not wanted now: put out every one;
Pack up the moon and dismantle the sun;
Pour away the ocean and sweep up the wood;
For nothing now can ever come to any good.

Epitaph on a Tyrant

Perfection, of a kind, was what he was after,
And the poetry he invented was easy to understand;

He knew human folly like the back of his hand,
And was greatly interested in armies and fleets;
When he laughed, respectable senators burst with laughter,
And when he cried the little children died in the streets.

FRANCIS BEAUMONT (1584–1616)

A Dance

Shake off your heavy trance!
And leap into a dance
Such as no mortals use to tread:
Fit only for Apollo
To play to, for the moon to lead,
And all the stars to follow!

HILAIRE BELLOC (1870–1953)

Ha'nacker Mill

Sally is gone that was so kindly
Sally is gone from Ha'nacker Hill.
And the Briar grows ever since then so blindly
And ever since then the clapper is still,
And the sweeps have fallen from Ha'nacker Mill.

Ha'nacker Hill is in Desolation:
Ruin a-top and a field unploughed.
And Spirits that call on a fallen nation
Spirits that loved her calling aloud:
Spirits abroad in a windy cloud.

Spirits that call and no one answers;
Ha'nacker's down and England's done.
Wind and Thistle for pipe and dancers
And never a ploughman under the Sun.
Never a ploughman. Never a one.

The World's a Stage

The world's a stage. The light is in one's eyes.
The Auditorium is extremely dark.
The more dishonest get the larger rise;
The more offensive make the greater mark.
The women on it prosper by their shape,
Some few by their vivacity. The men,
By tailoring in breeches and in cape.
The world's a stage—I say it once again.

The scenery is very much the best
Of what the wretched drama has to show,
Also the prompter happens to be dumb. .
We drink behind the scenes and pass a jest
On all our folly; then, before we go
Loud cries for 'Author' . . . but he doesn't come.

Ballade of Hell and of Mrs Roebeck

I'm going out to dine at Gray's
    With Bertie Morden, Charles and Kit,
And Manderly who never pays,
    And Jane who wins in spite of it,
    And Algernon who won't admit
The truth about his curious hair
    And teeth that very nearly fit:—
And Mrs Roebeck will be there.

And then tomorrow someone says
    That someone else has made a hit
In one of Mister Twister's plays.
    And off we go to yawn at it;
    And when it's petered out we quit
For number 20 Taunton Square,
    And smoke, and drink, and dance a bit:—
And Mrs Roebeck will be there.

And so through each declining phase
   Of emptied effort, jaded wit,
And day by day of London days
   Obscurely, more obscurely, lit;
   Until the uncertain shadows flit
Announcing to the shuddering air
   A Darkening, and the end of it:—
And Mrs Roebeck will be there.

Envoi

Prince, on their iron thrones they sit,
   Impassible to our despair,
The dreadful Guardians of the Pit:—
   And Mrs Roebeck will be there.

SIR JOHN BETJEMAN (1906–1984)

The Arrest of Oscar Wilde at the Cadogan Hotel

He sipped at a weak hock and seltzer
   As he gazed at the London skies
Through the Nottingham lace of the curtains
   Or was it his bees-winged eyes?

To the right and before him Pont Street
   Did tower in her new built red,
As hard as the morning gaslight
   That shone on his unmade bed.

'I want some more hock in my seltzer,
   And Robbie, please give me your hand—
Is this the end or beginning?
   How can I understand?

'So you've brought me the latest *Yellow Book*:
   And Buchan has got in it now:

Approval of what is approved of
    Is as false as a well-kept vow.

'More hock, Robbie—where is the seltzer?
    Dear boy, pull again at the bell!
They are all little better than *cretins*,
    Though this *is* the Cadogan Hotel.

'One astrakhan coat is at Willis's—
    Another one's at the Savoy:
Do fetch my morocco portmanteau,
    And bring them on later, dear boy.'

A thump, and a murmur of voices—
    ('Oh why must they make such a din?')
As the door of the bedroom swung open
    And Two Plain Clothes POLICEMEN came in:

'Mr Woilde, we 'ave come for tew take yew
    Where felons and criminals dwell:
We must ask yew tew leave with us quoietly
    For this *is* the Cadogan Hotel.'

He rose, and he put down *The Yellow Book*.
    He staggered—and, terrible-eyed,
He brushed past the palms on the staircase
    And was helped to a hansom outside.

In a Bath Teashop

'Let us not speak, for the love we bear one another—
    Let us hold hands and look.'
She, such a very ordinary little woman;
    He, such a thumping crook;
But both, for a moment, little lower than the angels
    In the teashop's ingle-nook

WILLIAM BLAKE (1757–1827)

The Tyger

Tyger! Tyger! burning bright
In the forests of the night,
What immortal hand or eye
Could frame thy fearful symmetry?

In what distant deeps or skies
Burnt the fire of thine eyes?
On what wings dare he aspire?
What the hand dare seize the fire?

And what shoulder, and what art,
Could twist the sinews of thy heart?
And when thy heart began to beat,
What dread hand? and what dread feet?

What the hammer? what the chain?
In what furnace was thy brain?
What the anvil? what dread grasp
Dare its deadly terrors clasp?

When the stars threw down their spears
And watered heaven with their tears,
Did he smile his work to see?
Did he who made the Lamb make thee?

Tyger! Tyger! burning bright
In the forests of the night,
What immortal hand or eye
Dare frame thy fearful symmetry?

The Lamb

Little Lamb, who made thee?
    Dost thou know who made thee?
Gave thee life and bid thee feed
By the stream and o'er the mead;

Gave thee clothing of delight,
Softest clothing, woolly, bright;
Gave thee such a tender voice
Making all the vales rejoice?
　　Little Lamb, who made thee?
　　Dost thou know who made thee?

　　Little Lamb, I'll tell thee,
　　Little Lamb, I'll tell thee:
He is callèd by thy name,
For he calls himself a Lamb.
He is meek and he is mild;
He became a little child.
I a child and thou a lamb,
We are callèd by his name.
　　Little Lamb, God bless thee.
　　Little Lamb, God bless thee.

The Sunflower

Ah, Sunflower! weary of time,
Who countest the steps of the Sun,
Seeking after that sweet golden clime
Where the traveller's journey is done:

Where the Youth pined away with desire,
And the pale Virgin shrouded in snow,
Arise from their graves and aspire
Where my Sunflower wishes to go.

The Sick Rose

O rose, thou art sick:
The invisible worm
That flies in the night
In the howling storm,

Has found out thy bed
Of crimson joy,
And his dark secret love
Does thy life destroy.

'How sweet I roamed'

How sweet I roamed from field to field
    And tasted all the summer's pride,
Till I the prince of love beheld
    Who in the sunny beams did glide!

He showed me lilies for my hair,
    And blushing roses for my brow;
He led me through his gardens fair
    Where all his golden pleasures grow.

With sweet May dews my wings were wet,
    And Phoebus fired my vocal rage;
He caught me in his silken net,
    And shut me in his golden cage.

He loves to sit and hear me sing,
    Then, laughing, sports and plays with me;
Then stretches out my golden wing,
    And mocks my loss of liberty.

Auguries of Innocence

To see a World in a Grain of Sand
And a Heaven in a Wild Flower,
Hold Infinity in the palm of your hand
And Eternity in an hour.

A Robin Redbreast in a Cage
Puts all Heaven in a Rage.
A Dove-house filled with Doves and Pigeons
Shudders Hell thro' all its regions.
A Dog starved at his Master's Gate
Predicts the ruin of the State.
A Horse misused upon the Road
Calls to Heaven for Human blood.
Each outcry of the hunted Hare
A fibre from the Brain does tear.
A Skylark wounded in the wing,

A Cherubim does cease to sing.
The Game Cock clipped and armed for fight
Does the Rising Sun affright.
Every Wolf's and Lion's howl
Raises from Hell a human Soul.
The wild Deer wand'ring here and there
Keeps the human Soul from Care.
The Lamb misused breeds public strife
And yet forgives the Butcher's Knife.
The Bat that flits at close of Eve
Has left the Brain that won't believe.
The Owl that calls upon the Night
Speaks the Unbeliever's fright.
He who shall hurt the little Wren
Shall never be beloved by Men.
He who the Ox to wrath had moved
Shall never be by Woman loved.
The wanton Boy that kills the Fly
Shall feel the Spider's enmity.
He who torments the Chafer's sprite
Weaves a Bower in endless Night.
The Caterpillar on the Leaf
Repeats to thee thy Mother's grief.
Kill not the Moth nor Butterfly
For the Last Judgement draweth nigh.
He who shall train the Horse to War
Shall never pass the Polar Bar.
The Begger's Dog and Widow's Cat,
Feed them and thou wilt grow fat.
The Gnat that sings his Summer's song
Poison gets from Slander's tongue.
The poison of the Snake and Newt
Is the sweat of Envy's Foot.
The Poison of the Honey Bee
Is the Artist's Jealousy.
The Prince's Robes and Beggar's Rags
Are Toadstools on the Miser's Bags.
A truth that's told with bad intent
Beats all the Lies you can invent.
It is right it should be so;
Man was made for Joy and Woe;
And when this we rightly know

Thro' the World we safely go.
Joy and Woe are woven fine,
A Clothing for the Soul divine;
Under every grief and pine
Runs a joy with silken twine.
The Babe is more than swadling Bands;
Throughout all these Human Lands
Tools were made, and born were hands,
Every Farmer Understands.
Every Tear from Every Eye
Becomes a Babe in Eternity;
This is caught by Females bright
And returned to its own delight.
The Bleat, the Bark, Bellow and Roar
Are Waves that Beat on Heaven's Shore.
The Babe that weeps the Rod beneath
Writes Revenge in realms of death.
The Beggar's Rags, fluttering in Air,
Does to Rags the Heavens tear.
The Soldier, armed with Sword and Gun,
Palsied strikes the Summer's Sun.
The poor Man's Farthing is worth more
Than all the Gold on Afric's Shore.
One Mite wrung from the Labrer's hands
Shall buy and sell the Miser's lands:
Or, if protected from on high,
Does that whole Nation sell and buy.
He who mocks the Infant's Faith
Shall be mocked in Age and Death.
He who shall teach the Child to Doubt
The rotting Grave shall ne'er get out.
He who respects the Infant's faith
Triumphs over Hell and Death.
The Child's Toys and the Old Man's Reasons
Are the Fruits of the Two seasons.
The Questioner who sits so sly
Shall never know how to Reply.
He who replies to words of Doubt
Doth put the Light of Knowledge out.
The Strongest Poison ever known
Came from Caesar's Laurel Crown.
Nought can deform the Human Race

Like to the Armour's iron brace.
When Gold and Gems adorn the Plow
To peaceful Arts shall Envy Bow.
A Riddle or the Cricket's Cry
Is to Doubt a fit Reply.
The Emmet's Inch and Eagle's Mile
Make Lame Philosophy to smile.
He who Doubts from what he sees
Will ne'er Believe, do what you Please.
If the Sun and Moon should doubt,
They'd immediately Go out.
To be in a Passion you Good may do,
But no Good if a Passion is in you.
The Whore and Gambler, by the State
Licensed, build that Nation's Fate.
The Harlot's cry from Street to Street
Shall weave Old England's winding Sheet.
The Winner's Shout, the Loser's Curse,
Dance before dead England's Hearse.
Every Night and every Morn
Some to Misery are Born.
Every Morn and every Night
Some are Born to sweet delight.
Some are Born to sweet delight,
Some are Born to Endless Night.
We are led to believe a Lie
When we see with, not thro' the Eye
Which was born in a Night, to perish in a Night,
When the Soul slept in Beams of Light.
God Appears and God is Light
To those poor Souls who dwell in Night,
But does a Human Form display
To those who dwell in Realms of Day.

'He who binds'

He who binds to himself a joy
Does the wingèd life destroy;
But he who kisses the joy as it flies
Lives in eternity's sunrise.

'And did those feet'

(from 'Milton')

And did those feet in ancient time
Walk upon England's mountains green?
And was the Holy Lamb of God
On England's pleasant pastures seen?

And did the countenance divine
Shine forth upon our clouded hills?
And was Jerusalem builded here
Among these dark satanic mills?

Bring me my bow of burning gold!
Bring me my arrows of desire!
Bring me my spear! O clouds, unfold!
Bring me my chariot of fire!

I will not cease from mental fight,
Nor shall my sword sleep in my hand,
Till we have built Jerusalem
In England's green and pleasant land.

'Never seek to tell thy love'

Never seek to tell thy love,
    Love that never told can be;
For the gentle wind does move
    Silently, invisibly.

I told my love, I told my love,
    I told her all my heart;
Trembling, cold, in ghastly fears,
    Ah! she doth depart!

Soon as she was gone from me
    A traveller came by,
Silently, invisibly—
    O, was no deny.

Epilogue from 'For the Sexes: The Gates of Paradise'

To the Accuser who is the God of the World

Truly, my Satan, thou art but a Dunce
And dost not know the Garment from the Man:
Every Harlot was a Virgin once,
Nor canst thou ever change Kate into Nan.

Though thou art Worshipped by the Names Divine
Of Jesus and Jehovah, thou art still
The Son of Morn in weary Night's decline,
The lost Traveller's Dream under the Hill.

EDMUND BLUNDEN (1896–1974)

Report on Experience

I have been young, and now am not too old;
And I have seen the righteous forsaken,
His health, his honour and his quality taken.
    This is not what we were formerly told.

I have seen a green country, useful to the race,
Knocked silly with guns and mines, its villages vanished,
Even the last rat and last kestrel banished—
    God bless us all, this was peculiar grace.

I knew Seraphina; Nature gave her hue,
Glance, sympathy, note, like one from Eden.
I saw her smile warp, heard her lyric deaden;
    She turned to harlotry;—this I took to be new.

Say what you will, our God sees how they run.
These disillusions are His curious proving
That He loves humanity, and will go on loving;
    Over there are faith, life, virtue in the sun.

NICHOLAS BRETON (1548?–1626?)

A Pastoral

On a hill there grows a flower,
    Fair befall the dainty sweet!
By that flower there is a bower
    Where the heavenly Muses meet.

In that bower there is a chair
    Fringèd all about with gold,
Where doth sit the fairest fair
    That did ever eye behold.

It is Phyllis fair and bright,
    She that is the shepherds' joy,
She that Venus did despite
    And did blind her little boy.

This is she, the wise, the rich,
    All the world desires to see;
This is *ipsa quae* the which
    There is none but only she.

Who would not this face admire?
    Who would not this saint adore?
Who would not this sight desire,
    Though he thought to see no more?

O fair eyes, yet let me see!
    One good look, and I am gone,
Look on me, for I am he—
    Thy poor silly Coridon.

Thou that art the shepherds' queen,
    Look upon thy silly swain;
By thy comfort have been seen
    Dead men brought to life again.

EMILY BRONTË (1818–1848)

Remembrance

Cold in the earth—and the deep snow piled above thee,
    Far, far removed, cold in the dreary grave!
Have I forgot, my only Love, to love thee,
    Severed at last by Time's all-severing wave?

Now, when alone, do my thoughts no longer hover
    Over the mountains, on that northern shore,
Resting their wings where heath and fern-leaves cover
    Thy noble heart for ever, ever more?

Cold in the earth—and fifteen wild Decembers
    From these brown hills have melted into spring:
Faithful, indeed, is the spirit that remembers
    After such years of change and suffering!

Sweet Love of youth, forgive, if I forget thee,
    While the world's tide is bearing me along;
Other desires and other hopes beset me,
    Hopes which obscure, but cannot do thee wrong!

No later light has lightened up my heaven,
    No second morn has ever shone for me;
All my life's bliss from thy dear life was given,
    All my life's bliss is in the grave with thee.

But, when the days of golden dreams had perished,
    And even Despair was powerless to destroy;
Then did I learn how existence could be cherished,
    Strengthened and fed without the aid of joy.

Then did I check the tears of useless passion—
    Weaned my young soul from yearning after thine;
Sternly denied its burning wish to hasten
    Down to that tomb already more than mine.

And, even yet, I dare not let it languish,
    Dare not indulge in memory's rapturous pain;
Once drinking deep of that divinest anguish,
    How could I seek the empty world again?

Last Lines

No coward soul is mine,
No trembler in the world's storm-troubled sphere:
    I see Heaven's glories shine,
And faith shines equal, arming me from fear.

O God within my breast.
Almighty, ever-present Deity!
    Life—that in me has rest,
As I—undying Life—have power in thee!

Vain are the thousand creeds
That move mens hearts: unutterably vain;
    Worthless as withered weeds,
Or idlest froth amid the boundless main,

To waken doubt in one
Holding so fast by thine infinity;
    So surely anchored on
The steadfast rock of immortality.

With wide-embracing love
Thy spirit animates eternal years,
    Pervades and broods above;
Changes, sustains, dissolves, creates, and rears.

Though earth and man were gone,
And suns and universes ceased to be,
    And Thou wert left alone,
Every existence would exist in Thee.

There is not room for Death,
Nor atom that his might could render void:
    Thou—Thou art being and breath,
And what Thou art may never be destroyed.

RUPERT BROOKE (1887–1915)

The Old Vicarage, Grantchester

(Café des Westens, Berlin, May 1912)

Just now the lilac is in bloom,
All before my little room;
And in my flowerbeds, I think,
Smile the carnation and the pink;
And down the borders, well I know,
The poppy and the pansy blow . . .
Oh! there the chestnuts, summer through,
Beside the river make for you
A tunnel of green gloom, and sleep
Deeply above; and green and deep
The stream mysterious glides beneath,
Green as a dream and deep as death.
—Oh, damn! I know it! and I know
How the May fields all golden show,
And when the day is young and sweet,
Gild gloriously the bare feet
That run to bathe . . .
                    'Du lieber Gott!'

Here am I, sweating, sick, and hot,
And there the shadowed waters fresh
Lean up to embrace the naked flesh.
Temperamentvoll German Jews
Drink beer around;—and *there* the dews
Are soft beneath a morn of gold.
Here tulips bloom as they are told;
Unkempt about those hedges blows
An English unofficial rose;
And there the unregulated sun
Slopes down to rest when day is done,
And wakes a vague unpunctual star,
A slippered Hesper; and there are
Meads towards Haslingfield and Coton
Where *das Betreten*'s not *verboten*.

Eithe genoimen . . . would I were
In Grantchester, in Grantchester!—

Some, it may be, can get in touch
With Nature there, or Earth, or such.
And clever modern men have seen
A Faun a-peeping through the green,
And felt the Classics were not dead,
To glimpse a Naiad's reedy head,
Or hear the Goat-foot piping low: . . .
But these are things I do not know.
I only know that you may lie
Day long and watch the Cambridge sky,
And, flower-lulled in sleepy grass,
Hear the cool lapse of hours pass,
Until the centuries blend and blur
In Grantchester, in Grantchester. . . .
Still in the dawnlit waters cool
His ghostly Lordship swims his pool,
And tries the strokes, essays the tricks,
Long learnt on Hellespont, or Styx.
Dan Chaucer hears his river still
Chatter beneath a phantom mill.
Tennyson notes, with studious eye,
How Cambridge waters hurry by . . .
And in that garden, black and white,
Creep whispers through the grass all night;
And spectral dance, before the dawn,
A hundred Vicars down the lawn;
Curates, long dust, will come and go
On lissom, clerical, printless toe;
And oft between the boughs is seen
The sly shade of a Rural Dean . . .
Till, at a shiver in the skies,
Vanishing with Satanic cries,
The prim ecclesiastic rout
Leaves but a startled sleeper-out,
Grey heavens, the first bird's drowsy calls,
The falling house that never falls.

God! I will pack, and take a train,
And get me to England once again!
For England's the one land, I know,
Where men with Splendid Hearts may go;
And Cambridgeshire, of all England,

The shire for Men who Understand;
And of *that* district I prefer
The lovely hamlet Grantchester.
For Cambridge people rarely smile,
Being urban, squat, and packed with guile;
And Royston men in the far South
Are black and fierce and strange of mouth;
At Over they fling oaths at one,
And worse than oaths at Trumpington,
And Ditton girls are mean and dirty,
And there's none in Harston under thirty,
And folks in Shelford and those parts
Have twisted lips and twisted hearts,
And Barton men make Cockney rhymes,
And Coton's full of nameless crimes,
And things are done you'd not believe
At Madingley on Christmas Eve.
Strong men have run for miles and miles,
When one from Cherry Hinton smiles;
Strong men have blanched, and shot their wives,
Rather than send them to St Ives;
Strong men have cried like babes, bydam,
To hear what happened at Babraham.
But Grantchester! ah, Grantchester!
There's peace and holy quiet there,
Great clouds along pacific skies,
And men and women with straight eyes,
Lithe children lovelier than a dream,
A bosky wood, a slumbrous stream,
And little kindly winds that creep
Round twilight corners, half asleep.
In Grantchester their skins are white;
They bathe by day, they bathe by night;
The women there do all they ought;
The men observe the Rules of Thought.
They love the Good; they worship Truth;
They laugh uproariously in youth;
(And when they get to feeling old,
They up and shoot themselves, I'm told) . . .

Ah God! to see the branches stir
Across the moon at Grantchester!

To smell the thrilling-sweet and rotten
Unforgettable, unforgotten
River-smell, and hear the breeze
Sobbing in the little trees.
Say, do the elm-clumps greatly stand
Still guardians of that holy land?
The chestnuts shade, in reverend dream,
The yet unacademic stream?
Is dawn a secret shy and cold
Anadyomene, silver-gold?
And sunset still a golden sea
From Haslingfield to Madingley?
And after, ere the night is born,
Do hares come out about the corn?
Oh, is the water sweet and cool,
Gentle and brown, above the pool?
And laughs the immortal river still
Under the mill, under the mill?
Say, is there Beauty yet to find?
And Certainty? and Quiet kind?
Deep meadows yet, for to forget
The lies, and truths, and pain? . . . oh! yet
Stands the Church clock at ten to three?
And is there honey still for tea?

The Soldier

If I should die, think only this of me:
    That there's some corner of a foreign field
That is for ever England. There shall be
    In that rich earth a richer dust concealed;
A dust whom England bore, shaped, made aware,
    Gave, once, her flowers to love, her ways to roam,
A body of England's, breathing English air,
    Washed by the rivers, blest by suns of home.

And think, this heart, all evil shed away,
    A pulse in the eternal mind, no less
        Gives somewhere back the thoughts by England given;
Her sights and sounds; dreams happy as her day;
    And laughter, learnt of friends; and gentleness,
        In hearts at peace, under an English heaven.

THOMAS EDWARD BROWN (1830–1897)

'I bended unto me'

I bended unto me a bough of May,
That I might see and smell:
It bore it in a sort of way,
It bore it very well.
But, when I let it backward sway,
Then it were hard to tell
With what a toss, with what a swing,
The dainty thing
Resumed its proper level,
And sent me to the devil.
I know it did—you doubt it?
I turned, and saw them whispering about it.

ELIZABETH BARRETT BROWNING (1806–1861)

from 'Sonnets from the Portuguese'

If thou must love me, let it be for nought
Except for love's sake only. Do not say,
'I love her for her smile—her look—her way
Of speaking gently—for a trick of thought
That falls in well with mine, and certes brought
A sense of pleasant ease on such a day.'
For these things in themselves, Belovèd, may
Be changed, or change for thee—and love, so wrought,
May be unwrought so. Neither love me for
Thine own dear pity's wiping my cheeks dry—
A creature might forget to weep, who bore
Thy comfort long, and lose thy love thereby!
But love me for love's sake, that evermore
Thou may'st love on, through love's eternity.

. . .

How do I love thee? Let me count the ways.
I love thee to the depth and breadth and height
My soul can reach, when feeling out of sight
For the ends of Being and ideal Grace.

I love thee to the level of every day's
Most quiet need, by sun and candlelight.
I love thee freely, as men strive for right;
I love thee purely, as they turn from praise.
I love thee with the passion put to use
In my old griefs, and with my childhood's faith.
I love thee with a love I seemed to lose
With my lost saints—I love thee with the breath,
Smiles, tears, of all my life!—and, if God choose,
I shall but love thee better after death.

ROBERT BROWNING (1812–1889)

My Last Duchess

Scene: Ferrara

That's my last Duchess painted on the wall,
Looking as if she were alive. I call
That piece a wonder, now: Fra Pandolf's hands
Worked busily a day, and there she stands.
Will'it please you sit and look at her? I said
'Fra Pandolf' by design, for never read
Strangers like you that pictured countenance,
The depth and passion of its earnest glance,
But to myself they turned (since none puts by
The curtain I have drawn for you, but I)
And seemed as they would ask me, if they durst,
How such a glance came there; so, not the first
Are you to turn and ask thus. Sir, 'twas not
Her husband's presence only, called that spot
Of joy into the Duchess' cheek: perhaps
Fra Pandolf chanced to say 'Her mantle laps
Over my Lady's wrist too much,' or 'Paint
Must never hope to reproduce the faint
Half-flush that dies along her throat'; such stuff
Was courtesy, she thought, and cause enough
For calling up that spot of joy. She had
A heart . . . how shall I say? . . . too soon made glad,
Too easily impressed; she liked whate'er
She looked on, and her looks went everywhere.

Sir, 'twas all one! My favour at her breast,
The drooping of the daylight in the West,
The bough of cherries some officious fool
Broke in the orchard for her, the white mule
She rode with round the terrace—all and each
Would draw from her alike the approving speech,
Or blush, at least. She thanked men,—good; but thanked
Somehow . . . I know not how . . . as if she ranked
My gift of a nine hundred years old name
With anybody's gift. Who'd stoop to blame
This sort of trifling. Even had you skill
In speech—(which I have not)—to make your will
Quite clear to such an one, and say 'Just this
Or that in you disgusts me; here you miss,
Or there exceed the mark'—and if she let
Herself be lessoned so, nor plaintly set
Her wits to yours forsooth, and made excuse,
—E'en then would be some stooping, and I choose
Never to stoop. Oh, Sir, she smiled, no doubt,
Whene'er I passed her; but who passed without
Much the same smile? This grew; I gave commands;
Then all smiles stopped together. There she stands
As if alive. Will'it please you rise? We'll meet
The company below, then. I repeat,
The Count your Master's known munificence
Is ample warrant that no just pretence
Of mine for dowry will be disallowed;
Though his fair daughter's self, as I avowed
At starting, is my object. Nay, we'll go
Together down, Sir! Notice Neptune, tho',
Taming a sea-horse, thought a rarity,
Which Claus of Innsbruck cast in bronze for me.

Home-Thoughts, from Abroad

Oh, to be in England
Now that April's there,
And whoever wakes in England
Sees, some morning, unaware,
That the lowest boughs and the brushwood sheaf
Round the elm-tree bole are in tiny leaf,

While the chaffinch sings on the orchard bough
In England—now!

And after April, when May follows,
And the whitethroat builds, and all the swallows—
Hark! where my blossomed pear tree in the hedge
Leans to the field and scatters on the clover
Blossoms and dewdrops—at the bent-spray's edge—
That's the wise thrush; he sings each song twice over,
Lest you should think he never could recapture
The first fine careless rapture!
And though the fields look rough with hoary dew,
All will be gay when noontide wakes anew
The buttercups, the little children's dower,
—Far brighter than this gaudy melon-flower!

Childe Roland to the Dark Tower Came

1

My first thought was, he lied in every word,
　　That hoary cripple, with the malicious eye
　　Askance to watch the working of his lie
On mine, and mouth scarce able to afford
Suppression of the glee, that pursed and scored
　　Its edge, at one more victim gained thereby.

2

What else should he be set for, with his staff?
　　What, save to waylay with his lies, ensnare
　　All travellers who might find him posted there,
And ask the road? I guessed what skull-like laugh
Would break, what crutch 'gin write my epitaph
　　For pastime in the dusty thoroughfare,

3

If at his counsel I should turn aside
　　Into that ominous tract which, all agree,
　　Hides the Dark Tower. Yet acquiesingly
I did turn as he pointed: neither pride

Nor hope rekindling at the end described,
    So much as gladness that some end might be.

4

For, what with my whole world-wide wandering,
    What with my search drawn out through years, my hope
    Dwindled into a ghost not fit to cope
With that obstreperous joy success would bring,—
I hardly tried now to rebuke the spring
    My heart made, finding failure in its scope.

5

As when a sick man very near to death
    Seems dead indeed, and feels begin and end
    The tears and takes the farewell of each friend,
And hears one bid the other go, draw breath
Freelier outside, ('since all is o'er,' he saith,
    'And the blow fallen no grieving can amend';)

6

While some discuss if near the other graves
    Be room enough for this, and when a day
    Suits best for carrying the corpse away,
With care about the banners, scarves and staves:
And still the man hears all, and only craves
    He may not shame such tender love and stay.

7

Thus, I had so long suffered in this quest,
    Heard failure prophesied so oft, been writ
    So many times among 'The Band'—to wit,
The knights who to the Dark Tower's search addressed
Their steps—that just to fail as they, seemed best,
    And all the doubt was now—should I be fit?

8

So, quiet as despair, I turned from him,
    That hateful cripple, out of his highway
    Into the path he pointed. All the day
Had been a dreary one at best, and dim
Was settling to its close, yet shot one grim
    Red leer to see the plain catch its estray.

9

For mark! no sooner was I fairly found
    Pledged to the plain, after a pace or two,
    Than, pausing to throw backward a last view
O'er the safe road, 'twas gone; grey plain all round:
Nothing but plain to the horizon's bound.
    I might go on; naught else remained to do.

10

So, on I went. I think I never saw
    Such starved ignoble nature; nothing throve:
    For flowers—as well expect a cedar grove!
But cockle, spurge, according to their law
Might propagate their kind, with none to awe,
    You'd think; a burr had been a treasure trove.

11

No! penury, inertness and grimace,
    In some strange sort, were the land's portion. 'See
    Or shut your eyes,' said Nature peevishly,
'It nothing skills: I cannot help my case:
'Tis the Last Judgment's fire must cure this place,
    Calcine its clods and set my prisoners free.'

12

If there pushed any ragged thistle-stalk
    Above its mates, the head was chopped; the bents
    Were jealous else. What made those holes and rents
In the dock's harsh swarth leaves, bruised as to balk
All hope of greenness? 'tis a brute must walk
    Pashing their life out, with a brute's intents.

13

As for the grass, it grew as scant as hair
    In leprosy; thin dry blades pricked the mud
    Which underneath looked kneaded up with blood.
One stiff blind horse, his every bone a-stare,
Stood stupefied, however he came there:
    Thrust out past service from the devil's stud!

14

Alive? he might be dead for aught I know,
    With that red gaunt and collapsed neck a-strain,

And shut eyes underneath the rusty mane;
Seldom went such grotesqueness with such woe;
I never saw a brute I hated so;
   He must be wicked to deserve such pain.

15

I shut my eyes and turned them on my heart.
   As a man calls for wine before he fights,
   I asked one draught of earlier, happier sights,
Ere fitly I could hope to play my part.
Think first, fight afterwards—the soldier's art:
   One taste of the old time sets all to rights.

16

Not it! I fancied Cuthbert's reddening face
   Beneath its garniture of curly gold,
   Dear fellow, till I almost felt him fold
An arm in mine to fix me to the place,
That way he used. Alas, one night's disgrace!
   Out went my heart's new fire and left it cold.

17

Giles then, the soul of honour—there he stands
   Frank as ten years ago when knighted first.
   What honest man should dare (he said) he durst.
Good —but the scene shifts —faugh! what hangman-hands
Pin to his breast a parchment? His own hands
   Read it. Poor traitor, spit upon and curst!

18

Better this present than a past like that;
   Back to my darkening path again!
   No sound, no sight as far as eye could strain.
Will the night send a howlet or a bat?
I asked: when something on the dismal flat
   Came to arrest my thoughts and change their train.

19

A sudden little river crossed my path
   As unexpected as a serpent comes.
   No sluggish tide congenial to the glooms;
This, as it frothed by, might have been a bath

For the fiend's glowing hoof—to see the wrath
    Of its black eddy bespate with flakes and spumes.

20

So petty yet so spiteful! All along,
    Low scrubby alders kneeled down over it;
    Drenched willows flung themselves headlong in a fit
Of mute despair, a suicidal throng:
The river which had done them all wrong,
    Whate'er that was, rolled by, deterred no whit.

21

Which, while I forded,—good saints, how I feared
    To set my foot upon a dead man's cheek,
    Each step, or feel the spear I thrust to seek
For hollows, tangled in his hair or beard!
—It may have been a water rat I speared,
    But, ugh! it sounded like a baby's shriek.

22

Glad was I when I reached the other bank.
    Now for a better country. Vain presage!
    Who were the strugglers, what war did they wage,
Whose savage trample thus could pad the dank
Soil to a plash? Toads in a poisoned tank,
    Or wild cats in a red-hot iron cage—

23

The fight must so have seemed in that fell cirque.
    What penned them there, with all the plain to choose?
    No footprint leading to that horrid mews,
None out of it. Mad brewage set to work
Their brains, no doubt, like galley-slaves the Turk
    Pits for his pastime, Christians against Jews.

24

And more than that—a furlong on—why, there!
    What bad use was that engine for, that wheel,
    Or brake, not wheel—that harrow fit to reel
Men's bodies out like silk? with all the air
Of Tophet's tool, on earth left unaware,
    Or brought to sharpen its rusty teeth of steel.

25

Then came a bit of stubbed ground, once a wood,
    Next a marsh, it would seem, and now mere earth
    Desperate and done with; (so a fool finds mirth,
Makes a thing and then mars it, till his mood
Changes and off he goes!) within a rood—
    Bog, clay and rubble, sand and stark black dearth.

26

Now blotches rankling, coloured gay and grim,
    Now patches where some leanness of the soil's
    Broke into moss or substance like boils;
Then came some palsied oak, a cleft in him
Like a disturbed mouth that splits its rim
    Gaping at death, and dies while it recoils.

27

And just as far as ever from the end!
    Naught in the distance but the evening, naught
    To point my footstep further! At the thought,
A great black bird, Apollyon's bosom-friend,
Sailed past, nor beat his wide wing dragon-penned
    That brushed my cap—perchance the guide I sought.

28

For, looking up, aware I somehow grew,
    'Spite of the dusk, the plain had given place
    All round to mountains—with such name to grace
Mere ugly heights and heaps now stolen in view.
How thus they had surprised me,—solve it, you!
    How to get from them was no clearer case.

29

Yet half I seemed to recognize some trick
    Of mischief happened to me, God knows when—
    In a bad dream perhaps. Here ended, then,
Progress this way. When, in the very nick
Of giving up, one more time, came a click
    As when a trap shuts—you're inside the den!

30

Burningly it came on me all at once,
    This was the place! those two hills on the right,
    Crouched like two bulls locked horn in horn in fight;
While to the left, a tall scalped mountain . . . Dunce,
Dotard, a-dozing at the very nonce,
    After a life spent training for the sight!

31

What in the midst lay but the Tower itself?
    The round squat turret, blind as the fool's heart,
    Built of brown stone, without a counterpart
In the whole world. The tempest's mocking elf
Points to the shipman thus the unseen self
    He strikes on, only when the timbers start.

32

Not see? because of night perhaps?—why, day
    Came back again for that! before it left,
    The dying sunset kindled through a cleft:
The hills, like giants at a hunting, lay,
Chin upon hand, to see the game at bay,—
    'Now stab and end the creature—to the heft!'

33

Not hear? when noise was everywhere! it tolled
    Increasing like a bell. Names in my ears
    Of all the lost adventurers my peers,—
How such a one was strong, and such was bold,
And such was fortunate, yet each of old
    Lost, lost! one moment knelled the woe of years.

34

There they stood, ranged along the hill-sides, met
    To view the last of me, a living frame
    For one more picture! in a sheet of flame
I saw them and I knew them all. And yet
Dauntless the slug-horn to my lips set,
    And blew. 'Childe Roland to the Dark Tower came.'

ROBERT BURNS (1759–1796)

The Banks O' Doon

Ye flowery banks o' bonnie Doon,
  How can ye blume sae fair?
How can ye chant, ye little birds,
  And I sae fu' o' care![3]

Thou'll break my heart, thou bonnie bird,
  That sings upon the bough;
Thou minds me o' the happy days
  When my fause Luve was true.[1]

Thou'll break my heart, thou bonnie bird
  That sings beside thy mate;
For sae I sat, and sae I sang,
  And wist na o' my fate.[2]

Aft hae I roved by bonnie Doon,[3]
  To see the woodbine twine,
And ilka bird sang o' its love;[4]
  And sae did I o' mine;

Wi' lightsome heart I pu'd a rose,
  Frae aff its thorny tree;[5]
And my fause Luver staw the rose,[6]
  But left the thorn wi' me.

Mary Morison

O Mary, at thy window be,
  It is the wished, the trysted hour!
Those smiles and glances let me see,
  That make the miser's treasure poor:
How blythely wad I bide the stour,[7]
  A weary slave frae sun to sun,

---

[1] fause = false. [2] wist na = wished not. [3] aft = oft, often; hae = have. [4] ilka = each.
[5] frae aff = from off. [6] staw = stole. [7] stour = struggle.

Could I the rich reward secure,
    The lovely Mary Morison.

Yestreen, when to the trembling string
    The dance gaed thro' the lighted ha',[1]
To thee my fancy took its wing,
    I sat, but neither heard nor saw:
Tho' this was fair, and that was braw,[2]
    And yon the toast of a' the town,
I sighed, and said amang them a',
    'Ye are na Mary Morison.'

Oh, Mary, canst thou wreck his peace,
    Wha for thy sake wad gladly die?
Or canst thou break that heart of his,
    Whose only faut is loving thee?[3]
If love for love thou wilt na gie,
    At least be pity to me shown;
A thought ungentle canna be
    The thought o' Mary Morison.

To a Mouse

On turning her up in her nest with the plough

Wee, sleekit, cowrin', tim'rous beastie,[4]
O, what a panic's in thy breastie!
Thou need na start awa sae hasty,
    Wi' bickering brattle![5]
I wad be laith to rin an' chase thee[6]
    Wi' murd'ring pattle![7]

I'm truly sorry man's dominion,
Has broken nature's social union,
An' justifies that ill opinion,
    Which makes thee startle
At me, thy poor, earth-born companion,
    An' fellow-mortal!

---

[1] gaed = went. [2] braw = fine. [3] faut = fault. [4] sleekit = smooth and glossy.
[5] bickering brattle = hurrying scamper. [6] = laith = loath; rin = run.
[7] pattle = plough staff.

I doubt na, whiles, but thou may thieve;
What then? poor beastie, thou maun live![1]
A daimen icker in a thrave[2]
    'S a sma' request:
I'll get a blessin wi' the lave,[3]
    An' never miss 't!

Thy wee bit housie, too, in ruin![4]
Its silly wa's the win's are strewin!
An' naething, now, to big a new ane,[5]
    O' foggage green![6]
An' bleak December's winds ensuin,
    Baith snell an' keen![7]

Thou saw the fields laid bare an' waste,
An' weary winter comin fast,
An' cosie here, beneath the blast,
    Thou thought to dwell—
Till crash! the cruel coulter past
    Out thro' thy cell.

That wee bit heap o' leaves an' stibble[8]
Has cost thee mony a weary nibble!
Now thou's turn'd out, for a' thy trouble,
    But house or hald,[9]
To thole the winter's sleety dribble[10]
    An' cranreuch cauld![11]

But, Mousie, thou art no thy lane,[12]
In proving foresight may be vain;
The best-laid schemes o' mice an' men
    Gang aft agley,[13]
An' lea'e us nought but grief an' pain,[8]
    For promised joy!

[1] maun = must. [2] daimen icker in a thrave = an odd ear of corn in a shock of grain.
[3] lave = the rest. [4] wee bit housie = dear little house. [5] big = build. [6] foggage = moss.
[7] snell = sharp and bitter. [8] stibble = stubble.
[9] but house or hald = without house or home. [10] thole = endure; dribble = drizzle.
[11] cranreuch cauld = hoarfrost. [12] no thy lane = no the only one.
[13] gang aft agley = often go wrong. [8] lea'e = leave.

Still thou art blest, compar'd wi' me;
 The present only toucheth thee:
But, och! I backward cast me e'e,[1]
  On prospects drear!
An' forward, tho' I canna see,
  I guess an' fear!

'John Anderson, my jo'

John Anderson, my jo, John,[2]
 When we were first acquent,[3]
Your locks were like the raven,
 Your bonie brow was brent;[4]
But now your brow is bald, John,
 Your locks are like the snow;
But blessings on your frosty pow,[5]
 John Anderson, my jo.

John Anderson, my jo, John,
 We clamb the hill thegither;
And mony a cantie day, John,[6]
 We've had wi' ane anither:[7]
Now we maun totter down, John;
 But hand in hand we'll go,
And sleep thegither at the foot,
 John Anderson, my jo.

Whistle an' I'll Come to Ye, My Lad

Chorus: O whistle an' I'll come to ye, my lad,
O whistle an' I'll come to ye, my lad;
Tho' father an' mother an' a' should gae mad,[8]
O whistle an' I'll come to ye, my lad.

But warily tent when ye come to court me,[9]
And come nae unless the back-yett be a-jee;[10]
Syne up the back stile and let naebody see,[11]

---

[1] e'e = eyes. [2] jo = sweetheart. [3] acquent = acquainted. [4] brent = smooth. [5] pow = head.
[6] cantie = cheery. [7] ane anither = one another. [8] gae = go. [9] tent = take care.
[10] back yett be a-jee = back gate be ajar. [11] syne = then.

And come as ye were na comin' to me,
And come as ye were na comin' to me.
    O whistle an' I'll come . . .

At kirk, or at market, whene'er ye meet me,
Gang by me as tho' that ye car'd nae a flea;
But steal me a blink o' your bonnie black e'e,
Yet look as ye were na lookin' at me,
Yet look as ye were na lookin' at me.
    O whistle an' I'll come . . .

Aye vow and protest that ye care na for me,
And whiles ye may lightly my beauty a-wee;[1]
But court nae anither, tho' jokin ye be,
For fear that she wile your fancy frae me,
For fear that she wile your fancy frae me.
    O whistle an' I'll come . . .

Tam O' Shanter

A Tale

'Of Brownyis and of Bogillis full is this Buke.' Gawin Douglas

When chapman billies leave the street,[2]
And drouthy neibors neibors meet;[3]
As market days are wearing late,
And folk begin to tak the gate,
While we sit bousing at the nappy,[4]
An' getting fou and unco happy,[5]
We think na on the lang Scots miles,
The mosses, waters, slaps and stiles,[6]
That lie between us and our hame,
Where sits our sulky, sullen dame,
Gathering her brows like gathering storm,
Nursing her wrath to keep it warm.

    This truth fand honest Tam o' Shanter,
As he frae Ayr ae night did canter

---

[1] a-wee = awhile. [2] chapman billies = pedlars. [3] drouthy neibor = thirsty neighbour.
[4] nappy = drinking ale. [5] fou = drunk; unco = very. [6] slaps = gaps.

(Auld Ayr, wham ne'er a town surpasses,
For honest men and bonnie lasses).

O Tam! had'st thou but been sae wise
As ta'en thy ain wife Kate's advice!
She tauld thee weel thou was a skellum,[1]
A blethering, blustering, drunken blellum;[2]
That frae November till October,
Ae market-day thou was na sober;
That ilka melder wi' the Miller,[3]
Thou sat as lang as thou had siller;[4]
That every naig was ca'd a shoe on[5]
The Smith and thee gat roaring fou on;
That at the Lord's house, ev'n on Sunday,[6]
Thou drank wi' Kirkton Jean till Monday;
She prophesied that late or soon,
Thou wad be found, deep drowned in Doon,
Or catch'd wi' warlocks in the mirk,[7]
By Alloway's auld, haunted kirk.

Ah, gentle dames! it gars me greet[8]
To think how mony counsels sweet,
How mony lengthened, sage advices,
The husband frae the wife despises!

But to our tale:—Ae market night,
Tam had got planted unco right,
Fast by an ingle, bleezing finely,[9]
Wi' reaming swats that drank divinely;[10]
And at his elbow, Souter Johnie,[11]
His ancient, trusty, drouthy crony:
Tam lo'ed him like a very brither;[12]
They had been fou for weeks thegither.
The night drave on wi' sangs an' clatter;
And aye the ale was growing better:

[1] skellum = rogue. [2] blellum = blusterer. [3] melder = the oats ground at one time.
[4] siller = (silver) money. [5] every nag had a shoe driven on.
[6] Lord's house = possibly an inn kept by the two sisters Kennedy, one of them called
Kirkton Jean; ev'n = even.
[7] warlocks = male witches; mirk = dark. [8] gars me greet = makes me weep.
[9] ingle = fireside; bleezing = blazing. [10] reaming swats = foaming tankards.
[11] souter = shoemaker. [12] brither = brother.

The Landlady and Tam grew gracious,
Wi' favours secret, sweet and precious:
The Souter tauld his queerest stories;
The Landlord's laugh was ready chorus:
The storm without might rair and rustle,
Tam did na mind the storm a whistle.

Care, mad to see a man sae happy,
E'en drown'd himsel amang the nappy.
As bees flee hame wi' lades o' treasure,[1]
The minutes winged their way wi' pleasure:
Kings may be blest, but Tam was glorious,
O'er a' the ills o' life victorious!

But pleasures are like poppies spread,
You seize the flow'r, its bloom is shed;
Or like the snow falls in the river,
A moment white—then melts for ever;
Or like the borealis race,
That flit ere you can point their place;
Or like the rainbow's lovely form
Evanishing amid the storm.
Nae man can tether time nor tide,—
The hour approaches Tam maun ride;
That hour, o' night's black arch the keystane,
That dreary hour he mounts his beast in;
And sic a night he taks the road in,
As ne'er poor sinner was abroad in.

The wind blew as 'twad blawn its last;
The rattling showers rose on the blast;
The speedy gleams the darkness swallowed;
Loud, deep, and lang, the thunder bellowed:
That night, a child might understand,
The Deil had business on his hand.[2]

Weel mounted on his grey mare, Meg,
A better never lifted leg,
Tam skelpit on through dub and mire,[3]
Despising wind, and rain, and fire;

<hr>

[1] lades = loads. [2] Deil = Devil. [3] skelpit = rushed; dub = puddle.

Whiles holding fast his guid blue bonnet;
Whiles crooning o'er some auld Scots sonnet;
Whiles glowering round wi' prudent cares,
Lest bogles catch him unawares;[1]
Kirk Alloway was drawing nigh,
Where ghaists and houlets nightly cry.[2]

By this time he was cross the ford,
Whare in the snaw the chapman smoored,[3]
And past the birks and meikle stane,[4]
Whare drunken Charlie brak's neckbane;
And through the whins, and by the cairn,[5]
Whare hunters fand the murdered bairn;[6]
And near the thorn, aboon the well,
Whare Mungo's mither hanged hersel.
Before him Doon pours all his floods;
The doubling storm roars through the woods;
The lightnings flash from pole to pole;
Near and more near the thunders roll:
When, glimmering thro' the groaning trees,
Kirk-Alloway seemed in a bleeze;[7]
Through ilka bore the beams were glancing;[8]
And loud resounded mirth and dancing.

Inspiring bold John Barleycorn!
What dangers thou canst make us scorn!
Wi' tippenny, we fear nae evil;[9]
Wi' usquabae, we'll face the Devil![10]
The swats sae reamed in Tammie's noddle,[11]
Fair play, he cared na deils a boddle.[12]
But Maggie stood right sair astonished,
Till, by the heel and hand admonished,
She ventured forward on the light;
And, wow! Tam saw an unco sight!
Warlocks and witches in a dance;
Nae cotillon brent-new frae France,
But hornpipes, jigs, strathspeys, and reels,

---

[1] bogles = goblins. [2] ghaists = ghosts; houlets = owls. [3] smoored = smothered.
[4] birks = birches; meikle stane = large stone. [5] whins = gorse; cairn = marker.
[6] bairn = child. [7] bleeze = blaze. [8] ilka bore = every chink. [9] tippenny = twopenny ale.
[10] usquabae = whisky. [11] noddle = head. [12] cared na deils a boddle = cared not a farthing.

Put life and mettle in their heels.
At winnock-bunker in the east,[1]
There sat Auld Nick, in shape o' beast;[2]
A towzie tyke, black, grim, and large,[3]
To gie them music was his charge:
He screwed the pipes and gart them skirl,[4]
Till roof and rafters a' did dirl.—[5]
Coffins stood round, like open presses,[6]
That shawed the dead in their last dresses;
And by some devilish cantrip sleight,[7]
Each in its cauld hand held a light,—
By which heroic Tam was able
To note upon the haly table[8]
A murderer's banes in gibbet airns;[9]
Twa span-lang, wee, unchristened bairns;
A thief, new-cutted frae a rape,[10]
Wi' his last gasp his gab did gape;[11]
Five tomahawks, wi' blude red-rusted;
Five scimitars, wi' murder crusted;
A garter which a babe had strangled;
A knife, a father's throat had mangled,
Whom his ain son of life bereft,
The grey hairs sticking to the heft;
Wi' mair of horrible and awfu',
Which even to name wad be unlawfu'.

As Tammie glowr'd, amaz'd and curious,
The mirth and fun grew fast and furious:
The Piper loud and louder blew,
The dancers quick and quicker flew;
They reeled, they set, they crossed, they cleekit,[12]
Till ilka carlin swat and reekit,[13]
And coost her duddies to the wark,[13]
And linkit at it in her sark![14]
. . .

---

[1] winnock-bunker = window seat. [2] Auld Nick = the Devil. [3] towzie tyke = shaggy cur.
[4] gart them skirl = made them sing shrilly. [5] dirl = rattle. [6] presses = cupboards.
[7] cantrip = magic. [8] haly table = altar. [9] gibbet-airns = gallows-irons. [10] rape = rope.
[11] gab = mouth. [12] cleekit = joined hands. [13] till every old woman sweated and reeked.
[13] cast off her clothes in the excitement. [14] danced in her shirt.

But Tam kent what was what fu' brawlie;[1]
There was ae winsome wench and waulie[2]
That night enlisted in the core,[3]
Lang after ken'd on Carrick shore
(For mony a beast to dead she shot,
And perished mony a bonie boat,
And shook baith meikle corn and bear,
And kept the countryside in fear);
Her cutty sark, o' Paisley harn,[4]
That while a lassie she had worn,
In longitude tho' sorely scanty,
It was her best, and she was vauntie.[3]
Ah! little ken'd thy reverend grannie,
That sark she coft for her wee Nannie,[6]
Wi twa pund Scots ('twas a' her riches),
Wad ever graced a dance of witches!

But here my Muse her wing maun cour.[7]
Sic flights are far beyond her power;
To sing how Nannie lap and flang[8]
(A souple jade she was and strang).
And how Tam stood, like ane bewitched,
And thought his very een enriched:
Even Satan glowr'd, and fidg'd fu' fain,[9]
And hotched and blew wi' might and main:[10]
Till first ae caper, syne anither,
Tam tint his reason a' thegither,[11]
And roars out, 'Weel done, Cutty-sark!'
And in an instant all was dark:
And scarcely had he Maggie rallied,
When out the hellish legion sallied.

As bees bizz out wi' angry fyke,[12]
When plundering herds assail their byke;[14]
As open pussie's mortal foes,[15]
When, pop! she starts before their nose;

---

[1] kent = knew; brawlie = fine. [2] waulie = jolly. [3] core = corps, company.
[4] cutty sark = short shirt; harn = linen. [5] vauntie = vain, proud of it. [6] coft = bought.
[7] maun cour = must cover. [8] lap = leapt; flang = flung.
[9] fidged fu' fain = fidgeted eagerly. [10] hotched = squirmed. [11] tint = lost.
[12] bizz = buzz; fyke = fuss. [13] byke = hive. [15] pussie's = hare's.

As eager runs the market crowd,
When 'Catch the thief!' resounds aloud;
So Maggie runs, the witches follow,
Wi' mony an eldritch skreich and hollo.[1]

Ah, Tam! Ah, Tam! thou'll get thy fairin![2]
In hell they'll roast thee like a herrin!
In vain thy Kate awaits thy comin!
Kate soon will be a woefu' woman!
Now, do thy speedy-utmost, Meg,
And win the keystane o' the brig[3]
There, at them thou thy tail may toss,
A running stream they dare na cross;
But ere the keystane she could make,
The fiend a tail she had to shake!
For Nannie, far before the rest,
Hard upon noble Maggie prest,
And flew at Tam wi' furious ettle;[4]
But little wist she Maggie's mettle![5]
Ae spring brought off her master hale,[6]
But left behind her ain grey tail:
The carlin claught her by the rump.
And left poor Maggie scarce a stump.

Now, wha this tale o' truth shall read,
Ilk' man and mother's son, take heed,
Whene'er to drink you are inclined,
Or cutty-sarks run in your mind,
Think, ye may buy the joys o'er dear,
Remember Tam o' Shanter's mare!

Sweet Afton

Flow gently, sweet Afton! among thy green braes,
Flow gently, I'll sing thee a song in thy praise;
My Mary's asleep by thy murmuring stream,
Flow gently, sweet Afton, disturb not her dream!

[1] eldritch skreich = unearthly scream. [2] fairin = reward. [3] brig = bridge. [4] ettle = intent.
[5] wist = knew. [6] hale = whole.

Thou stock dove whose echo resounds thro' the glen,
Ye wild whistling blackbirds in yon thorny den,
Thou green crested lapwing, thy screaming forbear,
I charge you, disturb not my slumbering Fair.

How lofty, sweet Afton, thy neighbouring hills,
Far marked with the courses of clear, winding rills;
There daily I wander as noon rises high,
My flocks and my Mary's sweet cot in my eye.

How pleasant thy banks and green valleys below,
Where, wild in the woodlands, the primroses blow;
There oft, as mild ev'ning weeps over the lea,
The sweet-scented birk shades my Mary and me.

Thy crystal stream, Afton, how lovely it glides,
And winds by the cot where my Mary resides;
How wanton thy waters her snowy feet lave,
As, gathering sweet flowerets she stems thy clear wave.

Flow gently, sweet Afton, among thy green braes,
Flow gently, sweet river, the theme of my lays;
My Mary's asleep by thy murmuring stream,
Flow gently, sweet Afton, disturb not her dream.

Bruce's March to Bannockburn

Scots, wha hae wi' Wallace bled,
Scots, wham Bruce has aften led,
Welcome to your gory bed,
  Or to victorie!

Now's the day, and now's the hour;
See the front o' battle lour:
See approach proud Edward's pow'r—
  Chains and slaverie!

Wha will be a traitor knave?
Wha can fill a coward's grave?

Wha sae base as be a slave?
　　Let him turn and flee!

Wha, for Scotland's King and Law,
Freedom's sword will strongly draw,
Free-man stand, or Free-man fa',
　　Let him on wi' me!

By oppression's woes and pains!
By your sons in servile chains!
We will drain our dearest veins,
　　But they shall be free!

Lay the proud usurpers low!
Tyrants fall in every foe!
Liberty's in every blow!—
　　Let us do or die!

My Luve

O my Luve is like a red, red rose
　　That's newly sprung in June:
O my Luve is like the melodie,
　　That's sweetly play'd in tune.

As fair art thou, my bonie lass,
　　So deep in luve am I;
And I will luve thee still, my dear,
　　Till a' the seas gang dry.

Till a' the seas gang dry, my dear,
　　And the rocks melt wi' the sun;
I will luve thee still, my dear,
　　While the sands o' life shall run.

And fare thee weel, my only Luve!
　　And fare thee weel awhile!
And I will come again, my Luve,
　　Tho' it were ten thousand mile.

'O wert thou in the cauld blast

O wert thou in the cauld blast,
   On yonder lea, on yonder lea,
My plaidie to the angry airt,[1]
   I'd shelter thee, I'd shelter thee.
Or did misfortune's bitter storms
   Around thee blaw, around thee blaw,
Thy bield should be my bosom,[2]
   To share it a', to share it a'!

O were I in the wildest waste,
   Sae black and bare, sae black and bare,
The desert were a Paradise,
   If thou wert there, if thou wert there;
Or were I monarch o' the globe,
   Wi' thee to reign, wi' thee to reign,
The brightest jewel in my crown
   Wad be my queen, wad be my queen!

GEORGE GORDON, LORD BYRON (1788–1824)

'She walks in beauty'

(from 'Hebrew Melodies')

She walks in beauty, like the night
Of cloudless climes and starry skies,
And all that's best of dark and bright
Meet in her aspect and her eyes;
Thus mellowed to that tender light
Which heaven to gaudy day denies.

One shade the more, one ray the less,
Had half impaired the nameless grace
Which waves in every raven tress
Or softly lightens o'er her face;

[1] plaidie = shawl; airt = wind. [2] bield = shelter.

Where thoughts serenely sweet express
How pure, how dear their dwelling-place.

And on that cheek, and o'er that brow,
So soft, so calm, yet eloquent,
The smiles that win, the tints that glow
But tell of days in goodness spent,
A mind at peace with all below,
A heart whose love is innocent!

'When we two parted'

When we two parted
In silence and tears,
Half broken-hearted,
To sever for years,
Pale grew thy cheek and cold,
Colder thy kiss;
Truly that hour foretold
Sorrow to this!

The dew of the morning
Sunk chill on my brow;
It felt like the warning
Of what I feel now.
Thy vows are all broken,
And light is thy fame:
I hear thy name spoken
And share in its shame.

They name thee before me,
A knell to mine ear;
A shudder comes o'er me—
Why wert thou so dear?
They know not I knew thee
Who knew thee too well:
Long, long shall I rue thee
Too deeply to tell.

In secret we met:
In silence I grieve

That thy heart could forget,
Thy spirit deceive.
If I should meet thee
After long years,
How should I greet thee?—
With silence and tears.

We'll Go No More A-roving

So, we'll go no more a–roving
     So late into the night,
Though the heart be still as loving,
     And the moon be still as bright.

For the sword outwears its sheath,
     And the soul wears out the breast,
And the heart must pause to breathe,
     And love itself have rest.

Though the night was made for loving,
     And the day returns too soon,
Yet we'll go no more a–roving
     By the light of the moon.

The Destruction of Sennacherib

The Assyrian came down like the wolf on the fold,
And his cohorts were gleaming in purple and gold;
And the sheen of their spears was like stars on the sea,
When the blue wave rolls nightly on deep Galilee.

Like the leaves of the forest when summer is green,
That host with their banners at sunset were seen:
Like the leaves of the forest when autumn hath blown,
That host on the morrow lay withered and strown.

For the Angel of Death spread his wings on the blast,
And breathed in the face of the foe as he passed;
And the eyes of the sleepers waxed deadly and chill,
And their hearts but once heaved, and for ever grew still!

And there lay the steed with his nostril all wide,
But through it there rolled not the breath of his pride:
And the foam of his gasping lay white on the turf,
And cold as the spray of the rock-beating surf.

And there lay the rider distorted and pale,
With the dew on his brow, and the rust on his mail,
And the tents were all silent, the banners alone,
The lances unlifted, the trumpet unblown.

And the widows of Ashur are loud in their wail,
And the idols are broke in the temple of Baal;
And the might of the Gentile, unsmote by the sword,
Hath melted like snow in the glance of the Lord!

Waterloo

(from 'Childe Harold's Pilgrimage', Canto 3)

There was a sound of revelry by night,
And Belgium's capital had gathered then
Her beauty and her chivalry, and bright
The lamps shone o'er fair women and brave men;
A thousand hearts beat happily; and when
Music arose with its voluptuous swell,
Soft eyes looked love to eyes which spake again,
And all went merry as a marriage bell;
But hush! hark! a deep sound strikes like a rising knell!

Did ye not hear it?—No; 'twas but the wind,
Or the car rattling o'er the stony street;
On with the dance! let joy be unconfined;
No sleep till morn, when Youth and Pleasure meet
To chase the glowing Hours with flying feet.—
But hark! that heavy sound breaks in once more,
As if the clouds its echo would repeat;
And nearer, clearer, deadlier than before!
Arm! Arm! it is—it is—the cannon's opening roar!

Within a windowed niche of that high hall
Sate Brunswick's fated chieftain; he did hear
That sound the first amidst the festival,
And caught its tone with Death's prophetic ear,
And when they smiled because he deemed it near,
His heart more truly knew that peal too well
Which stretched his father on a bloody bier,
And roused the vengeance blood alone could quell.
He rushed into the field, and, foremost fighting, fell.

Ah! then and there was hurrying to and fro,
And gathering tears, and tremblings of distress,
And cheeks all pale, which but an hour ago
Blushed at the praise of their own loveliness;
And there were sudden partings, such as press
The life from out young hearts, and choking sighs
Which ne'er might be repeated: who could guess
If ever more should meet those mutual eyes,
Since upon night so sweet such awful morn could rise!

And there was mounting in hot haste: the steed,
The mustering squadron, and the clattering car,
Went pouring forward with impetuous speed,
And swiftly forming in the ranks of war;
And the deep thunder peal on peal afar;
And near, the beat of the alarming drum
Roused up the soldier ere the morning star;
While thronged the citizens with terror dumb,
Or whispering, with white lips—'The foe! they come! they come!'

And wild and high the 'Cameron's Gathering' rose!
The war-note of Lochiel, which Albyn's hills
Have heard, and heard, too, have her Saxon foes:
How in the noon of night that pibroch thrills
Savage and shrill! But with the breath which fills
Their mountain-pipe, so fill the mountaineers
With the fierce native daring which instils
The stirring memory of a thousand years,
And Evan's, Donald's fame rings in each clansman's ears!

And Ardennes waves above them her green leaves,
Dewy with Nature's tear-drops, as they pass,
Grieving, if aught inanimate e'er grieves,
Over the unreturning brave—alas!
Ere evening to be trodden like the grass
Which now beneath them, but above shall grow
In its next verdure, when this fiery mass
Of living valour, rolling on the foe,
And burning with high hope, shall moulder cold and low.

Last noon beheld them full of lusty life,
Last eve in Beauty's circle proudly gay,
The midnight brought the signal-sound of strife,
The morn the marshalling arms, the day
Battle's magnificently stern array!
The thunder-clouds close o'er it, which when rent
The earth is covered thick with other clay,
Which her own clay shall cover, heaped and pent,
Rider and horse—friend, foe—in one red burial blent!

from Don Juan

from Canto the First

1

I want a hero: an uncommon want,
    When every year and month sends forth a new one,
Till, after cloying the gazettes with cant,
    The age discovers he is not the true one;
Of such as these I should not care to vaunt,
    I'll therefore take our ancient friend Don Juan—
We all have seen him, in the pantomime,
    Sent to the devil somewhat ere his time.

2

Vernon, the butcher Cumberland, Wolfe, Hawke,
    Prince Ferdinand, Granby, Burgoyne, Keppel, Howe,
Evil and good, have had their tithe of talk,
    And filled their signposts then, like Wellesley now;
Each in their turn like Banquo's monarchs stalk,
    Followers of fame, 'nine farrow' of that sow:

France, too, had Buonaparté and Dumourier
    Recorded in the Moniteur and Courier.

3

Barnave, Brissot, Condorcet, Mirabeau,
    Petion, Clootz, Danton, Marat, La Fayette,
Were French, and famous people, as we know:
    And there were others, scarce forgotten yet,
Joubert, Hoche, Marceau, Lannes, Desaix, Moreau,
    With many of the military set,
Exceedingly remarkable at times,
    But not at all adapted to my rhymes.

4

Nelson was once Britannia's god of war,
    And still should be so, but the tide is turned;
There's no more to be said of Trafalgar,
    'Tis with our hero quietly inurned;
Because the army's grown more popular,
    At which the naval people are concerned;
Besides, the prince is all for the land-service,
    Forgetting Duncan, Nelson, Howe, and Jervis.

5

Brave men were living before Agamemnon
    And since, exceeding valorous and sage,
A good deal like him too, though quite the same none;
    But then they shone not on the poet's page,
And so have been forgotten:—I condemn none,
    But can't find any in the present age
Fit for my poem (that is, for my new one);
    So, as I said, I'll take my friend Don Juan.

6

Most epic poets plunge 'in medias res'
    (Horace makes this the heroic turnpike road),
And then your hero tells, whene'er you please,
    What went before—by way of episode,
While seated after dinner at his ease,
    Beside his mistress in some soft abode,
Palace, or garden, paradise, or cavern,
    Which serves the happy couple for a tavern.

7

That is the usual method, but not mine—
　　My way is to begin with the beginning;
The regularity of my design
　　Forbids all wandering as the worst of sinning,
And therefore I shall open with a line
　　(Although it cost me half an hour in spinning)
Narrating somewhat of Don Juan's father,
　　And also of his mother, if you'd rather.

8

In Seville was he born, a pleasant city,
　　Famous for oranges and women—he
Who has not seen it will be much to pity,
　　So says the proverb—and I quite agree;
Of all the Spanish towns is none more pretty,
　　Cadiz perhaps—but that you soon may see;
Don Juan's parents lived beside the river,
　　A noble stream, and called the Guadalquivir.

9

His father's name was Jóse—Don, of course,—
　　A true Hidalgo, free from every stain
Of Moor or Hebrew blood, he traced his source
　　Through the most Gothic gentlemen of Spain;
A better cavalier ne'er mounted horse,
　　Or, being mounted, e'er got down again,
Than José, who begot our hero, who
　　Begot—but that's to come—Well, to renew:

10

His mother was a learnèd lady, famed
　　For every branch of every science known
In every Christian language ever named,
　　With virtues equalled by her wit alone,
She made the cleverest people quite ashamed,
　　And even the good with inward envy groan,
Finding themselves so very much exceeded
　　In their own way by all the things that she did.

11

Her memory was a mine: she knew by heart
　　All Calderón and greater part of Lopé,

So that if any actor missed his part
    She could have served him for the prompter's copy;
For her Feinagle's were an useless art,
    And he himself obliged to shut up shop—he
Could never make a memory so fine as
    That which adorned the brain of Donna Inez.

12

Her favourite science was the mathematical,
    Her noblest virtue was her magnanimity,
Her wit (she sometimes tried at wit) was Attic all,
    Her serious sayings darkened to sublimity;
In short, in all things she was fairly what I call
    A prodigy—her morning dress was dimity,
Her evening silk, or, in the summer, muslin,
    And other stuffs, with which I won't stay puzzling.

13

She knew the Latin—that is, 'the Lord's prayer',
    And Greek—the alphabet—I'm nearly sure;
She read some French romances here and there,
    Although her mode of speaking was not pure;
For native Spanish she had no great care,
    At least her conversation was obscure;
Her thoughts were theorems, her words a problem,
    As if she deemed that mystery would ennoble 'em.

14

She liked the English and the Hebrew tongue,
    And said there was analogy between 'em;
She proved it somehow out of sacred song,
    But I must leave the proofs to those who've seen 'em;
But this I heard her say, and can't be wrong
    And all may think which way their judgments lean 'em,
''Tis strange—the Hebrew noun which means "I am",
    The English always used to govern d——n.'

15

Some women use their tongues—she looked a lecture,
    Each eye a sermon, and her brow a homily,
An all-in-all sufficient self-director,
    Like the lamented late Sir Samuel Romilly

The Law's expounder, and the State's corrector,
    Whose suicide was almost an anomaly—
One sad example more, that 'All is vanity'
    (The jury brought their verdict in 'Insanity').

16

In short, she was a walking calculation,
    Miss Edgeworth's novels stepping from their covers,
Or Mrs Trimmer's books on education,
    Or 'Coelebs' Wife' set out in quest of lovers,
Morality's prim personification,
    In which not Envy's self a flaw discovers;
To others' share let 'female errors fall',
    For she had not even one—the worst of all.

17

Oh! she was perfect past all parallel—
    Of any modern female saint's comparison;
So far above the cunning powers of hell,
    Her guardian angel had given up his garrison;
Even her minutest motions went as well
    As those of the best timepiece made by Harrison:
In virtues nothing earthly could surpass her,
    Save thine 'incomparable oil', Macassar!

. . .

194

'Man's love is of man's life a thing apart,
    'Tis woman's whole existence; man may range
The court, camp, church, the vessel, and the mart;
    Sword, gown, gain, glory, offer in exchange
Pride, fame, ambition, to fill up his heart,
    And few there are whom these cannot estrange;
Men have all these resources, we but one,
    To love again, and be again undone.

195

'You will proceed in pleasure, and in pride,
    Beloved and loving many; all is o'er
For me on earth, except some years to hide
    My shame and sorrow deep in my heart's core;
These I could bear, but cannot cast aside
    The passion which still rages as before—

And so farewell—forgive me, love me—No,
  That word is idle now—but let it go.

196

'My breast has been all weakness, is so yet;
  But still I think I can collect my mind;
My blood still rushes where my spirit's set,
  As roll the waves before the settled wind;
My heart is feminine, nor can forget—
  To all, except one image, madly blind;
So shakes the needle, and so stands the pole,
  As vibrates my fond heart to my fixed soul.

197

'I have no more to say, but linger still,
  And dare not set my seal upon this sheet,
And yet I may as well the task fulfil,
  My misery can scarce be more complete:
I had not lived till now, could sorrow kill;
  Death shuns the wretch who fain the blow would meet,
And I must even survive this last adieu,
  And bear with life, to love and pray for you!'

198

This note was written upon gilt-edged paper
  With a neat little crow-quill, slight and new:
Her small white hand could hardly reach the taper,
  It trembled as magnetic needles do,
And yet she did not let one tear escape her;
  The seal a sunflower; 'Elle vous suit partout,'
The motto cut upon a white cornelian;
  The wax was superfine, its hue vermilion.

199

This was Don Juan's earliest scrape; but whether
  I shall proceed with his adventures is
Dependent on the public altogether;
  We'll see, however, what they say to this:
Their favour in an author's cap's a feather,
  And no great mischief's done by their caprice;
And if their approbation we experience,
  Perhaps they'll have some more about a year hence.

200

My poem's epic, and is meant to be
   Divided in twelve books; each book containing,
With love, and war, a heavy gale at sea,
   A list of ships, and captains, and kings reigning,
New characters; the episodes are three:
   A panoramic view of hell's in training,
After the style of Virgil and of Homer,
   So that my name of Epic's no misnomer.

201

All these things will be specified in time,
   With strict regard to Aristotle's rules,
The Vade Mecum of the true sublime,
   Which makes so many poets, and some fools:
Prose poets like blank-verse, I'm fond of rhyme,
   Good workmen never quarrel with their tools;
I've got new mythological machinery,
   And very handsome supernatural scenery.

202

There's only one slight difference between
   Me and my epic brethren gone before,
And here the advantage is my own, I ween
   (Not that I have not several merits more,
But this will more peculiarly be seen);
   They so embellish, that 'tis quite a bore
Their labyrinth of fables to thread through,
   Whereas this story's actually true.

203

If any person doubt it, I appeal
   To history, tradition, and to facts,
To newspapers, whose truth all know and feel,
   To plays in five, and operas in three acts;
All these confirm my statement a good deal,
   But that which more completely faith exacts
Is that myself, and several now in Seville,
   Saw Juan's last elopement with the devil.

204

If ever I should condescend to prose,
   I'll write poetical commandments, which

Shall supersede beyond all doubt all those
    That went before; in these I shall enrich
My text with many things that no one knows,
    And carry precept to the highest pitch:
I'll call the work 'Longinus o'er a Bottle,
    Or, Every Poet his own Aristotle.'

205

Thou shalt believe in Milton, Dryden, Pope;
    Thou shalt not set up Wordsworth, Coleridge, Southey;
Because the first is crazed beyond all hope,
    The second drunk, the third so quaint and mouthy:
With Crabbe it may be difficult to cope,
    And Campbell's Hippocrene is somewhat drouthy:
Thou shalt not steal from Samuel Rogers, nor
    Commit—flirtation with the muse of Moore.

206

Thou shalt not covet Mr Sotheby's Muse,
    His Pegasus, nor anything that's his;
Thou shalt not bear false witness like 'the Blues'
    (There's one, at least, is very fond of this);
Thou shalt not write, in short, but what I choose:
    This is true criticism, and you may kiss—
Exactly as you please, or not,—the rod;
    But if you don't, I'll lay it on, by G—d!

207

If any person should presume to assert
    This story is not moral, first, I pray,
That they will not cry out before they're hurt,
    Then that they'll read it o'er again, and say
(But, doubtless, nobody will be so pert)
    That this is not a moral tale, though gay;
Besides, in Canto Twelfth, I mean to show
    The very place where wicked people go.

. . .

221

But for the present, gentle reader! and
    Still gentler purchaser! the bard—that's I—
Must, with permission, shake you by the hand,
    And so your humble servant, and goodbye!

We meet again, if we should understand
    Each other; and if not, I shall not try
Your patience further than by this short sample—
    'Twere well if others followed my example.

222

'Go, little book, from this my solitude!
    I cast thee on the waters—go thy ways!
And if, as I believe, thy vein be good,
    The world will find thee after many days.'
When Southey's read, and Wordsworth understood,
    I can't help putting in my claim to praise—
The four first rhymes are Southey's, every line:
    For God's sake, reader, take them not for mine!

ROY CAMPBELL (1901–1957)

The Zulu Girl

When in the sun the hot red acres smoulder,
Down where the sweating gang its labour plies,
A girl flings down her hoe, and from her shoulder
Unslings her child tormented by the flies.

She takes him to a ring of shadow pooled
By thorn trees: purpled with the blood of ticks,
While her sharp nails, in slow caresses ruled,
Prowl through his hair with sharp electric clicks,

His sleepy mouth plugged by the heavy nipple,
Tugs like a puppy, grunting as he feeds:
Through his frail nerves her own deep langours ripple
Like a broad river sighing through its reeds.

Yet in that drowsy stream his flesh imbibes
An old unquenched unsmotherable heat—
The curbed ferocity of beaten tribes,
The sullen dignity of their defeat.

Her body looms above him like a hill
Within whose shade a village lies at rest,
Or the first cloud so terrible and still
That bears the coming harvest in its breast.

THOMAS CAMPION (1567–1620)

'There is a garden in her face'

There is a garden in her face
Where roses and white lilies grow;
   A heav'nly paradise is that place,
Wherein all pleasant fruits do flow.
   There cherries grow which none may buy,
   Till 'cherry-ripe' themselves do cry.

Those cherries fairly do enclose
Of orient pearls a double row,
   Which when her lovely laughter shows,
They look like rosebuds filled with snow;
   Yet them nor peer nor prince can buy,
   Till 'cherry-ripe' themselves do cry.

Her eyes like angels watch them still;
Her brows like bended bows do stand,
   Threat'ning with piercing frowns to kill
All that attempt with eye or hand
   Those sacred cherries to come nigh,
Till 'cherry-ripe' themselves do cry.

'Rose-cheeked Laura'

Rose-cheeked Laura, come,
Sing thou smoothly with thy beauty's
Silent music, either other
      Sweetly gracing.

Lovely forms do flow
From concent divinely framèd;[1]
Heav'n is music, and thy beauty's
      Birth is heavenly.

These dull notes we sing
Discords need for helps to grace them;

---

[1] concent = harmony.

Only beauty purely loving
Knows no discord,

But still moves delight,
Like clear springs renewed by flowing,
Ever perfect, ever in them-
Selves eternal.

It Shall Suffice

Follow your saint, follow with accents sweet!
Haste you, sad notes, fall at her flying feet!
There, wrapped in clouds of sorrow, pity move,
And tell the ravisher of my soul I perish for her love:
But, if she scorns my never-ceasing pain,
Then burst with sighing in her sight and ne'er return again.

All that I sang still to her praise did tend,
Still she was first, still she my songs did end;
Yet she my love and music both doth fly,
The music that her echo is and beauty's sympathy.
Then let my notes pursue her scornful flight!
It shall suffice that they were breathed and died for her delight.

LEWIS CARROLL (1832–1898)

Father William

'You are old, Father William,' the young man said,
    'And your hair has become very white;
And yet you incessantly stand on your head—
    Do you think, at your age, it is right?'

'In my youth,' Father William replied to his son,
    'I feared it might injure the brain;
But, now that I'm perfectly sure I have none,
    Why, I do it again and again.'

'You are old,' said the youth, 'as I mentioned before,
    And have grown most uncommonly fat;

Yet you turned a back-somersault in at the door—
    Pray, what is the reason of that?'

'In my youth,' said the sage, as he shook his grey locks,
    'I kept all my limbs very supple
By the use of this ointment—one shilling the box—
    Allow me to sell you a couple?'

'You are old,' said the youth, 'and your jaws are too weak
    For anything tougher than suet;
Yet you finished the goose, with the bones and the beak—
    Pray, how did you manage to do it?'

'In my youth,' said his father, 'I took to the law,
    And argued each case with my wife;
And the muscular strength which it gave to my jaw
    Has lasted the rest of my life.'

'You are old,' said the youth, 'one would hardly suppose
    That your eye was as steady as ever;
Yet you balanced an eel on the end of your nose—
    What made you so awfully clever?'

'I have answered three questions, and that is enough,'
    Said his father. 'Don't give yourself airs!
Do you think I can listen all day to such stuff?
    Be off, or I'll kick you downstairs!'

Jabberwocky

'Twas brillig, and the slithy toves
    Did gyre and gimble in the wabe:
All mimsy were the borogoves,
    And the mome raths outgrabe.

'Beward the Jabberwock, my son!
    The jaws that bite, the claws that catch!
Beward the Jubjub bird, and shun
    The frumious Bandersnatch!'

He took his vorpal sword in hand;
    Long time the manxome foe he sought—

So rested he by the Tumtum tree,
    And stood awhile in thought.

And, as in uffish thought he stood,
    The Jabberwock, with eyes of flame,
Came whiffling through the tulgey wood,
    And burbled as it came!

One, two! One, two! And through and through
    The vorpal blade went snicker-snack!
He left it dead, and with its head
    He went galumphing back.

'And hast thou slain the Jabberwock?
    Come to my arms, my beamish boy!
O frabjous day! Callooh, Callay!'
    He chortled in his joy.

'Twas brillig, and the slithy toves
    Did gyre and gimble in the wabe:
All mimsy were the borogoves,
    And the mome raths outgrabe.

The Walrus and the Carpenter

'The sun was shining on the sea,
    Shining with all his might:
He did his very best to make
    The billows smooth and bright—
And this was odd, because it was
    The middle of the night.

The moon was shining sulkily,
    Because she thought the sun
Had got no business to be there
    After the day was done—
"It's very rude of him," she said,
    "To come and spoil the fun!"

The sea was wet as wet could be,
    The sands were dry as dry.

You could not see a cloud, because
　　No cloud was in the sky:
No birds were flying over head—
　　There were no birds to fly.

The Walrus and the Carpenter
　　Were walking close at hand;
They wept like anything to see
　　Such quantities of sand:
"If this were only cleared away,"
　　They said, "it *would* be grand!"

"If seven maids with seven mops
　　Swept it for half a year,
Do you suppose," the Walrus said,
　　"That they could get it clear?"
"I doubt it," said the Carpenter,
　　And shed a bitter tear.

"O Oysters, come and walk with us!"
　　The Walrus did beseech.
"A pleasant walk, a pleasant talk,
　　Along the briny beach:
We cannot do with more than four,
　　To give a hand to each."

The eldest Oyster looked at him.
　　But never a word he said:
The eldest Oyster winked his eye,
　　And shook his heavy head—
Meaning to say he did not choose
　　To leave the oyster-bed.

But four young oysters hurried up,
　　All eager for the treat:
Their coats were brushed, their faces washed,
　　Their shoes were clean and neat—
And this was odd, because, you know,
　　They hadn't any feet.

Four other Oysters followed them,
　　And yet another four;

And thick and fast they came at last,
    And more, and more, and more—
All hopping through the frothy waves,
    And scrambling to the shore.

The Walrus and the Carpenter
    Walked on a mile or so,
And then they rested on a rock
    Conveniently low:
And all the little Oysters stood
    And waited in a row.

"The time has come," the Walrus said,
    "To talk of many things:
Of shoes—and ships—and sealing-wax—
    Of cabbages—and kings—
And why the sea is boiling hot—
    And whether pigs have wings."

"But wait a bit," the Oysters cried,
    "Before we have our chat;
For some of us are out of breath,
    And all of us are fat!"
"No hurry!" said the Carpenter.
    They thanked him much for that.

"A loaf of bread," the Walrus said,
    "Is what we chiefly need:
Pepper and vinegar besides
    Are very good indeed—
Now if you're ready Oysters dear,
    We can begin to feed."

"But not on us!" the Oysters cried,
    Turning a little blue,
"After such kindness, that would be
    A dismal thing to do!"
"The night is fine," the Walrus said
    "Do you admire the view?

"It was so kind of you to come!
    And you are very nice!"

The Carpenter said nothing but
  "Cut us another slice:
I wish you were not quite so deaf—
  I've had to ask you twice!"

"It seems a shame," the Walrus said,
  "To play them such a trick,
After we've brought them out so far,
  And made them trot so quick!"
The Carpenter said nothing but
  "The butter's spread too thick!"

"I weep for you," the Walrus said.
  "I deeply sympathize."
With sobs and tears he sorted out
  Those of the largest size.
Holding his pocket handkerchief
  Before his streaming eyes.

"O Oysters," said the Carpenter.
  "You've had a pleasant run!
Shall we be trotting home again?"
  But answer came there none—
And that was scarcely odd, because
  They'd eaten every one.'

GEOFFREY CHAUCER (1340?–1400)

Three Pilgrims

(from 'The Canterbury Tales')
A Knight

A Knight there was, and that a worthy man,
Who, from the moment when he first began
To ride forth, loved the code of chivalry:
Honour and truth, freedom and courtesy.
His lord's war had established him in worth;
He rode—and no man farther—ends of earth,
In heathen parts as well as Christendom,

Honoured wherever he might go or come. . . .
Of mortal battles he had seen fifteen,
And fought hard for our faith at Tramassene
Thrice in the lists, and always slain his foe.
This same worthy knight was even led to go
To Turkey where he fought most valiantly
Against the heathen hordes for Palaty.
Renowned he was; and, worthy, he was wise—
Prudence, with him, was more than mere disguise;
He was as meek in manner as a maid,
Vileness he shunned, rudeness he never said
In all his life, treating all persons right.
He was a very perfect, gentle knight.

A Prioress

There also was a nun, a Prioress,
Whose smile was full simple, quiet, even coy.
The only oath she swore was, 'By Saint Loy!'[1]
And she was called Sister Eglantine.
Full well she sang the services divine,
Intoning through her nose the melody.
And French she spake full fair and skilfully,
After the school of Stratford at-the-Bow,[2]
For French of Paris was not to her to know.
Precise at table and well-bred withal,
Her lips would never let a morsel fall;
She never wet her fingers in her sauce,
But carried every titbit without loss
Of even the smallest drop upon her breast.
Manners and good behaviour pleased her best.
She always wiped her upper lip so clean
That not a speck of grease was ever seen
Upon the cup from which she drank. Her food
Was reached for neatly; she was never rude.
Though her demeanour was the very best,
Her mood was amiable, she loved a jest,
She always tried to copy each report

---

[1] Saint Loy, or Saint Eligius, was not only the most fashionable but the mildest saints of
Chaucer's day. Thus the Prioress, when she swore at all, swore in the best and most
genteel tradition.
[2] A convent near London.

Of how the latest fashion ran at court,
And yet to hold herself with dignity.
But, speaking of her inner nature, she
Was so soft-hearted that she could not see
A mouse caught in a trap, if it had bled.
A few small dogs had she, and these she fed
With roasted flesh, and milk, and sweetened bread,
And she wept loud if one of them were dead,
Or if a person struck and made them smart—
She was all goodness and a tender heart.
Her wimple draped itself a modest way;
Her nose was straight, her eyes transparent grey,
Her mouth was small, but very soft and red;
Hers was a noble and a fair forehead,
Almost a span in breadth, one realised;
For she was small but scarcely undersized.
Her cloak was well designed, I was aware;
Her arm was graced with corals, and she bare
A string in which the green glass beads were bold,
And from it hung a brilliant brooch of gold
On which there was engraved a large, crowned *A*,
And after, *Amor vincit omnia.* . . .

A Wife of Bath

There was a wife from Bath, a well-appearing
Woman who was (alas!) quite hard of hearing.
She had such skill in making cloth that all
The weavers' guilds of Ypres and Ghent looked small.
In all the parish, not a soul dared offer
A thing to her, or, if they did, they'd suffer—
So loud she railed, so full of wrath was she
That she would lose all sense of charity.
The kerchiefs that she used were finely wound—
I'd take an oath they weighed above ten pound—
Which, of a Sunday, were upon her head.
Her stockings were the finest scarlet-red,
Tightly held up; her shoes were soft and new.
Bold was her face, and fair, and red of hue.
She was a worthy woman all her life;
She'd had five church-door husbands as a wife,
And others in her youth whom she'd allow—

But there's no need to mention such things now.
Thrice had she visited Jerusalem;
And she had crossed o'er many a foreign stream.
She'd been at Rome, she'd journeyed to Bologne,
To Saint James' in Galicia, to Cologne.
She'd gathered much from wandering by the way.
She was gap-toothed and loose-tongued, truth to say.
Upon an ambling mare she easily sat,
Her face half-veiled, and on her head a hat
Broad as a buckler, broader than a shield.
A mantle fell about her, but revealed
Large hips and feet equipped with sharpened spurs.
In company the laugh was always hers.
The remedies for love she knew, perchance—
She knew the the art of dancing that old dance.

JOHN CLARE (1793–1864)

Written in Northampton County Asylum

I am! yet what I am none cares, or knows?
　　My friends forsake me like a memory lost.
I am the self-consumer of my woes;
　　They rise and vanish, in oblivious host,
Shadows of life, whose very soul is lost.
And yet I am—I live—though I am tossed

Into the nothingness of scorn and noise,
　　Into the living sea of waking dream,
Where there is neither sense of life, nor joys,
　　But the huge shipwreck of my own esteem
And all that's dear. Even those I loved the best
Are strange—nay, they are stranger than the rest.

I long for scenes where man has never trod—
　　For scenes where woman never smil'd or wept—
There to abide with my Creator, God,
　　And sleep as I in childhood sweetly slept,
Full of high thoughts, unborn. So let me lie,—
The grass below; above, the vaulted sky.

'I lost the love of heaven'

I lost the love of heaven above,
　　I spurned the lust of earth below,
I felt the sweets of fancied love.
　　And hell itself my only foe.

I lost earth's joys, but felt the glow
　　Of heaven's flame abound in me,
Till loveliness and I did grow
　　The bard of immortality.

I loved, but woman fell away;
　　I hid me from her faded flame.
I snatched the sun's eternal ray
　　And wrote till earth was but a name.

In every language upon earth,
　　On every shore, o'er every sea,
I gave my name immortal birth
　　And kept my spirit with the free.

ARTHUR HUGH CLOUGH (1819–1861)

'Say not the struggle naught availeth'

Say not the struggle naught availeth,
　　The labour and the wounds are vain,
The enemy faints not, nor faileth,
　　And as things have been, things remain.

If hopes were dupes, fears may be liars;
　　It may be, in yon smoke concealed,
Your comrades chase e'en now the fliers,
　　And, but for you, possess the field.

For while the tired waves, vainly breaking,
　　Seem here no painful inch to gain,
Far back through creeks and inlets making
　　Comes silent, flooding in, the main.

And not by eastern windows only,
    When daylight comes, comes in the light,
In front the sun climbs slow, how slowly,
    But westward, look, the land is bright.

from 'Amours de Voyage', Canto 2

ii Claude to Eustace

Dulce it is, and *decorum*, no doubt, for the country to fall,—to
Offer one's blood an oblation to Freedom, and die for the Cause; yet
Still, individual culture is also something, and no man
Finds quite distinct the assurance that he of all others is called on,
Or would be justified, even, in taking away from the world that
Precious creature, himself. Nature sent him here to abide here;
Else why sent him at all? Nature wants him still, it is likely.
On the whole, we are meant to look after ourselves; it is certain
Each has to eat for himself, digest for himself, and in general
Care for his own dear life, and see to his own preservation;
Nature's intentions, in most things uncertain, in this are decisive;
These, on the whole, I conjecture the Romans will follow, and I shall.
    So we cling to our rocks like limpets; Ocean may bluster,
Over and under and round us; we open our shells to imbibe our
Nourishment, close them again, and are safe, fulfilling the purpose
Nature intended,—a wise one, of course, and a noble, we doubt not.
Sweet it may be and decorous, perhaps, for the country to die; but,
On the whole, we conclude the Romans won't do it, and I sha'n't.
. . .

iii Claude to Eustace

Will they fight? They say so. And will the French? I can hardly,
Hardly think so; and yet—He is come, they say, to Palo,
He is passed from Monterone, at Santa Severa
He hath laid up his guns. But the Virgin, the Daughter of Roma,
She hath despised thee and laughed thee to scorn,—The Daughter of
    Tiber,
She hath shaken her head and built barricades against thee!
Will they fight? I believe it. Alas! 'tis ephemeral folly,
Vain and ephemeral folly, of course, compared with pictures,
Statues, and antique gems!—Indeed: and yet indeed too,

Yet, methought, in broad day did I dream,—tell it not in St. James's,
Whisper it not in thy courts, O Christ Church!—yet did I, waking,
Dream of a cadence that sings, *Si tombent nos jeunes héros, la*
Terre en produit de nouveaux contre vous tous prêts à se battre;
Dreamt of great indignations and angers transcendental,
Dreamt of a sword at my side and a battle-horse underneath me.

iv Claude to Eustace

Now supposing the French or the Neapolitan soldier
Should by some evil chance come exploring the Maison Serny
(Where the family English are all to assemble for safety),
Am I prepared to lay down my life for the British female?
Really, who knows? One has bowed and talked, till, little by little,
All the natural heat has escaped of the chivalrous spirit.
Oh, one conformed, of course; but one doesn't die for good manners,
Stab or shoot, or be shot, by way of graceful attention.
No, if it should be at all, it should be on the barricades there;
Should I incarnadine ever this inky pacifical finger,
Sooner far should it be for this vapour of Italy's freedom,
Sooner far by the side of the d——d and dirty plebeians.
Ah, for a child in the street I could strike; for the full-blown lady—
Somehow, Eustace, alas! I have not felt the vocation.
Yet these people of course will expect, as of course, my protection,
Vernon in radiant arms stand forth for the lovely Georgina,
And to appear, I suppose, were but common civility. Yes, and
Truly I do not desire they should either be killed or offended.
Oh, and of course, you will say, 'When the time comes, you will be ready.'
Ah, but before it comes, am I to presume it will be so?
What I cannot feel now, am I to suppose that I shall feel?
Am I not free to attend for the ripe and indubious instinct?
Am I forbidden to wait for the clear and lawful perception?
Is it the calling of man to surrender his knowledge and insight,
For the mere venture of what may, perhaps, be the virtuous action?
Must we, walking our earth, discerning a little, and hoping
Some plain visible task shall yet for our hands be assigned us,—
Must we abandon the future for fear of omitting the present,
Quit our own fireside hopes at the alien call of a neighbour,
To the mere possible shadow of Deity offer the victim?
And is all this, my friend, but a weak and ignoble refining,
Wholly unworthy the head or the heart of Your Own Correspondent?

from 'Dipsychus'

'There is no God,' the wicked saith,
    'And truly it's a blessing,
For what He might have done with us
    It's better only guessing.'

'There is no God,' a youngster thinks,
    'or really, if there may be,
He surely did not mean a man
    Always to be a baby.'

'There is no God, or if there is,'
    The tradesman thinks, ''twere funny
If He should take it ill in me
    To make a little money.'

'Whether there be,' the rich man says,
    'It matters very little,
For I and mine, thank somebody,
    Are not in want of victual.'

Some others, also, to themselves,
    Who scarce so much as doubt it,
Think there is none, when they are well,
    And do not think about it.

But country folks who live beneath
    The shadow of the steeple;
The parson and the parson's wife,
    And mostly married people;

Youths green and happy in first love,
    So thankful for illusion;
And men caught out in what the world
    Calls guilt, in first confusion;

And almost everyone when age,
    Disease, or sorrows strike him,
Inclines to think there is a God,
    Or something very like Him.

SAMUEL TAYLOR COLERIDGE (1772–1834)

Kubla Khan

In Xanadu did Kubla Khan
    A stately pleasure-dome decree:
Where Alph, the sacred river, ran
Through caverns measureless to man
    Down to a sunless sea.

So twice five miles of fertile ground
With walls and towers were girdled round:
And there were gardens bright with sinuous rills,
Where blossomed many an incense-bearing tree,
And here were forests ancient as the hills,
Enfolding sunny spots of greenery.

But oh! that deep romantic chasm which slanted
Down the green hill athwart a cedarn cover!
A savage place; as holy and enchanted
As e'er beneath a waning moon was haunted
By woman wailing for her demon-lover!
And from this chasm, with ceaseless turmoil seething,
As if this earth in fast thick pants were breathing,
A mighty fountain momently was forced,
Amid whose swift half-intermitted burst
Huge fragments vaulted like rebounding hail,
Or chaffy grain beneath the thresher's flail:
And 'mid these dancing rocks at once and ever
It flung up momently the sacred river.
Five miles meandering with a mazy motion
Through wood and dale the sacred river ran,
Then reached the caverns measureless to man,
And sank in tumult to a lifeless ocean:
And 'mid this tumult Kubla heard from far
Ancestral voices prophesying war!

    The shadow of the dome of pleasure
    Floated midway on the waves;
    Where was heard the mingled measure
    From the fountain and the caves.

It was a miracle of rare device,
A sunny pleasure-dome with caves of ice!

    A damsel with a dulcimer
    In a vision once I saw:
    It was an Abyssinian maid,
    And on her dulcimer she played,
    Singing of Mount Abora.
    Could I revive within me
    Her symphony and song,
To such a deep delight 'twould win me,
That with music loud and long,
I would build that dome in air,
That sunny dome! those caves of ice!
And all who heard should see them there,
And all should cry, Beware! Beware!
His flashing eyes, his floating hair!
Weave a circle round him thrice,
And close your eyes with holy dread,
For he on honey-dew hath fed,
And drunk the milk of Paradise.

Frost at Midnight

The Frost performs its secret ministry,
Unhelped by any wind. The owlet's cry
Came loud—and hark, again! loud as before.
The inmates of my cottage, all at rest,
Have left me to that solitude, which suits
Abstruser musings: save that at my side
My cradled infant slumbers peacefully.
'Tis calm indeed! so calm, that it disturbs
And vexes meditation with its strange
And extreme silentness. Sea, hill, and wood,
    This populous village! Sea, and hill, and wood,
With all the numberless goings-on of life,
Inaudible as dreams! the thin blue flame
Lies on my low-burnt fire, and quivers not;
Only that film, which fluttered on the grate,
Still flutters there, the sole unquiet thing.
Methinks, its motion in this hush of nature

Gives it dim sympathies with me who live,
Making it a companionable form,
Whose puny flaps and freaks the idling Spirit
By its own moods interprets, every where
Echo or mirror seeking of itself,
And makes a toy of Thought.
    But O! how oft,
How oft, at school, with most believing mind,
Presageful, have I gazed upon the bars,
To watch that fluttering stranger ! and as oft
With unclosed lids, already had I dreamt
Of my sweet birth-place, and the old church-tower,
Whose bells, the poor man's only music, rang
From morn to evening, all the hot Fair-day,
So sweetly, that they stirred and haunted me
With a wild pleasure, falling on mine ear
Most like articulate sounds of things to come!
So gazed I, till the soothing things, I dreamt,
Lulled me to sleep, and sleep prolonged my dreams!
And so I brooded all the following morn,
Awed by the stern preceptor's face, mine eye
Fixed with mock study on my swimming book:
Save if the door half opened, and I snatched
A hasty glance, and still my heart leaped up,
For still I hoped to see the stranger's face,
Townsman, or aunt, or sister more beloved,
My play-mate when we both were clothed alike!
Dear Babe, that sleepest cradled by my side,
Whose gentle breathings, heard in this deep calm,
    Fill up the interspers'd vacancies
And momentary pauses of the thought!
My babe so beautiful! it thrills my heart
With tender gladness, thus to look at thee,
And think that thou shalt learn far other lore,
And in far other scenes! For I was reared
In the great city, pent 'mid cloisters dim,
And saw nought lovely but the sky and stars.
But thouß, my babe! shalt wander like a breeze
By lakes and sandy shores, beneath the crags
Of ancient mountain, and beneath the clouds,
Which image in their bulk both lakes and shores
And mountain crags: so shalt thou see and hear

The lovely shapes and sounds intelligible
Of that eternal language, which thy God
Utters, who from eternity doth teach
Himself in all, and all things in himself.
Great universal Teacher! he shall mould
Thy spirit, and by giving make it ask.
Therefore all seasons shall be sweet to thee,
Whether the summer clothe the general earth
With greenness, or the redbreast sit and sing
Betwixt the tufts of snow on the bare branch
Of mossy apple-tree, while the nigh thatch
Smokes in the sun-thaw; whether the eave-drops fall
Heard only in the trances of the blast,
Or if the secret ministry of frost
Shall hang them up in silent icicles,
    Quietly shining to the quiet Moon.

The Rime of the Ancient Mariner

Part 1

An ancient Mariner meeteth three Gallants biddeth to a wedding-feast, and detaineth one.

It is an ancient Mariner,
And he stoppeth one of three.
'By thy long grey beard and glittering eye,
Now wherefore stopp'st thou me?

'The Bridegroom's doors are opened wide,
And I am next of kin;
The guests are met, the feast is set:
May'st hear the merry din.'

The Wedding-Guest is spellbound by the old seafaring man, and constrained to hear his tale.

He holds him with his skinny hand,
'There was a ship,' quoth he.
'Hold off! unhand me, grey-beard loon!'
Eftsoons his hand dropt he.[1]

He holds him with his glittering eye—
The Wedding-Guest stood still,
And listens like a three years child:
The Mariner hath his will.

[1] eftsoons = forthwith.

The Wedding-Guest sat on a stone:
He cannot choose but hear;
And thus spake on that ancient man,
The bright-eyed Mariner.

'The ship was cheered, the harbour cleared,
Merrily did we drop
Below the kirk, below the hill,
Below the lighthouse top.

The Mariner tells how the ship sailed southward with a good wind and fair weather, till it reached the Line.

'The sun came up upon the left,
Out of the sea came he!
And he shone bright, and on the right
Went down into the sea.

'Higher and higher every day,
Till over the mast at noon—'
The Wedding-Guest here beat his breast,
For he heard the loud bassoon.

The Wedding-Guest heareth the bridal music; but the Mariner continueth his tale.

The bride hath paced into the hall,
Red as a rose is she;
Nodding their heads before her goes
The merry minstrelsy.

The Wedding-Guest he beat his breast,
Yet he cannot choose but hear;
And thus spake on that ancient man,
The bright-eyed Mariner.

The ship drawn by a storm toward the South Pole.

'And now the Storm-blast came, and he
Was tyrannous and strong:
He struck with his o'ertaking wings,
And chased us south along.

'With sloping masts and dipping prow,
As who pursued with yell and blow
Still treads the shadow of his foe,
And forward bends his head,
The ship drove fast, loud roared the blast,
And southward aye we fled.

'And now there came both mist and snow,
And it grew wondrous cold:
And ice, mast-high, came floating by,
As green as emerald.

The land of ice, and of fearful sounds where no living thing was to be seen.

'And through the drifts the snowy clifts
Did send a dismal sheen:
Nor shapes of men nor beasts we ken—
The ice was all between.

'The ice was here, the ice was there,
The ice was all around:
It cracked and growled, and roared and howled,
Like noises in a swound![1]

Till a great sea-bird, called the Albatross, came through the snow-fog, and was received with great joy and hospitality.

'At length did cross an Albatross:
Thorough the fog it came;
As if it had been a Christian soul,
We hailed it in God's name.

'It ate the food it ne'er had eat,
And round and round it flew.
The ice did split with a thunder-fit;
The helmsman steered us through!

And lo! the Albatross proveth a bird of good omen, and followeth the ship as it returned northward through fog and floating ice.

'And a good south wind sprung up behind;
The Albatross did follow,
And every day, for food or play,
Came to the mariners' hollo!

'In mist or cloud, on mast or shroud,
It perched for vespers nine;
Whiles all the night, through fog-smoke white,
Glimmered the white moonshine.'

The ancient Mariner inhospitably killeth the pious bird of good omen.

'God save thee, ancient Mariner!
From the fiends, that plague thee thus!—
Why look'st thou so?'—'With my crossbow
I shot the Albatross.'

[1] swound = swoon, fainting fit.

Part 2

The Sun now rose upon the right:
Out of the sea came he,
Still hid in mist, and on the left
Went down into the sea.

And the good south wind still blew behind,
But no sweet bird did follow,
Nor any day for food or play
Came to the mariners' hollo!

His shipmates
cry out against
the Mariner, for
killing the bird
of good luck.

And I had done a hellish thing,
And it would work 'em woe:
For all averred, I had killed the bird
That made the breeze to blow.
'Ah wretch!' said they, 'the bird to slay
That made the breeze to blow!'

But when the
fog cleared off,
they justify the
same, and thus
make themselves
accomplices in
the crime.

Nor dim nor red, like God's own head,
The glorious Sun uprist:
Then all averred, I had killed the bird
That brought the fog and mist.
'Twas right, said they, such birds to slay,
That bring the fog and mist.

The fair breeze
continues; the
ship enters the
Pacific Ocean,
and sails north-
ward, even till it
reaches the Line.

The fair breeze blew, the white foam flew,
The furrow followed free;
We were the first that ever burst
Into that silent sea.

Down dropt the breeze, the sails dropt down,
'Twas sad as sad could be;

The ship hath
been suddenly
becalmed.

And we did speak only to break
The silence of the sea!

All in a hot and copper sky,
The bloody Sun, at noon,
Right up above the mast did stand,
No bigger than the Moon.

Day after day, day after day,
We stuck, nor breath nor motion;
As idle as a painted ship
Upon a painted ocean.

And the Albatross
begins to be avenged.

Water, water, everywhere,
And all the boards did shrink;
Water, water, everywhere,
Nor any drop to drink.

The very deep did rot: O Christ!
That ever this should be!
Yea, slimy things did crawl with legs
Upon the slimy sea.

About, about, in reel and rout
The death-fires danced at night;
The water, like a witch's oils,
Burnt green, and blue and white.

A Spirit had followed
them; one of the
invisible inhabitants of
this planet, neither
departed souls nor
angels; concerning
whom the learned Jew,
Josephus, and the
Platonic Constantino-
politan, Michael Psellus,
may be consulted. They
are very numerous, and
there is no climate or
element without one or
more.

And some in dreams assuréd were
Of the Spirit that plagued us so,
Nine fathom deep he had followed us
From the land of mist and snow.

And every tongue, through utter drought,
Was withered at the root;
We could not speak, no more than if
We had been choked with soot.

The shipmates, in their
sore distress, would fain
throw the whole guilt
on the ancient Mariner:
in sign whereof they
hang the dead sea-bird
round his neck.

Ah! well a-day! what evil looks
Had I from old and young!
Instead of the cross, the Albatross
About my neck was hung.

Part 3

There passed a weary time. Each throat
Was parched, and glazed each eye.
A weary time! a weary time!
How glazed each weary eye,

The ancient Mariner
beholdeth a sign in
the element afar off.

When looking westward, I beheld
A something in the sky.

At first it seemed a little speck,
And then it seemed a mist;
It moved and moved, and took at last
A certain shape, I wist.

A speck, a mist, a shape, I wist!
And still it neared and neared:
As if it dodged a water-sprite,
It plunged and tacked and veered.

At its nearer
approach, it seemeth
him to be a ship; and
at a dear ransom he
freeth his speech
from the bonds of
thirst.

With throats unslaked, with black lips baked,
We could nor laugh nor wail;
Through utter drought all dumb we stood!
I bit my arm, I sucked the blood,
And cried, A sail! a sail!

With throats unslaked, with black lips baked,
Agape they heard me call;
A flash of joy.
Gramercy! they for joy did grin,
And all at once their breath drew in,
As they were drinking all.

And horror follows.
For can it be a ship
that comes onward
without wind or
tide?

See! see! (I cried) she tacks no more!
Hither to work us weal;
Without a breeze, without a tide,
She steadies with upright keel!

The western wave was all a-flame.
The day was well nigh done!
Almost upon the western wave
Rested the broad bright Sun;
When that strange shape drove suddenly
Betwixt us and the Sun.

It seemeth him but
the skeleton of a ship.

And straight the Sun was flecked with bars,
(Heaven's Mother send us grace!)
As if through a dungeon-grate he peered
With broad and burning face.

Alas! (thought I, and my heart beat loud)
How fast she nears and nears!
Are those her sails that glance in the Sun,
Like restless gossameres!

And its ribs are seen as bars on the face of the setting Sun. The Spectre-Woman and her Deathmate, and no other on board the skeleton-ship. Like vessel, like crew!

Are those her ribs through which the Sun
Did peer, as through a grate?
And is that Woman all her crew?
Is that a Death? and are there two?
Is Death that woman's mate?

Her lips were red, her looks were free,
Her locks were yellow as gold:
Her skin was as white as leprosy,
The nightmare Life-in-Death was she,
Who thicks man's blood with cold.

Death and Life-in-Death have diced for the ship's crew, and she (the latter) winneth the ancient Mariner.

The naked hulk alongside came,
And the twain were casting dice;
'The game is done! I've won! I've won!'
Quoth she, and whistles thrice.

No twilight within the courts of the Sun.

The Sun's rim dips; the stars rush out:
At one stride comes the dark;
With far-heard whisper, o'er the sea,
Off shot the spectre-bark.

At the rising of the Moon,

We listened and looked sideways up!
Fear at my heart, as at a cup,
My life-blood seemed to sip!
The stars were dim, and thick the night,
The steersman's face by his lamp gleamed white;
From the sails the dew did drip—
Till clomb above the eastern bar
The hornèd Moon, with one bright star
Within the nether tip.

One after another, His shipmates drop down dead.

One after one, by the star-dogged Moon
Too quick for groan or sigh,
Each turned his face with a ghastly pang,
And cursed me with his eye.

Four times fifty living men,
(And I heard nor sigh nor groan)
With heavy thump, a lifeless lump,
They dropped down one by one.

But Life-in-Death
begins her work on
the ancient Mariner.

The souls did from their bodies fly,—
They fled to bliss or woe!
And every soul, it passed me by,
Like the whizz of my crossbow!

Part 4

The Wedding-Guest
feareth that a Spirit is
talking to him.

'I fear thee, ancient Mariner!
I fear thy skinny hand!
And thou art long, and lank, and brown,
As is the ribbed sea-sand.

'I fear thee and thy glittering eye,
And thy skinny hand, so brown.'—
Fear not, fear not, thou Wedding-Guest!
This body dropt not down.

But the ancient
Mariner assureth him
of his bodily life, and
proceedeth to relate
his horrible penance.

Alone, alone, all, all alone,
Alone on a wide, wide sea!
And never a saint took pity on
My soul in agony.

He despiseth the
creatures of the calm.

The many men, so beautiful!
And they all dead did lie:
And a thousand thousand slimy things
Lived on; and so did I.

And envieth that they
should live and so
many lie dead.

I looked upon the rotting sea,
And drew my eyes away;
I looked upon the rotting deck,
And there the dead men lay.

I looked to heaven, and tried to pray;
But or ever a prayer had gusht,[1]
A wicked whisper came, and made
My heart as dry as dust.

[1] or ever = before.

I closed my lids, and kept them close,
And the balls like pulses beat;
For the sky and the sea, and the sea and the sky
Lay like a load on my weary eye,
And the dead were at my feet.

But the curse liveth for him in the eye of the dead men.

The cold sweat melted from their limbs,
Nor rot nor reek did they:
The look with which they looked on me
Had never passed away.

An orphan's curse would drag to hell
A spirit from on high;
But oh! more horrible than that
Is the curse in a dead man's eye!
Seven days, seven nights, I saw that curse,
And yet I could not die.

In his loneliness and fixedness he yearneth towards the journeying Moon, and the stars that still sojourn, yet still move onward; and everywhere the blue sky belongs to them, and is their appointed rest, and their native country, and their own natural homes, which they enter unannounced, as lords that are certainly expected and yet there us a silent joy at their arrival.

The moving Moon went up the sky,
And nowhere did abide:
Softly she was going up,
And a star or two beside—

Her beams bemocked the sultry main,
Like April hoar-frost spread;
But where the ship's huge shadow lay,
The charmèd water burnt alway
A still and awful red.

By the light of the Moon he beholdeth God's creatures of the great calm.

Beyond the shadow of the ship,
I watched the water-snakes:
They moved in tracks of shining white,
And when they reared, the elfish light
Fell off in hoary flakes.

Within the shadow of the ship
I watched their rich attire:
Blue, glossy green, and velvet black,
They coiled and swam: and every track
Was a flash of golden fire.

Their beauty and their happiness.

O happy living things! no tongue
Their beauty might declare:
A spring of love gushed from my heart,

He blesseth them in his heart.

And I blessed them unaware:
Sure my kind saint took pity on me,
And I blessed them unaware.

The spell begins to break.

The selfsame moment I could pray;
And from my neck so free
The Albatross fell off, and sank
Like lead into the sea.

Part 5

Oh sleep! it is a gentle thing,
Beloved from pole to pole!
To Mary Queen the praise be given!
She sent the gentle sleep from Heaven,
That slid into my soul.

By grace of the holy Mother, the ancient Mariner is refreshed with rain.

The silly buckets on the deck,[1]
That had so long remained,
I dreamt that they were filled with dew;
And when I awoke, it rained.

My lips were wet, my throat was cold,
My garments all were dank;
Sure I had drunken in my dreams,
And still my body drank.

I moved, and could not feel my limbs;
I was so light—almost
I thought that I had died in sleep,
And was a blessèd ghost.

He heareth sounds and seeth strange sights and commotions in the sky and the elment.

And soon I heard a roaring wind:
It did not come anear;
But with its sound it shook the sails,
That were so thin and sere.

[1] silly = poor, helpless.

The upper air burst into life!
And a hundred fire-flags sheen,[1]
To and fro they were hurried about!
And to and fro, and in and out,
The wan stars danced between.

And the coming wind did roar more loud,
And the sails did sigh like sedge;
And the rain poured down from one black cloud;
The Moon was at its edge.

The thick black cloud was cleft, and still
The Moon was at its side:
Like waters shot from some high crag,
The lightning fell with never a jag,
A river steep and wide.

The loud wind never reached the ship,
Yet now the ship moved on!
Beneath the lightning and the Moon
The dead men gave a groan.

The bodies of the ship's crew are inspired, and the ship moves on;

They groaned, they stirred, they all uprose,
Nor spake, nor moved their eyes;
It had been strange, even in a dream,
To have seen those dead men rise.

The helmsman steered, the ship moved on;
Yet never a breeze up blew;
The mariners all 'gan work the ropes,
Where they were wont to do;
They raised their limbs like lifeless tools—
We were a ghastly crew.

The body of my brother's son
Stood by me, knee to knee:
The body and I pulled at one rope
But he said nought to me.

But not by the souls of the men, nor by daemons of earth or

'I fear thee, ancient Mariner!'
Be calm, thou Wedding-Guest!

[1] sheen = bright.

middle air, but by a blessed troop of angelic spirits, sent down by the invocation of the gusardian Saint.

'Twas not those souls that fled in pain,
Which to their corses came again,
But a troop of spirits blest:

For when it dawned—they dropped their arms,
And clustered round the mast;
Sweet sounds rose slowly through their mouths,
And from their bodies passed.

Around, around, flew each sweet sound,
Then darted to the Sun;
Slowly the sounds came back again,
Now mixed, now one by one.

Sometimes a-dropping from the sky
I heard the skylark sing;
Sometimes all little birds that are,
How they seemed to fill the sea and air
With their sweet jargoning!

And now 'twas like all instruments,
Now like a lonely flute;
And now it is an angel's song,
That makes the heavens be mute.

It ceased; yet still the sails made on
A pleasant noise till noon,
A noise like of a hidden brook
In the leafy month of June,
That to the sleeping woods all night
Singeth a quiet tune.

Till noon we quietly sailed on,
Yet never a breeze did breathe:
Slowly and smoothly went the ship,
Moved onward from beneath.

The lonesome Spirit from the South Pole carries on the ship as far as the Line, in obedience to the angelic troop, but still requireth vengeance.

Under the keel nine fathom deep,
From the land of mist and snow,
The spirit slid: and it was he
That made the ship to go.
The sails at noon left off their tune,
And the ship stood still also.

The Sun, right up above the mast,
Had fixed her to the ocean:
But in a minute she 'gan stir,
With a short uneasy motion—
Backwards and forwards half her length
With a short uneasy motion.

Then like a pawing horse let go,
She made a sudden bound:
It flung the blood into my head,
And I fell down in a swound.

The Polar Spirit's
fellow-daemons, the
invisible inhabitants of
the element, take part
in his wrong; and two
of them relate, one to
the other, that penance
long and heavy for the
ancient Mariner has
been accorded to the
Polar Spirit, who
returneth southward.

How long in that same fit I lay,
I have not to declare;
But ere my living life returned,
I heard and in my soul discerned
Two voices in the air.

'Is it he?' quoth one, 'Is this the man?
By him who died on cross,
With his cruel bow he laid full low
The harmless Albatross.

'The Spirit who bideth by himself
In the land of mist and snow,
He loved the bird that loved the man
Who shot him with a bow.'

The other was a softer voice,
As soft as honey-dew:
Quoth he, 'The man hath penance done,
And penance more will do.'

Part 6

First Voice
'But tell me, tell me! speak again,
Thy soft response renewing—
What makes that ship drive on so fast?
What is the ocean doing?'

Second Voice
'Still as a slave before his lord,
The ocean hath no blast;
His great bright eye most silently
Up to the moon is cast—

'If he may know which way to go;
For she guides him smooth or grim.
See, brother, see! how graciously
She looketh down on him.'

First Voice
'But why drives on that ship so fast,
Without or wave or wind?'

The Mariner hath
been cast into a
trance; for the
angelic power
causeth the vessel
to drive northward
faster than human
life could endure.

Second Voice
'The air is cut away before,
And closes from behind.

'Fly, brother, fly! more high, more high!
Or we shall be belated:
For slow and slow that ship will go,
When the Mariner's trance is abated.'

The supernatural
motion is retarded;
the Mariner
awakes, and his
penance begins
anew.

I woke, and we were sailing on
As in a gentle weather:
'Twas night, calm night, the moon was high,
The dead men stood together.

All stood together on the deck,
For a charnel-dungeon fitter:
All fixed on me their stony eyes,
That in the moon did glitter.

The pang, the curse, with which they died,
Had never passed away:
I could not draw my eyes from theirs,
Nor turn them up to pray.

The curse is finally
expiated.

And now this spell was snapt: once more
I viewed the ocean green,
And looked far forth, yet little saw
Of what had else been seen—

Like one, that on a lonesome road
Doth walk in fear and dread,
And having once turned round walks on,
And turns no more his head;
Because he knows, a frightful fiend
Doth close behind him tread.

But soon there breathed a wind on me,
Nor sound nor motion made:
Its path was not upon the sea,
In ripple or in shade.

It raised my hair, it fanned my cheek
Like a meadow-gale of spring—
It mingled strangely with my fears,
Yet it felt like a welcoming.

Swiftly, swiftly flew the ship,
Yet she sailed softly too:
Sweetly, sweetly blew the breeze—
On me alone it blew.

And the ancient
Mariner beholdeth
his native country.

Oh! dream of joy! is this indeed
The lighthouse top I see?
Is this the hill? is this the kirk?
Is this mine own countree!

We drifted o'er the harbour-bar,
And I with sobs did pray—
O let me be awake, my God!
Or let me sleep alway.

The harbour-bay was clear as glass,
So smoothly it was strewn!
And on the bay the moonlight lay,
And the shadow of the moon.

The rock shone bright, the kirk no less,
That stands above the rock:
The moonlight steeped in silentness
The steady weathercock.

And the bay was white with silent light
Till rising from the same,
Full many shapes, that shadows were,
In crimson colours came.

The Angelic spirits
leave the dead
bodies,

A little distance from the prow
Those crimson shadows were:
I turned my eyes upon the deck—
Oh, Christ! what saw I there!

And appear in their
own forms of light.

Each corse lay flat, lifeless and flat,
And, by the holy rood!
A man all light, a seraph-man,
On every corse there stood.

This seraph-band, each waved his hand;
It was a heavenly sight!
They stood as signals to the land,
Each one a lovely light;

This seraph-band, each waved his hand;
No voice did they impart—
No voice; but oh! the silence sank
Like music on my heart.

But soon I heard the dash of oars,
I heard the Pilot's cheer;
My head was turned perforce away,
And I saw a boat appear.

The Pilot and the Pilot's boy,
I heard them coming fast:
Dear Lord in Heaven! it was a joy
The dead men could not blast.

I saw a third—I heard his voice:
It is the Hermit good!
He singeth loud his godly hymns
That he makes in the wood.
He'll shrieve my soul, he'll wash away
The Albatross's blood.

Part 7

The Hermit of
the Wood

This Hermit good lives in that wood
Which slopes down to the sea.
How loudly his sweet voice he rears!
He loves to talk with marineres
That come from a far countree.

He kneels at morn, and noon, and eve—
He hath a cushion plump:
It is the moss that wholly hides
The rotted old oak-stump.

The skiff-boat neared: I heard them talk,
'Why this is strange, I trow!
Where are those lights so many and fair,
That signal made but now?'

Approacheth
the ship with
wonder.

'Strange, by my faith!' the Hermit said—
'And they answered not our cheer!
The planks looked warped! and see those sails,
How thin they are and sere!
I never saw aught like to them,
Unless perchance it were

'Brown skeletons of leaves that lag
My forest-brook along;
When the ivy-tod is heavy with snow,[1]
And the owlet whoops to the wolf below,
That eats the she-wolf's young.'

'Dear Lord! it hath a fiendish look—
(The Pilot made reply)
I am a-feared'—'Push on, push on!'
Said the Hermit cheerily.

The boat came closer to the ship,
But I nor spake nor stirred;
The boat came close beneath the ship,
And straight a sound was heard.

[1] ivy-tod = ivy bush.

The ship suddenly
sinketh.

Under the water it rumbled on,
Still louder and more dread:
It reached the ship, it split the bay;
The ship went down like lead.

The ancient Mariner
is saved in the Pilot's
boat.

Stunned by that loud and dreadful sound,
Which sky and ocean smote,
Like one that hath been seven days drowned
My body lay afloat;
But swift as dreams, myself I found
Within the Pilot's boat.

Upon the whirl, where sank the ship,
The boat spun round and round;
And all was still, save that the hill
Was telling of the sound.

I moved my lips—the Pilot shrieked
And fell down in a fit;
The holy Hermit raised his eyes,
And prayed where he did sit.

I took the oars: the Pilot's boy,
Who now doth crazy go,
Laughed loud and long, and all the while
His eyes went to and fro.
'Ha! ha!' quoth he, 'full plain I see,
The Devil knows how to row.'

And now, all in my own countree,
I stood on the firm land!
The Hermit stepped forth from the boat,
And scarcely he could stand.

The ancient Mariner
earnestly entreateth
the Hermit to
shrieve him; and the
penance of life falls
on him.

'O shrieve me, shrieve me, holy man!'
The Hermit crossed his brow.
'Say quick,' quoth he, 'I bid thee say—
What manner of man art thou?'

Forthwith this frame of mine was wrenched
With a woful agony,
Which forced me to begin my tale;
And then it left me free.

And ever and anon throughout his future life an agony constraineth him to travel from land to land.

Since then, at an uncertain hour,
That agony returns:
And till my ghastly tale is told,
This heart within me burns.

I pass, like night, from land to land;
I have strange power of speech;
That moment that his face I see,
I know the man that must hear me:
To him my tale I teach.

What loud uproar bursts from that door!
The Wedding-guests are there:
But in the garden-bower the bride
And bride-maids singing are:
And hark the little vesper bell
Which biddeth me to prayer!

O Wedding-Guest! this soul hath been
Alone on a wide, wide sea:
So lonely 'twas, that God himself
Scarce seemèd there to be.

O sweeter than the marriage-feast,
'Tis sweeter far to me,
To walk together to the kirk
With a goodly company!—

To walk together to the kirk,
And all together pray,
While each to his great Father bends,
Old men, and babes, and loving friends,
And youths and maidens gay!

And to teach, by his own example, love and reference to all things that Gd made and loveth.

Farewell, farewell! but this I tell
To thee, thou Wedding-Guest!
He prayeth well, who loveth well
Both man and bird and beast.

He prayeth best, who loveth best
All things both great and small;
For the dear God who loveth us,
He made and loveth all.

The Mariner, whose eye is bright,
Whose beard with age is hoar,
Is gone: and now the Wedding-Guest
Turned from the bridegroom's door.

He went like one that hath been stunned,
And is of sense forlorn:
A sadder and a wiser man,
He rose the morrow morn.

WILLIAM COLLINS (1721–1759)

Ode to Evening

If ought of oaten stop, or pastoral song
May hope, O pensive Eve, to soothe thine ear,
    Like thy own solemn springs,
    Thy springs, and dying gales,
O nymph reserved, while now the bright-haired sun
Sits in yon western tent, whose cloudy skirts,
    With braid ethereal wove,
    O'erhang his wavy bed:

Now air is hushed,[1] save where the weak-eyed bat,
With short shrill shriek, flits by on leathern wing,
    Or where the beetle winds
    His small but sullen horn,
As oft he rises 'midst the twilight path,
Against the pilgrim borne in heedless hum:
    Now teach me, maid composed,
    To breathe some softened strain,
Whose numbers stealing thro' thy darkening vale,
May not unseemly with its stillness suit,
    As musing slow, I hail
    Thy genial loved return!

For when thy folding-star arising shows
His paly circlet, at his warning lamp[1]
    The fragrant hours, and elves
    Who slept in buds the day,

[1] paly = vertically striped.

And many a nymph who wreathes her brows with sedge,
And sheds the fresh'ning dew, and lovelier still,
    The pensive pleasures sweet
    Prepare thy shadowy car.

Then let me rove some wild and heathy scene,
Or find some ruin 'midst its dreary dells,
    Whose walls more awful nod
    By thy religious gleams.
Or if chill blust'ring winds, or driving rain,
Prevent my willing feet, be mine the hut,
    That from the mountain's side,
    Views wilds, and swelling floods,
And hamlets brown, and dim-discovered spires,
And hears their simple bell, and marks o'er all
    Thy dewy fingers draw
    The gradual dusky veil.

While Spring shall pour his showers, as oft he wont,
And bathe thy breathing tresses, meekest Eve!
    While Summer loves to sport
    Beneath thy lingering light;
While sallow Autumn fills thy lap with leaves;
Or Winter, yelling through the troublous air,
    Affrights thy shrinking train
    And rudely rends thy robes;
So long, regardful of thy quiet rule,
Shall fancy, friendship, science, smiling peace,
    Thy gentlest influence own,
    And love thy favourite name!

WENDY COPE (1945–)

Triolet

I used to think all poets were Byronic—
Mad, bad and dangerous to know.
And then I met a few. Yes it's ironic—
I used to think all poets were Byronic.
They're mostly wicked as a ginless tonic
And wild as pension plans. Not long ago

I used to think all poets were Byronic—
Mad, bad and dangerous to know.

RICHARD CORBET (1582–1635)

The Fairies' Farewell

Farewell, rewards and fairies,
    Good housewives now may say,
For now foul sluts in dairies
    Do fare as well as they.
And though they sweep their hearths no less
    Than maids were wont to do,
Yet who of late, for cleanliness,
    Finds sixpence in her shoe?
Lament, lament, old Abbeys,
    The fairies' lost command;
They did not change priests' babies,
    But some have changed your land!
And all your children sprung from thence
    Are now grown Puritans,
Who live as changelings ever since,
    For love of your domains.

At morning and at evening both
    You merry were and glad;
So little care of sleep or sloth
    These pretty ladies had;
When Tom came home from labour,
    Or Ciss to milking rose,
Then merrily went their tabor
    And nimbly went their toes.

Witness those rings and roundelays
    Of theirs, which yet remain,
Were footed in Queen Mary's days
    On many a grassy plain;
But since of late, Elizabeth
    And, later, James came in,
They never danced on any heath
    As when the time hath been.

By which we note the fairies
  Were of the old profession;
Their songs were *Ave-Maries*,
  Their dances were procession.
But now, alas! they all are dead,
  Or gone beyond the seas;
Or farther for religion fled;
  Or else they take their ease.

A tell-tale in their company
  They never could endure;
And whoso kept not secretly
  Their mirth, was punished sure;
It was a most just Christian deed
  To pinch such black and blue:
Oh, how the Commonwealth doth need
  Such justices as you!

WILLIAM (JOHNSON) CORY (1823–1892)

Heraclitus

They told me, Heraclitus, they told me you were dead,
They brought me bitter news to hear and bitter tears to shed.
I wept as I remembered how often you and I
Had tired the sun with talking and sent him down the sky.
And now that thou art lying, my dear old Carian guest,
A handful of grey ashes, long, long ago at rest,
Still are thy pleasant voices, thy nightingales, awake;
For Death, he taketh all away, but them he cannot take.

ABRAHAM COWLEY (1618–1667)

The Wish

Well then! I now do plainly see
This busy world and I shall ne'er agree.
The very honey of all earthly joy
Does of all meats the soonest cloy;
  And they, methinks, deserve my pity

Who for it can endure the stings,
The crowd and buzz and murmurings
    Of this great hive, the city.

Ah, yet, ere I descend to th' grave
May I a small house and large garden have;
And a few friends, and many books, both true,
Both wise, and both delightful too!
    And since love ne'er will from me flee,
A mistress moderately fair,
And good as guardian angels are,
    Only beloved, and loving me.

O fountains! when in you shall I
Myself eased of unpeaceful thoughts espy?
O fields! O woods! when, when shall I be made
The happy tenant of your shade?
    Here's the spring-head of Pleasure's flood:
Here's wealthy Nature's treasury,
Where all the riches lie that she
    Has coined and stamped for good.

Pride and Ambition here
Only in far-fetched metaphors appear;
Here nought but winds can hurtful murmurs scatter,
And nought but Echo flatter.
    The gods, when they descended, hither
From heaven did always choose their way:
And therefore we may boldly say
    That 'tis the way, too, thither.

How happy here should I
And one dear She live, and embracing die!
She who is all the world, and can exclude
In deserts solitude.
    I should have then this only fear:
Lest men, when they my pleasure see,
Should hither throng to live like me,
    And make a city here.

WILLIAM COWPER (1731–1800)

'God moves in a mysterious way'
(from 'Olney Hymns')

God moves in a mysterious way,
    His wonders to perform;
He plants His footsteps in the sea,
    And rides upon the storm.

Deep in unfathomable mines,
    With never-failing skill,
He treasures up His bright designs,
    And works his sovereign will.

Ye fearful saints, fresh courage take;
    The clouds ye so much dread
Are big with mercy, and shall break
    In blessings on your head.

Judge not the Lord by feeble sense,
    But trust Him for His grace;
Behind a frowning providence
    He hides a smiling face.

His purposes will ripen fast,
    Unfolding every hour;
The bud may have a bitter taste,
    But sweet will be the flower.

Blind unbelief is sure to err,
    And scan his work in vain;
God is His own interpreter,
    And He will make it plain.

The Poplar Field

The poplars are felled, farewell to the shade
And the whispering sound of the cool colonnade:
The winds play no longer and sing in the leaves,
Nor Ouse on his bosom their image receives.

Twelve years have elapsed since I first took a view
Of my favourite field, and the bank where they grew,
And now in the grass behold they are laid,
And the tree is my seat that once lent me a shade.

The blackbird has fled to another retreat
Where the hazels afford him a screen from the heat;
And the scene where his melody charmed me before
Resounds with his sweet-flowing ditty no more.

My fugitive years are all hasting away,
And I must ere long lie as lowly as they,
With a turf on my breast and a stone at my head,
Ere another such grove shall arise in its stead.

'Tis a sight to engage me, if anything can,
To muse on the perishing pleasures of man;
Short-lived as we are, our enjoyments, I see,
Have a still shorter date, and die sooner than we.

Epitaph on a Hare

Here lies, whom hound did ne'er pursue,
    Nor swifter greyhound follow,
Whose footprints ne'er tainted morning dew,
    Nor ear heard huntsman's 'Hallo,'

Old Tiny, surliest of his kind,
    Who, nursed with tender care,
And to domestic bounds confin'd,
    Was still a wild jack-hare.

Though duly from my hand he took
    His pittance ev'ry night,
He did it with a jealous look,
    And, when he could, would bite.

His diet was of wheaten bread,
    And milk, and oats, and straw,
Thistles, or lettuces instead,
    With sand to scour his maw.

On twigs of hawthorn he regaled,
　　On pippins' russet peel;
And, when his juicy salads failed,
　　Slic'd carrot pleased him well.

A Turkey carpet was his lawn,
　　Whereon he loved to bound,
To skip and gambol like a fawn,
　　And swing his rump around.

His frisking was at evening hours,
　　For then he lost his fear;
But most before approaching showers,
　　Or when a storm drew near.

Eight years and five round-rolling moons
　　He thus saw steal away,
Dozing out his idle noons,
　　And every night at play.

I kept him for his humour's sake,
　　For he would oft beguile
My heart of thoughts that made it ache,
　　And force me to a smile.

But now, beneath this walnut-shade
　　He finds his long, last home,
And waits in snug concealment laid,
　　Till gentler Puss shall come.

He, still more aged, feels the shocks
　　From which no care can save,
And, partner once of Tiny's box,
　　Must soon partake his grave.

The Castaway

Obscurest night involved the sky,
　　Th' Atlantic billows roared,
When such a destined wretch as I,
　　Washed headlong from on board,

Of friends, of hope, of all bereft,
His floating home for ever left.

No braver chief could Albion boast
    Than he with whom he went,
Nor ever ship left Albion's coast,
    With warmer wishes sent.
He loved them both, but both in vain,
Nor him beheld, nor her again.

Not long beneath the whelming brine,
    Expert to swim, he lay;
Nor soon he felt his strength decline,
    Or courage die away;
But waged with death a lasting strife,
Supported by despair of life.

He shouted: nor his friends had failed
    To check the vessel's course,
But so the furious blast prevailed
    That, pitiless perforce,
They left their outcast mate behind,
And scudded still before the wind.

Some succour yet they could afford;
    And such as storms allow,
The cask, the coop, the floated cord,
    Delayed not to bestow.
But he (they knew) nor ship, nor shore,
Whate'er they gave, should visit more.

Nor, cruel as it seemed, could he
    Their haste himself condemn,
Aware that flight, in such a sea,
    Alone could rescue them;
Yet bitter felt it still to die
Deserted, and his friends so nigh.

He long survives, who lives an hour
    In ocean, self-upheld;
And so long he, with unspent power,
    His destiny repelled;

And ever, as the minutes flew,
Entreated help, or cried—Adieu!

At length, his transient respite past,
    His comrades, who before
Had heard his voice in ev'ry blast,
    Could catch the sound no more.
For then, by toil subdued, he drank
The stifling wave, and then he sank.

No poet wept him: but the page
    Of narrative sincere,
That tells his name, his worth, his age,
    Is wet with Anson's tear.
And tears by bards or heroes shed
Alike immortalise the dead.

I therefore purpose not, or dream,
    Descanting on his fate,
To give the melancholy theme
    A more enduring date:
But misery still delights to trace
Its semblance in another's case.

No voice divine the storm allayed,
    No light propitious shone;
When, snatched from all effectual aid,
    We perished, each alone:
But I beneath a rougher sea,
And whelm'd in deeper gulphs than he.

RICHARD CRASHAW (1613–1649)

from 'Wishes for the Supposed Mistress'

Whoe'er she be
That not impossible She
That shall command my heart and me;

Where'er she lie,
Locked up from mortal eye
In shady leaves of destiny:

Till that ripe birth
Of studied Fate stand forth,
And teach her fair steps tread our earth:

Till that divine
Idea take a shrine
Of crystal flesh, through which to shine:

Meet you her, my wishes,
Bespeak her to my blisses,
And be ye called my absent kisses.

I wish her beauty
That owes not all its duty
To gaudy tire, or glist'ring shoe-tie:

A face that's best
By its own beauty drest,
And can alone commend the rest.

Something more than
Taffeta or tissue can,
Or rampant feather, or rich fan.

More than the spoil
Of shop, or silkworm's toil,
Or a bought blush, or a set smile.

A face made up
Out of no other shop
Than what nature's white hand sets ope.

A cheek where youth,
And blood, with pen of truth
Write, what the reader sweetly ru'th.

A cheek, where grows
More than a morning rose:
Which to no box his being owes.

Lips, where all day
A lover's kiss may play,
Yet carry nothing thence away.

Looks that oppress
Their richest tires, but dress
And clothe their simplest nakedness.

Eyes, that displaces
The neighbour diamond, and outfaces
That sungshine by their own sweet graces.

Tresses that wear
Jewels, but to declare
How much themselves more precious are:

Whose native ray
Can tame the wanton day
Of gems, that in their bright shades play.

Each ruby there,
Or pearl that dare appear,
Be its own blush, be its own tear.

A well-tamed heart,
For whose more noble smart
Love may be long choosing a dart.

Eyes, that bestow
Full quivers on love's bow;
Yet pay less arrows than they owe.

Smiles, that can warm
The blood, yet teach a charm,
That chastity shall take no harm.

Blushes, that bin
The burnish of no sin,
Nor flames of aught too hot within.

Joys, that confess
Virtue their mistress,
And have no other head to dress.

Fears, fond and slight,
As the coy bride's, when night
First does the longing lover right.

Tears, quickly fled,
And vain, as those are shed
For a dying maidenhead.

Days, that need borrow
No part of their good-morrow
From a fore-spent night of sorrow.

Days, that in spite
Of darkness, by the light
Of a clear mind are day all night.

Nights, sweet as they,
Made short by lovers' play,
Yet long by th' absence of the day.

Life, that dares send
A challenge to his end,
And when it comes say, 'Welcome friend!'

Sydneian showers
Of sweet discourse, whose powers
Can crown old winter's head with flowers.

Soft silken hours,
Open suns, shady bowers,
'Bove all, nothing within that lowers.

Whate'er delight
Can make day's forehead bright;
Or give down to the wings of night.
. . .

I wish her store
Of worth may leave her poor
Of wishes, and I wish—no more.

Now if time knows
That Her whose radiant brows
Weave them a garland of my vows;
. . .

Her that dares be
What these lines wish to see:
I seek no further, it is she.

'Tis she, and here,
Lo! I unclothe and clear
My wishes' cloudy character.

May she enjoy it,
Whose merit dare apply it,
But modesty dares still deny it.

Such worth as this is
Shall fix my flying wishes,
And determine them to kisses.

Let her full glory,
My fancies, fly before ye;
Be ye my fictions—but her story.

JOHN PHILPOT CURRAN (1750–1817)

Let Us Be Merry

If sadly thinking, with spirits sinking,
Could, more than drinking, my cares compose
A cure for sorrow from sighs I'd borrow,
And hope tomorrow would end my woes.
But as in wailing, there's nought availing,
And Death unfailing will strike the blow;
Then for that reasons, and for a season,
Let us be merry before we go.

To joy a stranger, a wayworn ranger,
In every danger my course I've run;
Now hope all ending, and death befriending,
His last aid lending, my cares are done.
No more a rover, or hapless lover,
My griefs are over—my glass runs low;
Then for that reason, and for a season,
Let us be merry before we go.

S<small>AMUEL</small> D<small>ANIEL</small> (1562–1619)

'Care-charmer Sleep'

Care-charmer Sleep, son of the sable Night,
Brother to Death, in silent darkness born,
Relieve my languish, and restore the light;
With dark forgetting of my care return.

And let the day be time enough to mourn
The shipwreck of my ill-adventured youth:
Let waking eyes suffice to wail their scorn,
Without the torment of the night's untruth.

Cease, dreams, the the images of day-desires,
To model forth the passions of the morrow;
Never let rising Sun approve you liars,
To add more grief to aggravate my sorrow:
Still let me sleep, embracing clouds in vain,
And never wake to feel the day's disdain.

Then and Now

When men shall find thy flower, thy glory, pass,
And thou, with careful brow sitting alone,
Receivèd hast this message from thy glass,
That tells the truth and says that all is gone;
Fresh shalt thou see in me the wounds thou madest,
Thou spent thy flame, in me the heat remaining;
I that have loved thee thus before thou fadest,
My faith shall wax when thou art in thy waning.

The world shall find this miracle in me,
That fire can burn when all the matter's spent;
Then what my faith hath been, thyself shall see,
And that thou wast unkind, thou mayst repent.
Thou mayst repent that thou hast scorned my tears,
When winter snows upon thy sable hairs.

GEORGE DARLEY (1795–1846)

The Mermaids' Vesper Hymn

Troop home to silent grots and caves!
Troop home! and mimic as you go
The mournful winding of the waves
Which to their dark abysses flow.

At this sweet hour, all things beside
In amorous pairs to covert creep:
The swans that brushed the evening tide
Homeward in snowy couples keep.

In his green den the murmuring seal
Close by his sleek companion lies;
While singly we to bedward steal,
And close in fruitless sleep our eyes.

In bowers of love men take their rest,
In loveless bowers we sigh alone,
With bosom friends are others blest—
But we have none! but we have none!

WILLIAM DAVENANT (1606–1668)

Awake! Awake!

The lark now leaves his watery nest,
    And, climbing, shakes his dewy wings.
He takes this window for the East,
    And to implore your light he sings—
Awake! awake! The morn will never rise
Till she can dress her beauty at your eyes.

The merchant bows unto the seaman's star,
    The ploughman from the sun his season takes;
But still the lover wonders what they are
    Who look for day before his mistress wakes.
Awake! awake! Break thro' your veils of lawn!
Then draw your curtains, and begin the dawn!

John Davidson (1857–1909)

Thirty Bob a Week

I couldn't touch a stop and turn a screw,
    And set the blooming world a-work for me,
Like such as cut their teeth—I hope, like you—
    On the handle of a skeleton gold key;
I cut mine on a leek, which I eat it every week:
    I'm a clerk at thirty bob as you can see.

But I don't allow it's luck and all a toss;
    There's no such thing as being starred and crossed;
It's just the power of some to be a boss,
    And the bally power of others to be bossed:
I face the music, sir; you bet I ain't a cur;
    Strike me lucky if I don't believe I'm lost!

For like a mole I journey in the dark,
    A-travelling along the underground
From my Pillar'd Halls and broad Suburban Park,
    To come the daily dull official round;
And home again at night with my pipe all alight,
    A-scheming how to count ten bob a pound.

And it's often very cold and very wet,
    And my missus stitches towels for a hunks;
And the Pillar'd Halls is half of it to let—
    Three rooms about the size of travelling trunks.
And we cough, my wife and I, to dislocate a sigh,
    When the noisy little kids are in their bunks.

But you never hear her do a growl or whine,
    For she's made of flint and roses, very odd;
And I've got to cut my meaning rather fine,
    Or I'd blubber, for I'm made of greens and sod:
So p'r'haps we are in Hell for all that I can tell,
    And lost and damn'd and served up hot to God.

I ain't blaspheming, Mr Silver-tongue;
    I'm saying things a bit beyond your art:
Of all the rummy starts you ever sprung,

Thirty bob a week's the rummiest start!
With your science and your books and your the'ries about spooks,
   Did you ever hear of looking in your heart?

I didn't mean your pocket, Mr, no:
   I mean that having children and a wife,
With thirty bob on which to come and go,
   Isn't dancing to the tabor and the fife:
When it doesn't make you drink, by Heaven! it makes you think,
   And notice curious items about life.

I step into my heart and there I meet
   A god-almighty devil singing small,
Who would like to shout and whistle in the street,
   And squelch the passers flat against the wall;
If the whole world was a cake he had the power to take,
   He would take it, ask for more, and eat them all.

And I meet a sort of simpleton beside,
   The kind that life is always giving beans;
With thirty bob a week to keep a bride
   He fell in love and married in his teens:
At thirty bob he stuck; but he knows it isn't luck:
   He knows the seas are deeper than tureens.

And the god-almighty devil and the fool
   That meet me in the High Street on the strike,
When I walk about my heart a-gathering wool,
   Are my good and evil angels if you like.
And both of them together in every kind of weather
   Ride me like a double-seated bike.

That's rough a bit and needs its meaning curled.
   But I have a high old hot 'un in my mind—
A most engrugious notion of the world,
   That leaves your lightning 'rithmetic behind:
I give it at a glance when I say 'There ain't no chance,
   Nor nothing of the lucky-lottery kind.'

And it's this way that I make it out to be:
   No fathers, mothers, countries, climates—none;
Not Adam was responsible for me,
   Nor society, nor systems, nary one:

A little sleeping seed, I woke—I did, indeed—
    A million years before the blooming sun.

I woke because I thought the time had come;
    Beyond my will there was no other cause;
And everywhere I found myself at home,
    Because I chose to be the thing I was;
And in whatever shape of mollusc or of ape
    I always went according to the laws.

I was the love that chose my mother out;
    I joined two lives and from the union burst;
My weakness and my strength without a doubt
    Are mine alone for ever from the first:
It's just the very same with a difference in the name
    As 'Thy will be done.' You say it if you durst!

They say it daily up and down the land
    As easy as you take a drink, it's true;
But the difficultest go to understand,
    And the difficultest job a man can do,
Is to come it brave and meek with thirty bob a week,
    And feel that that's the proper thing for you.

It's a naked child against a hungry wolf;
    It's playing bowls upon a splitting wreck;
It's walking on a string across a gulf
    With millstones fore-and-aft about your neck;
But the thing is daily done by many and many a one;
    And we fall, face forward, fighting, on the deck.

DANIEL DEFOE (1660–1731)

from 'The True-born Englishman'

    The western Angles all the rest subdued;
    A bloody nation, barbarous and rude:
    Who by the tenure of the sword possest
    One part of Britain, and subdued the rest
    And as great things denominate the small,
    The conquering part gave title to the whole.

The Scot, Pict, Britain, Roman, Dane, submit,
And with the English-Saxon all unite:
And these the mixture have so close pursued,
The very name and memory's subdued:
No Roman now, no Britain does remain;
Wales strove to separate, but strove in vain:
The silent nations undistinguished fall,
And Englishman's the common name for all.
Fate jumbled them together, God knows how;
What e'er they were they're true-born English now.
The wonder which remains is at our pride,
To value that which all wise men deride.
For Englishmen to boast of generation,
Cancels their knowledge, and lampoons the nation.
A true-born Englishman's a contradiction,
A banter made to be a test of fools,
Which those that use it justly ridicules.
A metaphor invented to express
A man akin to all the universe.
For as the Scots, as learnèd men ha' said,
Throughout the world their wandering seed ha' spread;
So open-handed England, 'tis believed,
Has all the gleanings of the world received.
Some think of England 'twas our Saviour meant,
The Gospel should to all the world be sent:
Since, when the blessèd sound did hither reach,
They to all nations might be said to preach.
'Tis well that virtue gives nobility,
How shall we else the want of birth and blood supply?
Since scarce one family is left alive,
Which does not from some foreigner derive.

THOMAS DEKKER (1570?–1641?)

Lullaby

Golden slumbers kiss your eyes;
Smiles awake you when you rise.
Sleep, pretty wantons, do not cry,
And I will sing a lullaby:
Rock them, rock them, lullaby.

Care is heavy, therefore sleep you;
You are care, and care must keep you.
Sleep, pretty wantons, do not cry,
And I will sing a lullaby:
Rock them, rock them, lullaby.

WALTER DE LA MARE (1873–1956)

The Listeners

'Is there anybody there?' said the Traveller,
  Knocking on the moonlit door;
And his horse in the silence champed the grasses
  Of the forest's ferny floor.
And a bird flew up out of the turret,
  Above the Traveller's head:
And he smote upon the door again a second time;
  'Is there anybody there?' he said.
But no one descended to the Traveller;
  No head from the leaf-fringed sill
Leaned over and looked into his grey eyes,
  Where he stood perplexed and still.
But only a host of phantom listeners
  That dwelt in the lone house then
Stood listening in the quiet of the moonlight
  To that voice from the world of men:
Stood thronging the faint moonbeams on the dark stair
  That goes down to the empty hall,
Hearkening in an air stirred and shaken
  By the lonely Traveller's call.
And he felt in his heart their strangeness,
  Their stillness answering his cry,
While his horse moved, cropping the dark turf,
  'Neath the starred and leafy sky;
For he suddenly smote on the door, even
  Louder, and lifted his head:—
'Tell them I came, and no one answered,
  That I kept my word,' he said.
Never the least stir made the listeners,
  Though every word he spake

Fell echoing through the shadowiness of the still house
    From the one man left awake:
Aye, they heard his foot upon the stirrup,
    And the sound of iron on stone,
And how the silence surged softly backward,
    When the plunging hoofs were gone.

An Epitaph

Here lies a most beautiful lady,
Light of step and heart was she;
I think she was the most beautiful lady
That ever was in the West Country.
But beauty vanishes; beauty passes;
However rare—rare it be;
And when I crumble, who will remember
This lady of the West Country?

Napoleon

'What is the world, O soldiers?
    It is I:
I, this incessant snow,
    This northern sky;
Soldiers, this solitude
    Through which we go
      Is I.'

EMILY DICKINSON (1830–1886)

The Only News I Know

The only news I know
Is bulletins all day
From Immortality.

The only shows I see,
Tomorrow and Today,
Perchance Eternity.

The only One I meet
Is God,—the only street,
Existence; this traversed

If other news there be,
Or admirabler show—
I'll tell it you.

Snake

A narrow fellow in the grass
Occasionally rides;
You may have met him,—did you not,
His notice sudden is.

The grass divides as with a comb,
A spotted shaft is seen;
And then it closes at your feet
And opens further on.

He likes a boggy acre,
A floor too cool for corn.
Yet when a child, and barefoot,
I more than once, at morn,

Have passed, I thought, a whip-lash
Unbraiding in the sun,—
When, stooping to secure it,
It wrinkled, and was gone.

Several of nature's people
I know, and they know me;
I feel for them a transport
Of cordiality;

But never met this fellow,
Attended or alone,
Without a tighter breathing,
And zero at the bone.

'I've known a Heaven like a tent'

I've known a Heaven like a tent
To wrap its shining yards,
Pluck up its stakes and disappear
Without the sound of boards
Or rip of nail, or carpenter,
But just the miles of stare
That signalize a show's retreat
In North America.

No trace, no figment of the thing
That dazzled yesterday,
No ring, no marvel;
Men and feats
Dissolved as utterly
As birds' far navigation
Discloses just a hue;
A plash of oars—a gaiety,
Then swallowed up to view.

'There's a certain slant of light'

There's a certain slant of light,
On winter afternoons,
That oppresses, like the weight
Of cathedral tunes.

Heavenly hurt it gives us;
We can find no scar,
But internal difference
Where the meanings are.

None may teach it anything,
'Tis the seal, despair,—
An imperial affliction
Sent us of the air.

When it comes, the landscape listens,
Shadows hold their breath;

When it goes, 'tis like the distance
On the look of death.

'There's been a death'

There's been a death in the opposite house
    As lately as today.
I know it by the numb look
    Such houses have alway.

The neighbours rustle in and out,
    The doctor drives away.
A window opens like a pod,
    Abrupt, mechanically;

Somebody flings a mattress out,—
    The children hurry by;
They wonder if It died on that,—
    I used to when a boy.

The minister goes stiffly in
    As if the house were his,
And he owned all the mourners now,
    And little boys besides;

And then the milliner, and the man
    Of the appalling trade,
To take the measure of the house,
    There'll be that dark parade.

Of tassels and of coaches soon;
    It's easy as a sign,—
The intuition of the news
    In just a country town.

The Immortality She Gave

The Immortality she gave
We borrowed at her grave;
For just one plaudit banishing
The might of human love.

'Love's stricken "why"'

Love's stricken 'why'
Is all that love can speak—
Built of but just a syllable
The hugest hearts that break.

'Go not too near a house of rose'

Go not too near a house of rose,
The depredation of a breeze
Or inundation of a dew
Alarm its walls away;

Nor try to tie the butterfly;
Nor climb the bars of ecstasy.
In insecurity to lie
Is joy's insuring quality.

'My life closed twice before its close'

My life closed twice before its close;
It yet remains to see
If Immortality unveil
A third event to me,

So huge, so hopeless to conceive,
As these that twice befell.
Parting is all we know of heaven,
And all we need of hell.

HENRY AUSTIN DOBSON (1840–1921)

'In after days'

In after days when grasses high
O'ertop the stone where I shall lie,
    Though ill or well the world adjust

My slender claim to honoured dust,
I shall not question or reply.

I shall not see the morning sky;
I shall not hear the night-wind's sigh;
    I shall be mute, as all men must
      In after days!

But yet, now living, fain were I
That some one then should testify,
    Saying—'He held his pen in trust
    To Art, not serving shame or lust.'
Will none?—Then let my memory die
      In after days.

JOHN DONNE (1573–1631)

A Hymn to God the Father

Wilt thou forgive that sin where I begun,
    Which is my sin, though it were done before?
Wilt Thou forgive that sin, through which I run,
    And do run still: though still I do deplore?
      When Thou hast done, Thou hast not done,
      For I have more.

Wilt Thou forgive that sin which I have won
    Others to sin, and made my sin their door?
Wilt Thou forgive that sin which I did shun
    A year or two: but wallowed in, a score?
      When thou hast done, thou hast not done,
      For I have more.

I have a sin of fear, that when I have spun
    My last thread, I shall perish on the shore;
But swear by Thyself, that at my death Thy son
    Shall shine as He shines now, and heretofore;
      And, having done that, Thou hast done;
      I fear no more.

The Sun Rising

Busy old fool, unruly Sun,
　　Why dost thou thus,
Through windows, and through curtains, call on us?
Must to thy motions lovers' seasons run?
　　Saucy pedantic wretch, go chide
　　Late schoolboys, and sour prentices,
　Go tell court-huntsmen that the king will ride,
　Call country ants to harvest offices;
Love, all alike, no season knows, nor clime,
Nor hours, days, months, which are the rags of time.

Thy beams, so reverend and strong
　　Why shouldst thou think?
I could eclipse and cloud them with a wink,
But that I would not lose her sight so long:
　　If her eyes have not blinded thine,
　　Look, and tomorrow late, tell me
　Whether both th' Indias of spice and mine
　Be where thou left'st them, or lie here with me.
Ask for those kings whom thou saw'st yesterday,
And thou shalt hear, 'All here in one bed lay.'

She is all states, and all princes I:
　　Nothing else is;
Princes do but play us; compared to this,
All honour's mimic, all wealth alchemy.
　　Thou, Sun, art half as happy as are we,
　　In that the world's contracted thus;
　Thine age asks ease, and since thy duties be
　To warm the world, that's done in warming us.
Shine here to us, and thou art everywhere;
This bed thy centre is, these walls, thy sphere.

The Burned Ship

Out of a fired ship, which by no way
But drowning could be rescued from the flame,
Some men leaped forth, and ever as they came

Near the foes' ships, did by their shot decay;
So all were lost, which in the ship were found,
They in the sea being burnt, they in the burnt ship drowned.

The Good Morrow

I wonder by my troth, what thou and I
Did, till we loved? Were we not weaned till then?
But sucked on country pleasures, childishly?
Or snorted we in the Seven Sleepers' den?
'Twas so; but this, all pleasures fancies be;
If ever any beauty I did see,
Which I desired, and got, 'twas but a dream of thee.

And now good morrow to our waking souls,
Which watch not one another out of fear;
For love all love of other sights controls,
And makes one little room an everywhere.
Let sea-discoverers to new worlds have gone;
Let maps to other, worlds on worlds have shown;
Let us possess one world; each hath one, and is one.

My face in thine eye, thine in mine appears,
And true plain hearts do in the faces rest;
Where can we find two better hemispheres
Without sharp north, without declining west?
Whatever dies, was not mixed equally;
If our two loves be one, or thou and I
Love so alike that none do slacken, none can die.

To His Mistress Going to Bed
(from Elegy 19)

Come, Madam, come, all rest my powers defy,
Until I labour, I in labour lie.
The foe oft-times having the foe in sight,
Is tired with standing though he never fight.
Off with that girdle, like heaven's Zone glistering,
But a far fairer world encompassing.
Unpin that spangled breastplate which you wear,

That the eyes of busy fools may be stopt there.
Unlace yourself, for that harmonious chime
Tells me from you, that now it is bed time.
Off with that happy busk, which I envy,
That still can be, and still can stand so nigh.
Your gown going off, such beauteous state reveals,
As when from flowery meads th' hill's shadow steals. . . .
    Licence my roving hands, and let them go,
Before, behind, between, above, below.
O my America! my new-found-land,
My kingdom, safeliest when with one man manned,
My Mine of precious stones, my Empery,
How blest am I in this discovering thee!
To enter in these bonds, is to be free;
Then where my hand is set, my seal shall be.
    Full nakedness! All joys are due to thee,
As souls unbodied, bodies unclothed must be,
To taste whole joys.

ERNEST DOWSON (1867–1900)

Cynara

Non Sum Qualis Eram Bonae Sub Regno Cynarae

Last night, ah, yesternight, betwixt her lips and mine
There fell thy shadow, Cynara! thy breath was shed
Upon my soul between the kisses and the wine;
And I was desolate and sick of an old passion,
    Yea, I was desolate and bowed my head:
I have been faithful to thee, Cynara! in my fashion.

All night upon mine heart I felt her warm heart beat,
Night-long within mine arms in love and sleep she lay;
Surely the kisses of her bought red mouth were sweet;
But I was desolate and sick of an old passion,
    When I awoke and found the dawn was grey:
I have been faithful to thee, Cynara! in my fashion.

I have forgot much, Cynara! gone with the wind,
Flung roses, roses riotously with the throng,
Dancing, to put thy pale, lost lilies out of mind;

But I was desolate and sick of an old passion,
    Yea, all the time, because the dance was long:
I have been faithful to thee, Cynara! in my fashion.

I cried for madder music and for stronger wine,
But when the feast is finished and the lamps expire,
Then falls thy shadow, Cynara! the night is thine;
And I am desolate and sick of an old passion,
    Yea hungry for the lips of my desire:
I have been faithful to thee, Cynara! in my fashion.

Days of Wine and Roses

Vitae Summa Brevis Spem Nos Vetat Incohare Longam

They are not long, the weeping and the laughter,
Love and desire and hate:
I think they have no portion in us after
We pass the gate.

They are not long, the days of wine and roses:
Out of a misty dream
Our path merges for a while, then closes
Within a dream.

MICHAEL DRAYTON (1563–1631)

Parting

Since there's no help, come let us kiss and part;
Nay, I have done, you get no more of me;
And I am glad, yea glad with all my heart,
That thus so cleanly I myself can free.

Shake hands for ever, cancel all our vows,
And, when we meet at any time again,
Be it not seen in either of our brows
That we one jot of former love retain.

Now at the last gasp of Love's latest breath,
When, his pulse failing, Passion speechless lies,
When Faith is kneeling by his bed of death,

And Innocence is closing up his eyes—
    Now, if thou wouldst, when all have given him over,
    From death to life thou might'st him yet recover!

'How many paltry, foolish, painted things'

How many paltry, foolish, painted things,
That now in coaches trouble every street,
Shall be forgotten, whom no poet sings,
Ere they be well wrapped in their winding-sheet?
Where I to thee eternity shall give,
When nothing else remaineth of these days,
And queens hereafter shall be glad to live
Upon the alms of thy superfluous praise.

Virgins and matrons reading these my rhymes
Shall be so much delighted with thy story,
That they shall grieve they lived not in these times
To have seen thee, their sex's only glory.
    So shalt thou fly above the vulgar throng,
    Still to survive in my immortal song.

The Paradox

When first I ended, then I first began;
Then more I travelled further from my rest.
Where most I lost, there most of all I won;
Pinèd with hunger, rising from a feast.
Methinks I fly, yet want I legs to go;
Wise in conceit, in act a very sot;
Ravished with joy amidst a hell of woe;
What most I seem that surest I am not.

I build my hopes a world above the sky,
Yet with the mole I creep into the earth;
In plenty, I am starved with penury,
And yet I surfeit in the greatest dearth.
    I have, I want; despair, and yet desire;
    Burned in a sea of ice, and drowned amidst a fire.

JOHN DRYDEN (1631–1700)

The Secular Masque

Enter Janus

Janus:	Chronos, Chronos, mend thy pace:
	An hundred times the rolling sun
	Around the radiant belt has run
	In his revolving race.
	Behold, behold, the goal in sight;
	Spread thy fans, and wing thy flight.

Enter Chronos, *with a scythe in his hand, and a great globe on his back,*
which he sets down at his entrance

Chronos:	Weary, weary of my weight,
	Let me, let me drop my freight,
	And leave the world behind.
	I could not bear
	Another year
	The load of human-kind.

Enter Momus, *laughing*

Momus:	Ha! ha! ha! Ha! ha! ha! well hast thou done,
	To lay down thy pack,
	And lighten thy back.
	The world was a fool, e'er since it begun,
	And since neither Janus, nor Chronos, nor I,
	Can hinder the crimes,
	Or mend the bad times,
	'Tis better to laugh than to cry.

Chorus of all three:	'Tis better to laugh than to cry

Janus:	Since Momus comes to laugh below,
	Old Time begin the show,
	That he may see, in every scene,
	What changes in this age have been,

Chronos:	Then goddess of the silver bow begin.

                                         [Horns, or hunting-music within]

Enter Diana

Diana:	With horns and with hounds I waken the day,

And hie to my woodland walks away;
I tuck up my robe, and am buskined soon,
And tie to my forehead a waxing Moon.
I course the fleet stag, unkennel the fox,
And chase the wild goats o'er summits of rocks,
With shouting and hooting we pierce thro' the sky;
And Echo turns hunter, and doubles the cry.

Chorus of all: With shouting and hooting, we pierce through the sky,
And Echo turns hunter, and doubles the cry.

Janus: Then our age was in its prime:

Chronos: Free from rage,

Diana: —And free from crime.

Momus: A very merry, dancing, drinking,
Laughing, quaffing, and unthinking time.

Chorus of all: Then our age was in its prime,
Free from rage, and free from crime,
A very merry, dancing, drinking,
Laughing, quaffing, and unthinking time.

[*Dance of* Diana's *attendants*]

Enter Mars

Mars: Inspire the vocal brass, inspire;
The world is past its infant age:
    Arms and honour,
    Arms and honour,
Set the martial mind on fire,
And kindle manly rage.
    Mars has looked the sky to red;
And peace, the lazy good, is fled.
Plenty, peace, and pleasure fly;
    The sprightly green
In woodland-walks no more is seen;
The sprightly green has drunk the Tyrian dye.

Chorus of all: Plenty, peace, etc.

Mars: Sound the trumpet, beat the drum;
    Through all the world around,
    Sound a reveille, sound, sound,
The Warrior God is come.

Chorus of all: Sound the trumpet, etc.

Momus:	Thy sword within the scabbard keep,
	    And let mankind agree;
	Better the world were fast asleep,
	    Than kept awake by thee.
	The fools are only thinner,
	    With all our cost and care;
	But neither side a winner,
	    For things are as they were.

Chorus of all:	The fools are only, etc

Enter Venus

Venus	Calms appear, when storms are past; Love will have his hour at last: Nature is my kindly care; Mars destroys, and I repair; Take me, take me, while you may, Venus comes not ev'ry day.
Chorus of all:	Take her, take her, etc.

Chronos:	The world was then so light,
	    I scarcely felt the weight;
	Joy rul'd the day, and love the night.
	But since the queen of pleasure left the ground,
	    I faint, I lag,
	    And feebly drag
	The pond'rous orb around.

Momus:	All, all of a piece throughout: (*pointing to Diana*) Thy chase had a beast in view; (—*to Mars*) Thy wars brought nothing about; (—*to Venus*) Thy lovers were all untrue.
Janus:	'Tis well an old age is out,
Chronos:	And time to begin a new.

Chorus of all:	All, all of a piece throughout;
	    Thy chase had a beast in view;
	Thy wars brought nothing about;
	    Thy lovers were all untrue.
	'Tis well an old age is out,
	    And time to begin a new.

[*Dance of huntsmen, nymphs, warriors, and lovers*]

A Song for St Cecilia's Day

From harmony, from heavenly harmony
  This universal frame began;
  When Nature underneath a heap
   Of jarring atoms lay,
  And could not heave her head,
The tuneful voice was heard from high,
  Arise, ye more than dead.
Then cold and hot and moist and dry
  In order to their stations leap,
   And Music's power obey.
From harmony, from heavenly harmony
  This universal frame began:
  From harmony to harmony
Through all the compass of the notes it ran,
The diapason closing full in Man.
What passion cannot music raise and quell?
   When Jubal struck the corded shell,
  His listening brethren stood around,
   And wondering, on their faces fell
To worship that celestial sound:
Less than a god they thought there could not dwell
   Within the hollow of that shell,
   That spoke so sweetly, and so well.
What passion cannot Music raise and quell!
  The trumpet's loud clangour
   Excites us to arms
  With shrill notes of anger
   And mortal alarms.
  The double double double beat
   Of the thundering drum
   Cries, Hark! the foes come;
Charge, charge, 'tis too late to retreat.
  The soft complaining flute
  In dying notes discovers
  The woes of hopeless lovers,
Whose dirge is whispered by the warbling lute.
  Sharp violins proclaim
  Their jealous pangs and desperation,

Fury, frantic indignation,
Depth of pains and height of passion,
    For the fair, disdainful dame.

But oh! what art can teach
What human voice can reach
    The sacred organ's praise?
Notes inspiring holy love,
Notes that wing their heavenly ways
    To mend the choirs above.

Orpheus could lead the savage race,
And trees unrooted left their place,
    Sequacious of the lyre:
But bright Cecilia raised the wonder higher.
When to her organ vocal breath was given,
An angel heard, and straight appeared
    Mistaking earth for heaven.

Grand Chorus
    As from the power of sacred lays
        The spheres began to move,
    And sung the great Creator's praise
        To all the Blest above;
    So, when the last and dreadful hour
    This crumbling pageant shall devour,
    The trumpet shall be heard on high,
    The dead shall live, the living die,
    And music shall untune the sky.

Alexander's Feast

or *The Power of Music*

'Twas at the royal feast, for Persia won
By Philip's warlike son—
Aloft in awful state
The godlike hero sate
On his imperial throne;
His valiant peers were placed around,
Their brows with roses and with myrtles bound,

(So should desert in arms be crowned);
The lovely Thais, by his side,
Sate like a blooming eastern bride
In flower of youth and beauty's pride:—
Happy, happy, happy pair!
None but the brave,
None but the brave,
None but the brave deserves the fair.

Timotheus, placèd on high
Amid the tuneful choir,
With flying fingers touched the lyre:
The trembling notes ascend the sky,
And heavenly joys inspire.
The song began from Jove,
Who left his blissful seats above—
Such is the power of mighty love!
A dragon's fiery form belied the god;
Sublime on radiant spires he rode
When he to fair Olympia prest,
And while he sought her snowy breast:
Then, round her slender waist he curled,
And stamped an image of himself, a sovereign of the world.
—The listening crowd admire the lofty sound!
'A present deity!' they shout around:
'A present deity!' the vaulted roofs rebound!
With ravished ears
The monarch hears,
Assumes the god;
Affects to nod
And seems to shake the spheres.
The praise of Bacchus then the sweet musician sung,
Of Bacchus ever fair and ever young:
The jolly god in triumph comes;
Sound the trumpets; beat the drums;
Flushed with a purple grace
He shows his honest face;
Now give the hautboys breath. He comes! he comes!
Bacchus, ever fair and young,
Drinking joys did first ordain;
Bacchus' blessings are a treasure,
Drinking is the soldier's pleasure:

Rich the treasure,
Sweet the pleasure,
Sweet is pleasure after pain.

Soothed with the sound, the king grew vain;
Fought all his battles o'er again;
And thrice he routed all his foes; and thrice he slew the slain!
The master saw the madness rise,
His glowing cheeks, his ardent eyes;
And while he heaven and earth defied,
Changed his hand, and checked his pride.
He chose a mournful Muse
Soft pity to infuse:
He sung Darius great and good,
By too severe a fate
Fallen, fallen, fallen, fallen,
Fallen from his high estate,
And weltering in his blood;
Deserted at his utmost need
By those his former bounty fed;
On the bare earth exposed he lies
With not a friend to close his eyes.
—With downcast looks the joyless victor sat,
Revolving in his altered soul
The various turns of chance below;
And now and then a sigh he stole,
And tears began to flow.

The mighty master smiled to see
That love was in the next degree;
'Twas but a kindred sound to move,
For pity melts the mind to love.
Softly sweet, in Lydian measures
Soon he soothed his soul to pleasures.
'War,' he sung, 'is toil and trouble,
Honour, but an empty bubble;
Never ending, still beginning,
Fighting still, and still destroying;
If the world be worth thy winning,
Think, O think, it worth enjoying:
Lovely Thais sits beside thee,
Take the good the gods provide thee.'

—The many rend the skies with loud applause;
So Love was crowned, but Music won the cause.
The prince, unable to conceal his pain,
Gazed on the fair
Who caused his care,
And sighed and looked, sighed and looked again:
Sighed and looked, and sighed again:
At length with love and wine at once opprest
The vanquished victor sunk upon her breast.

Now strike the golden lyre again:
A louder yet, and yet a louder strain!
Break his bands of sleep asunder
And rouse him like a rattling peal of thunder.
Hark! hark! the horrid sound
Has raisèd up his head:
As wakèd from the dead
And amazed, he stares around.
'Revenge, revenge,' Timotheus cries,
'See the Furies arise!
See the snakes that they rear!
How they hiss in their hair,
And the sparkles that flash from their eyes!
Behold a ghastly band,
Each a torch in his hand!
Those are Grecian ghosts, that in battle were slain
And unburied remain
Inglorious on the plain:
Give the vengeance due
To the valiant crew!
Behold how they toss their torches on high,
How they point to the Persian abodes,
And glittering temples of their hostile gods!'
—The princes applaud with a furious joy;
And the king seized a flambeau with zeal to destroy;
Thais led the way
To light him to his prey,
And, like another Helen, fired another Troy.

—Thus long ago,
Ere heaving bellows learned to blow,
While organs yet were mute,

Timotheus, to his breathing flute
And sounding lyre
Could swell the soul to rage, or kindle soft desire.
At last divine Cecilia came,
Inventress of the vocal frame;
The sweet enthusiast from her sacred store,
Enlarged the former narrow bounds,
And added length to solemn sounds,
With Nature's mother wit, and arts unknown before.

Let old Timotheus yield the prize,
Or both divide the crown:
He raised a mortal to the skies;
She drew an angel down!

Milton

Three poets, in three distant ages born,
Greece, Italy, and England did adorn.
The first in loftiness of thought surpassed,
The next in majesty, in both the last.
The force of Nature could no further go—
To make a third she joined the other two.

WILLIAM DUNBAR (1456?–1513?)

Lament for the Makaris[1]

I that in heill was and gladnèss[2]
Am trublit now with great sickness
And feblit with infirmitie:
  Timor Mortis conturbat me.[3]

Our plesance here is all vain glory,
This fals world is but transitory,
The flesh is bruckle, the Feynd is slee:[4]
  Timor Mortis conturbat me.

[1] makaris = makers (poets). [2] heill = health. [3] Fear of death disquiets me.
[4] bruckle = brittle, feeble. slee = sly.

The state of man does change and vary,
Now sound, now sick, now blyth, now sary,
Now dansand mirry, now like to die:[1]
    Timor Mortis conturbat me.

No state in Erd here standis sicker;[2]
As with the wynd wavis the wicker[3]
So wannis this world's vanitie:[4]
    Timor Mortis conturbat me.

Unto the Death gois all Estatis,
Princis, Prelatis, and Potestatis,
Baith rich and poor of all degree:
    Timor Mortis conturbat me.

He takis the knichtis in to the field
Enarmit under helm and scheild;
Victor he is at all mellie:[5]
    Timor Mortis conturbat me.

That strong unmerciful tyrand
Takis, on the motheris breast sowkand,[6]
The babe full of benignitie:
    Timor Mortis conturbat me.

He takis the campion in the stour,[7]
The captain closit in the tour,
The lady in bour full of bewtie:
    Timor Mortis conturbat me.

He spairis no lord for his piscence,[8]
Na clerk for his intelligence;
His awful straik may no man flee:[9]
    Timor Mortis conturbat me.

Art-magicianis and astrologgis,
Rethoris, logicianis, and theologgis,
Them helpis no conclusionis slee:
    Timor Mortis conturbat me.

---

[1] dansand = dancing. [2] sicker = sure. [3] wicker = willow. [4] wannis = wanes.
[5] mellie = close combat. [6] sowkand = sucking. [7] campion = champion; stour = fight.
[8] piscence = puissance. [9] straik = stroke.

In medecine the most practicianis,
Leechis, surrigianis, and physicianis,
Themself from Death may not supplee:[1]
    Timor Mortis conturbat me.

I see that makaris amang the lave[2]
Playis here their padyanis, syne gois to grave;[3]
Sparit is nocht their facultie:
    Timor Mortis conturbat me.

He has done petuously devour
The noble Chaucer, of makaris flour,
The Monk of Bury, and Gower, all three:
    Timor Mortis conturbat me.

The good Sir Hew of Eglintoun,
Ettrick, Heriot, and Wintoun,
He has tane out of this cuntrie:
    Timor Mortis conturbat me.

That scorpion fell has done infeck
Maister John Clerk, and James Afflek,
Fra ballat-making and tragedie:
    Timor Mortis conturbat me.

Holland and Barbour he has berevit;
Alas! that he not with us levit
Sir Mungo Lockart of the Lee:
    Timor Mortis conturbat me.

Clerk of Tranent eke he has tane,
That made the anteris of Gawaine;[4]
Sir Gilbert Hay endit has he:
    Timor Mortis conturbat me.

He has Blind Harry and Sandy Traill
Slain with his schour of mortal hail,[5]
Quhilk Patrick Johnstoun might nought flee:
    Timor Mortis conturbat me.

[1] supplee = save. [2] the lave = the leave, the rest. [3] padyanis = pageants.
[4] anteris = adventures. [5] schour = shower.

He has reft Merseir his endite,[1]
That did in luve so lively write,
So short, so quick, of sentence hie:
    Timor Mortis conturbat me.

He has tane Rowll of Aberdene,
And gentill Rowll of Corstorphine;
Two better fallowis did no man see:[2]
    Timor Mortis conturbat me.

In Dunfermline he has tane Broun
With Maister Robert Henrysoun;
Sir John the Ross enbrast has he:
    Timor Mortis conturbat me.

And he has now tane, last of a,
Good gentil Stobo and Quintin Shaw,
Of quhom all wichtis hes pitie:[3]
    Timor Mortis conturbat me.

Good Maister Walter Kennedy
In point of Death lies verily;
Great ruth it were that so suld be:
    Timor Mortis conturbat me.

Sen he has all my brether tane,
He will naught let me live alane;
Of force I man his next prey be:[4]
    Timor Mortis conturbat me.

Since for the Death remeid is none,
Best is that we for Death dispone,[5]
After our death that live may we:
    Timor Mortis conturbat me.

---

[1] endite = inditing. [2] fallowis = fellows. [3] quhom = whom wichtis = wights, persons.
[4] man = must. [5] dispone = make disposition.

T. S. ELIOT (1888–1965)

Preludes

1

The winter evening settles down
With smell of steaks in passageways.
Six o' clock.
The burnt-out ends of smoky days,
And now a gusty shower wraps
The grimy scraps
Of withered leaves about your feet
And newspapers from vacant lots;
The showers beat
On broken blinds and chimney-pots,
And at the corner of the street
A lonely cab-horse steams and stamps.

And then the lighting of the lamps.

2

The morning comes to consciousness
Of faint stale smells of beer
From the sawdust-trampled street
With all its muddy feet that press
To early coffee-stands.

With the other masquerades
That time resumes,
One thinks of all the hands
That are raising dingy shades
In a thousand furnished rooms.

3

You tossed a blanket from the bed,
You lay upon your back, and waited;
You dozed, and watched the night revealing
The thousand sordid images
Of which your soul was constituted;
They flickered against the ceiling.

And when all the world came back
And the light crept up between the shutters
And you heard the sparrows in the gutters,
You had such a vision of the street
As the street hardly understands;
Sitting along the bed's edge, where
You curled the papers from your hair,
Or clasped the yellow soles of feet
In the palms of both soiled hands.

4

His soul stretched tight across the skies
That fade behind a city block,
Or trampled by insistent feet
At four and five and six o'clock;
And short square fingers stuffing pipes,
And evening newspapers, and eyes
Assured of certain certainties,
The conscience of a blackened street
Impatient to assume the world.

I am moved by fancies that are curled
Around these images, and cling:
The notion of some infinitely gentle
Infinitely suffering thing.

Wipe your hand across your mouth, and laugh;
The worlds revolve like ancient women
Gathering fuel in vacant lots.

U. A. Fanthorpe (1929–)

BC:AD

This was the moment when Before
Turned into After, and the future's
Uninvented timekeepers presented arms.

This was the moment when nothing
Happened. Only dull peace
Sprawled boringly over the earth.

This was the moment when even energetic Romans
Could find nothing better to do
Than counting beads in remote provinces.

And this was the moment
When a few farm workers and three
Members of an obscure Persian sect

Walked haphazard by starlight straight
Into the kingdom of heaven.

EDWARD FITZGERALD (1809–1883)

Rubáiyát of Omar Khayyám

The First Edition, 1859

1

Awake! for Morning in the Bowl of Night
Has flung the Stone that puts the Stars to Flight:
    And Lo! the Hunter of the East has caught
The Sultan's Turret in a Noose of Light.

2

Dreaming when Dawn's Left Hand was in the Sky
I heard a Voice within the Tavern cry,
    'Awake, my Little ones, and fill the Cup
Before Life's Liquor in its Cup be dry.'

3

And, as the Cock crew, those who stood before
The Tavern shouted—'Open then the Door!
    You know how little while we have to stay,
And, once departed, may return no more.'

4

Now the New Year reviving old Desires,
The thoughtful Soul to Solitude retires,
    Where the WHITE HAND OF MOSES on the Bough
Puts out, and Jesus from the Ground suspires.

5

Iram indeed is gone with all its Rose,
And Jamsh´yd's Sev'n-ring'd Cup where no one knows;
    But still the Vine her ancient Ruby yields,
And still a Garden by the Water blows.

6

And David's Lips are lock't; but in divine
High-piping Pehlevi, with 'Wine! Wine! Wine!
    Red Wine!'—the Nightingale cries to the Rose
That yellow Cheek of hers to incardine.

7

Come, fill the Cup, and in the fire of Spring
The Winter-garment of Repentance fling:
    The Bird of Time has but a little way
To fly—and Lo! the Bird is on the Wing.

8

And look—a thousand Blossoms with the Day
Woke—and a thousand scatter'd into Clay:
    And this first Summer Month that brings the Rose
Shall take Jamsh´yd and Kaikobád away.

9

But come with old Khayyám, and leave the Lot
Of Kaikobád and Kaikhosrú forgot:
    Let Rustum lay about him as he will,
Or Hátim Tai cry Supper—heed them not.

10

With me along some Strip of Herbage strown
That just divides the desert from the sown,
    Where name of Slave and Sultán scarce is known,
And pity Sultán Mahmud on his Throne.

11

Here with a Loaf of Bread beneath the Bough,
A Flask of Wine, a Book of Verse—and Thou
    Beside me singing in the Wilderness—
And Wilderness is Paradise enow.

12

'How sweet is mortal Sovranty!'—think some:
Others—'How blest the Paradise to come!'
  Ah, take the Cash in hand and waive the Rest;
Oh, the brave Music of a *distant* Drum!

13

Look to the Rose that blows about us—'Lo,
Laughing,' she says, 'into the World I blow:
  At once the silken Tassel of my Purse
Tear, and its Treasures on the Garden throw.'

14

The Wordly Hope men set their Hearts upon
Turns Ashes—or it prospers; and anon,
  Like Snow upon the Desert's dusty Face
Lighting a little Hour or two—is gone.

15

And those who husbanded the Golden Grain,
And those who flung it to the Winds like Rain,
  Alike to no such aureate Earth are turn'd
As, buried once, Men want dug up again.

16

Think, in this battered Caravanserai
Whose Doorways are alternative Night and Day,
  How Sultán after Sultán with his Pomp
Abode his Hour or two and went his way.

17

They say the Lion and the Lizard keep
The Courts where Jamsh'yd gloried and drank deep:
  And Bahrám, that great Hunter—the Wild Ass
Stamps o'er his Head, and he lies fast asleep.

18

I sometimes think that never blows so red
The Rose as where some buried Caesar bled;
  That every Hyacinth the Garden wears
Dropt in its Lap from some once lovely Head.

19

And this delightful Herb whose tender Green
Fledges the River's Lip on which we lean—
   Ah, lean upon it lightly! for who knows
From what once lovely Lip it springs unseen!

20

Ah, my Belovèd, fill the Cup that clears
TODAY of past Regrets and future Fears—
   Tomorrow?—Why, Tomorrow I may be
Myself with Yesterday's Sev'n Thousand Years.

21

Lo! some we loved, the loveliest and best
That Time and Fate of all their Vintage prest,
   Have drunk their Cup a Round or two before,
And one by one crept silently to Rest.

22

And we, that now make merry in the Room
They left, and Summer dresses in new Bloom,
   Ourselves must we beneath the Couch of Earth
Descend, ourselves to make a Couch—for whom?

23

Ah, make the most of what we yet may spend,
Before we too into the Dust descend;
   Dust into Dust, and under Dust, to lie,
Sans Wine, sans Song, sans Singer, and—sans End!

24

Alike for those who for TODAY prepare,
And those that after a TOMORROW stare,
   A Muezzin from the Tower of Darkness cries,
'Fools! your Reward is neither Here nor There!'

25

Why, all the Saints and Sages who discussed
Of the Two Worlds so learnedly, are thrust
   Like foolish Prophets forth; their Words to Scorn
Are scattered, and their Mouths are stopt with Dust.

26

Oh, come with old Khayyám, and leave the Wise
To talk; one thing is certain, that Life flies;
    One thing is certain, and the Rest is Lies;
The Flower that once has blown for ever dies.

27

Myself when young did eagerly frequent
Doctor and Saint, and heard great Argument
    About it and about; but evermore
Came out by the same Door as in I went.

28

With them the Seed of Wisdom did I sow,
And with my own hand laboured it to grow:
    And this was all the Harvest that I reaped—
'I came like Water and like Wind I go.'

29

Into this Universe, and *why* not knowing,
Nor *whence*, like Water willy-nilly flowing:
    And out of it, as Wind along the Waste,
I know not *whither*, willy-nilly blowing.

30

What, without asking, hither hurried *whence*?
And, without asking, *whither* hurried hence!
    Another and another Cup to drown
The Memory of this Impertinence!

31

Up from Earth's Centre, through the Seventh Gate
I rose, and on the Throne of Saturn sate,
    And many Knots unravelled by the Road;
But not the Knot of Human Death and Fate.

32

There was a Door to which I found no Key:
There was a Veil past which I could not see:
    Some little Talk awhile of ME and THEE
There seemed—and then no more of THEE and ME.

33

Then to the rolling Heav'n itself I cried,
Asking, 'What Lamp had Destiny to guide
    Her little Children stumbling in the Dark?'
And—'A blind Understanding!' Heav'n replied.

34

Then to this earthen Bowl did I adjourn
My Lip the secret Well of Life to learn:
    And Lip to Lip it murmured—'While you live
Drink!—for once dead you never shall return.'

35

I think the Vessel, that with fugitive
Articulation answered, once did live,
    And merry-make; and the cold Lip I kissed
How many Kisses might it take—and give!

36

For in the Marketplace, one Dusk of Day,
I watch'd the Potter thumping his wet Clay:
    And with its all obliterated Tongue
It murmured—'Gently, Brother, gently, pray!'

37

Ah, fill the Cup:—what boots it to repeat
How Time is slipping underneath our Feet:
    Unborn TOMORROW, and dead YESTERDAY,
Why fret about them if TODAY be sweet.

38

One Moment in Annihilation's Waste,
One Moment, of the Well of Life to taste—
    The Stars are setting and the Caravan
Starts for the Dawn of Nothing—Oh, make haste!

39

How long, how long, in infinite Pursuit
Of This and That endeavour and dispute?
    Better be merry with the fruitful Grape
Than sadden after none, or bitter, Fruit.

40

You know, my Friends, how long since in my House
For a new Marriage I did make Carouse:
    Divorced old barren Reason from my Bed,
And took the Daughter of the Vine to Spouse.

41

For 'Is' and 'Is-NOT' though *with* Rule and Line,
And 'UP-AND-DOWN' *without* I could define,
    I yet in all I only cared to know,
Was never deep in anything but—Wine.

42

And lately, by the Tavern Door agape,
Came stealing though the Dusk an Angel Shape
    Bearing a Vessel on his Shoulder; and
He bid me taste of it; and 'twas—the Grape!

43

The Grape that can with Logic absolute
The Two-and-Seventy jarring Sects confute:
    The subtle Alchemist that in a Trice
Life's leaden Metal into Gold transmute.

44

The might Mahmud, the victorious Lord,
That all the misbelieving and black Horde
    Of Fears and Sorrows that infest the Soul
Scatters and slays with his enchanted Sword.

45

But leave the Wise to wrangle, and with me
The Quarrel of the Universe let be:
    And, in some corner of the Hubbub coucht,
Make Game of that which makes as much of Thee.

46

For in and out, above, about, below,
'Tis nothing but a Magic Shadow-show,
    Play'd in a Box whose Candle is the Sun,
Round which we Phantom Figures come and go.

47

And if the Wine you drink, the Lip you press,
End in the Nothing all Things end in—Yes—
   Then fancy while Thou art, Thou art but what
Thou shalt be—Nothing—Thou shalt not be less.

48

While the Rose blows along the River Brink,
With old Khayyám the Ruby Vintage drink:
   And when the Angel with his darker Draught
Draws up to Thee—take that, and do not shrink.

49

'Tis all a Chequerboard of Nights and Days
Where Destiny with Men for Pieces plays:
   Hither and thither moves, and mates, and slays,
And one by one back in the Closet lays.

50

The Ball no Question makes of Ayes and Noes,
But Right or Left, as strikes the Player goes;
   And He that toss'd Thee down into the Field,
He knows about it all—HE knows—HE knows!

51

The Moving Finger writes; and, having writ,
Moves on: nor all thy Piety nor Wit
   Shall lure it back to cancel half a Line,
Nor all thy Tears wash out a Word of it.

52

And that inverted Bowl we call The Sky,
Whereunder crawling coop't we live and die,
   Lift not thy hands to *It* for help—for It
Rolls impotently on as Thou or I.

53

With Earth's first Clay They did the Last Man's knead,
And then of the Last Harvest sow'd the Seed:
   Yea, the first Morning of Creation wrote
What the Last Dawn of Reckoning shall read.

54

I tell Thee this—When, starting from the Goal,
Over the shoulders of the flaming Foal
  Of Heav'n Parwín and Mushtara they flung,
In my predestin'd Plot of Dust and Soul.

55

The Vine had struck a Fibre; which about
If clings my Being—let the Sufi flout;
  Of my Base Metal may be filed a Key,
That shall unlock the Door he howls without.

56

And this I know: whether the one True Light,
Kindle to Love, or Wrath consume me quite,
  One Glimpse of It within the Tavern caught
Better than in the Temple lost outright.

57

Oh, Thou, who didst with Pitfall and with Gin
Beset the Road I was to wander in,
  Thou wilt not with Predestination round
Enmesh me, and impute my Fall to Sin?

58

Oh, Thou, who Man of baser Earth didst make
And who with Eden didst devise the Snake;
  For all the Sin wherewith the Face of Man
Is blacken'd, Man's Forgiveness give—and take!

Kuza-Nama

59

Listen again. One Evening at the Close
Of Ramazán, ere the better Moon arose,
  In that old Potter's Shop I stood alone
With the clay Population round in Rows.

60

And, strange to tell, among that Earthen Lot
Some could articulate, while others not:
  And suddenly one more impatient cried—
'Who *is* the Potter, pray, and who the Pot?'

61

Then said another—'Surely not in vain
My Substance from the common Earth was ta'en,
    That He who subtly wrought me into Shape
Should stamp me back to common Earth again.'

62

Another said—'Why, ne'er a peevish Boy,
Would break the Bowl from which he drank in Joy;
    Shall He that *made* the Vessel in pure Love
And Fancy, in an after Rage destroy!'

63

None answer'd this; but after Silence spake
A Vessel of a more ungainly Make:
    'They sneer at me for leaning all awry;
What! did the Hand then of the Potter shake?'

64

Said one—'Folks of a surly Tapster tell,
And daub his Visage with the Smoke of Hell;
    They talk of some strict Testing of us—Pish!
He's a Good Fellow, and 'twill all be well.'

65

Then said another with a long-drawn Sigh,
'My Clay with long oblivion is gone dry:
    But, fill me with the old familiar Juice,
Methinks I might recover by and by!'

66

So while the Vessels one by one were speaking,
One spied the little Crescent all were seeking:
    And then they jogg'd each other, 'Brother! Brother!
Hark to the Porter's Shoulder-knot a-creaking!'

67

Ah, with the Grape my fading Life provide
And wash my Body whence the Life has died,
    And in a Winding-sheet of Vine-leaf wrapt,
So bury me by some sweet Garden-side.

68

That ev'n my buried Ashes such a Snare
Of Perfume shall fling up into the Air,
　　As not a True Believer passing by
But shall be overtaken unaware.

69

Indeed the Idols I have loved so long
Have done my Credit in Men's Eyes much wrong:
　　Have drown'd my Honour in a shallow Cup,
And sold my Reputation for a Song.

70

Indeed, indeed, Repentance oft before
I swore—but was I sober when I swore?
　　And then and then came Spring, and Rose-in-hand
My threadbare Penitence apieces tore.

71

And much as Wine has play'd the Infidel,
And robb'd me of my Robe of Honour—well,
　　I often wonder what the Vintners buy
One half so precious as the Goods they sell.

72

Alas, that Spring should vanish with the Rose!
That Youth's sweet-scented Manuscript should close!
　　The Nightingale that in the Branches sang,
Ah, whence, and whither flown again, who knows!

73

Ah Love! could thou and I with Fate conspire
To grasp this sorry Scheme of Things entire,
　　Would not we shatter it to bits—and then
Remould it nearer to the Heart's Desire!

74

Ah, Moon of my Delight who know'st no wane,
The Moon of Heav'n is rising once again:
　　How oft hereafter rising shall she look
Through this same Garden after me—in vain!

75

And when Thyself with shining Foot shall pass
Among the Guests Star-scatter'd on the Grass,
    And in thy joyous Errand reach the Spot
Where I made one—turn down an empty Glass!

Tamám Shud

JOHN FLETCHER (1579–1625)

Mourn No More

Weep no more, nor sigh, nor groan,
Sorrow calls no time that's gone:
Violets plucked the sweetest rain
Makes not fresh nor grow again.
Trim thy locks, look cheerfully;
Fate's hid ends eyes cannot see.
Joys as wingèd dreams fly fast;
Why should sadness longer last?
Grief is but a wound to woe:
Gentlest fair, mourn, mourn no more!

'Care-charming Sleep'

Care-charming Sleep, thou easer of all woes,
Brother to Death, sweetly thyself dispose
On this afflicted prince. Fall like a cloud
In gentle showers. Give nothing that is loud,
Or painful to his slumbers; easy, sweet,
And as a purling stream, thou son of Night,
Pass by his troubled senses. Sing his pain,
Like hollow murmuring wind or silver rain.
Into this prince gently, oh gently slide,
And kiss him into slumbers like a bride.

SIR W. S. GILBERT (1836–1911)

from 'HMS Pinafore'
The Englishman

He is an Englishman!
　　For he himself has said it,
　　And it's greatly to his credit,
That he is an Englishman!
　　For he might have been a Roosian,
　　A French, or Turk, or Proosian,
Or perhaps Itali–an!
　　But in spite of all temptations,
　　To belong to other nations,
He remains an Englishman!
　　　　Hurrah!
For the true-born Englishman!

from 'The Pirates of Penzance'
Song of the Major General

I am the very model of a modern Major-General,
I've information vegetable, animal and mineral;
I know the kings of England, and I quote the fights historical,
From Marathon to Waterloo, in order categorical;
I'm very well acquainted, too, with matters mathematical,
I understand equations, both the simple and quadratical;
About binomial theorem I'm teeming with a lot o' news,
With many cheerful facts about the square of the hypotenuse.
I'm very good at integral and differential calculus,
I know the scientific names of beings animalculous;
In short, in matters vegetable, animal and mineral,
I am the very model of a modern Major-General.

I know our mythic history, King Arthur's and Sir Caradoc's,
I answer hard acrostics, I've a pretty taste for paradox.
I quote in elegiacs all the crimes of Heliogabalus,
In conics I can floor peculiarities parabolus.
I can tell undoubted Raphaels from Gerard Dows and Zoffanies,

I know the croaking chorus from the 'Frogs' of Aristophanes;
Then I can hum a fugue of which I've heard the music's din afore,
And whistle all the airs from that infernal nonsense 'Pinafore'.
Then I can write a washing bill in Babylonic cuneiform,
And tell you every detail of Caractacus's uniform.
In short, in matters vegetable, animal and mineral,
I am the very model of a modern Major-General.

In fact, when I know what is meant by 'mamelon' and 'ravelin',
When I can tell at sight a Chassepôt rifle from a javelin,
When such affairs as *sorties* and surprises I'm more wary at,
And when I know precisely what is meant by Commissariat,
When I have learnt what progress has been made in modern gunnery,
When I know more of tactics than a novice in a nunnery,
In short, when I've a smattering of elemental strategy,
You'll say a better Major-General has never sat a gee—
For my military knowledge, though I'm plucky and adventury,
Has only been brought down to the beginning of the century;
But still in matters vegetable, animal and mineral,
I am the very model of a modern Major-General.

The Policeman's Lot

When a felon's not engaged in his employment
    Or maturing his felonious little plans,
His capacity for innocent enjoyment
    Is just as great as any honest man's.
Our feelings we with difficulty smother
    When constabulary duty's to be done:
Ah, take one consideration with another,
    A policeman's lot is not a happy one!

When the enterprising burglar isn't burgling,
    When the cut-throat isn't occupied in crime,
He loves to hear the little brook a-gurgling,
    And listen to the merry village chime.
When the coster's finished jumping on his mother,
    He loves to lie a-basking in the sun:
Ah, take one consideration with another,
    The policeman's lot is not a happy one!

OLIVER GOLDSMITH (1730?–1774)

The Deserted Village

Sweet Auburn! loveliest village of the plain,
Where health and plenty cheered the labouring swain,
Where smiling spring its earliest visit paid,
And parting summer's lingering blooms delayed:
Dear lovely bowers of innocence and ease,
Seats of my youth, when every sport could please,
How often have I loitered o'er thy green,
Where humble happiness endeared each scene!
How often have I paused on every charm,
The sheltered cot, the cultivated farm,
The never-failing brook, the busy mill,
The decent church that topt the neighbouring hill,
The hawthorn bush, with seats beneath the shade,
For talking age and whispering lovers made!
How often have I blest the coming day,
When toil remitting lent its turn to play,
And all the village train, from labour free,
Led up their sports beneath the spreading tree;
While many a pastime circled in the shade,
The young contending as the old surveyed;
And many a gambol frolicked o'er the ground,
And sleights of art and feats of strength went round;
And still, as each repeated pleasure tired,
Succeeding sports the mirthful band inspired;
The dancing pair that simply sought renown
By holding out to tire each other down:
The swain mistrustless of his smutted face,
While secret laughter tittered round the place;
The bashful virgin's sidelong looks of love,
The matron's glance that would those looks reprove:
These were thy charms, sweet village! sports like these
With sweet succession, taught e'en toil to please:
These round thy bowers their cheerful influence shed,
These were thy charms—but all these charms are fled.

Sweet smiling village, loveliest of the lawn,
Thy sports are fled, and all thy charms withdrawn;

Amidst thy bowers the tyrant's hand is seen,
And desolation saddens all thy green:
One only master grasps the whole domain,
And half a tillage stints thy smiling plain.
No more thy glassy brook reflects the day,
But, choked with sedges, works its weedy way;
Along thy glades, a solitary guest,
The hollow-sounding bittern guards its nest;
Amidst thy desert walks the lapwing flies,
And tires their echoes with unvaried cries;
Sunk are thy bowers in shapeless ruin all,
And the long grass o'ertops the mouldering wall;
And trembling, shrinking from the spoiler's hand,
Far, far away, thy children leave the land.

Ill fares the land, to hastening ills a prey,
Where wealth accumulates, and men decay:
Princes and lords may flourish, or may fade;
A breath can make them, as a breath has made:
But a bold peasantry, their country's pride,
When once destroyed, can never be supplied.

A time there was, ere England's griefs began,
When every rood of ground maintained its man;
For him light labour spread her wholesome store,
Just gave what life required, but gave no more:
His best companions, innocence and health;
And his best riches, ignorance of wealth.

But times are altered; trade's unfeeling train
Usurp the land and dispossess the swain;
Along the lawn, where scattered hamlets rose,
Unwieldy wealth and cumbrous pomp repose,
And every want to opulence allied,
And every pang that folly pays to pride.
Those gentle hours that plenty bade to bloom,
Those calm desires that asked but little room,
Those healthful sports that graced the peaceful scene,
Lived in each look, and brightened all the green,—
These, far departing, seek a kinder shore,
And rural mirth and manners are no more.

Sweet Auburn! parent of the blissful hour,
Thy glades forlorn confess the tyrant's power.
Here, as I take my solitary rounds,
Amidst thy tangling walks and ruined grounds,
And, many a year elapsed, return to view
Where once the cottage stood, the hawthorn grew,
Remembrance wakes with all her busy train,
Swells at my breast, and turns the past to pain.

In all my wanderings round this world of care,
In all my griefs—and God has given my share—
I still had hopes, my latest hours to crown,
Amidst these humble bowers to lay me down;
To husband out life's taper at the close,
And keep the flame from wasting by repose:
I still had hopes, for pride attends us still,
Amidst the swains to show my book-learned skill,
Around my fire an evening group to draw,
And tell of all I felt and all I saw;
And as a hare whom hounds and horns pursue,
Pants to the place from whence at first she flew,
I still had hopes, my long vexations past,
Here to return, and die at home at last.

O blest retirement, friend to life's decline,
Retreats from care, that never must be mine,
How happy he who crowns in shades like these,
A youth of labour with an age of ease;
Who quits a world where strong temptations try,
And, since 'tis hard to combat, learns to fly!
For him no wretches, born to work and weep,
Explore the mine, or tempt the dangerous deep;
No surly porter stands in guilty state
To spurn imploring famine from the gate,
But on he moves to meet his latter end,
Angels around befriending virtue's friend;
Bends to the grave with unperceived decay,
While resignation gently slopes the way;
And, all his prospects brightening to the last,
His Heaven commences ere the world be past!

Sweet was the sound when oft at evening's close,
Up yonder hill the village murmur rose;
There, as I past with careless steps and slow,
The mingling notes came softened from below;
The swain responsive as the milk-maid sung,
The sober herd that lowed to meet their young,
The noisy geese that gabbled o'er the pool,
The playful children just let loose from school,
The watch-dog's voice that bayed the whispering wind,
And the loud laugh that spoke the vacant mind,
These all in sweet confusion sought the shade,
And filled each pause the nightingale had made.
But now the sounds of population fail,
No cheerful murmurs fluctuate in the gale,
No busy steps the grass-grown foot-way tread,
For all the bloomy flush of life is fled.
All but yon widowed, solitary thing,
That feebly bends beside the plashy spring;
She, wretched matron, forced in age for bread,
To strip the brook with mantling cresses spread,
To pick her wintry faggot from the thorn,
To seek her nightly shed, and weep till morn;
She only left of all the harmless train,
The sad historian of the pensive plain.

Near yonder copse, where once the garden smiled,
And still where many a garden flower grows wild;
There, where a few torn shrubs the place disclose,
The village preacher's modest mansion rose.
A man he was, to all the country dear,
And passing rich with forty pounds a year;
Remote from towns he ran his godly race,
Nor e'er had changed, nor wished to change his place;
Unpractised he to fawn, or seek for power,
By doctrines fashioned to the varying hour;
Far other aims his heart had learned to prize,
More skilled to raise the wretched than to rise.
His house was known to all the vagrant train,
He chid their wanderings, but relieved their pain;
The long-remembered beggar was his guest,
Whose beard descending swept his agèd breast;
The ruined spendthrift, now no longer proud,

Claimed kindred there, and had his claims allowed;
The broken soldier, kindly bade to stay,
Sate by his fire, and talked the night away;
Wept o'er his wounds, or, tales of sorrow done,
Shouldered his crutch and showed how fields were won.
Pleased with his guests, the good man learned to glow,
And quite forgot their vices in their woe;
Careless their merits, or their faults to scan,
His pity gave ere charity began.

Thus to relieve the wretched was his pride,
And even his failings leaned to Virtue's side;
But in his duty prompt at every call,
He watched and wept, he prayed and felt, for all.
And, as a bird each fond endearment tries
To tempt its new-fledged offspring to the skies;
He tried each art, reproved each dull delay,
Allured to brighter worlds, and led the way.

Beside the bed where parting life was laid,
And sorrow, guilt, and pain, by turns, dismayed
The reverend champion stood. At his control,
Despair and anguish fled the struggling soul;
Comfort came down the trembling wretch to raise,
And his last faltering accents whispered praise.

At church, with meek and unaffected grace,
His looks adorned the venerable place;
Truth from his lips prevailed with double sway,
And fools, who came to scoff, remained to pray.
The service past, around the pious man,
With steady zeal, each honest rustic ran;
Even children followed with endearing wile,
And plucked his gown, to share the good man's smile.
His ready smile a parent's warmth exprest,
Their welfare pleased him, and their cares distrest;
To them his heart, his love, his griefs were given,
But all his serious thoughts had rest in Heaven.
As some tall cliff that lifts its awful form,
Swells from the vale, and midway leaves the storm,
Tho' round its breast the rolling clouds are spread,
Eternal sunshine settles on its head.

Beside yon straggling fence that skirts the way,
With blossomed furze unprofitably gay,
There, in his noisy mansion, skill'd to rule,
The village master taught his little school;
A man severe he was, and stern to view,
I knew him well, and every truant knew;
Well had the boding tremblers learned to trace
The day's disasters in his morning face;
Full well they laughed with counterfeited glee
At all his jokes, for many a joke had he:
Full well the busy whisper circling round,
Conveyed the dismal tidings when he frowned;
Yet he was kind, or if severe in aught,
The love he bore to learning was in fault;
The village all declared how much he knew;
'Twas certain he could write, and cypher too;
Lands he could measure, terms and tides presage,
And even the story ran that he could gauge.
In arguing too, the parson owned his skill,
For even tho' vanquished, he could argue still;
While words of learnèd length and thundering sound
Amazed the gazing rustics ranged around;
And still they gazed, and still the wonder grew,
That one small head could carry all he knew.

But past is all his fame. The very spot
Where many a time he triumphed is forgot.
Near yonder thorn, that lifts its head on high,
Where once the signpost caught the passing eye,
Low lies that house where nut-brown draughts inspired,
Where grey-beard mirth and smiling toil retired,
Where village statesmen talked with looks profound,
And news much older than their ale went round.
Imagination fondly stoops to trace
The parlour splendours of that festive place;
The white-washed wall, the nicely sanded floor,
The varnished clock that clicked behind the door;
The chest contrived a double debt to pay,
A bed by night, a chest of drawers by day;
The pictures placed for ornament and use,
The twelve good rules, the royal game of goose;
The hearth, except when winter chilled the day,

With aspen boughs, and flowers, and fennel gay;
While broken tea-cups, wisely kept for show,
Ranged o'er the chimney, glistened in a row.

Vain transitory splendours! could not all
Reprieve the tottering mansion from its fall?
Obscure it sinks, nor shall it more impart
An hour's importance to the poor man's heart;
Thither no more the peasant shall repair
To sweet oblivion of his daily care;
No more the farmer's news, the barber's tale,
No more the woodman's ballad shall prevail;
No more the smith his dusky brow shall clear,
Relax his pond'rous strength, and lean to hear;
The host himself no longer shall be found
Careful to see the mantling bliss go round;
Nor the coy maid, half willing to be prest,
Shall kiss the cup to pass it to the rest.

Yes! let the rich deride, the proud disdain,
These simple blessings of the lowly train;
To me more dear, congenial to my heart,
One native charm, than all the gloss of art;
Spontaneous joys, where nature has its play,
The soul adopts, and owns their first-born sway;
Lightly they frolic o'er the vacant mind,
Unenvied, unmolested, unconfined:
But the long pomp, the midnight masquerade,
With all the freaks of wanton wealth arrayed,
In these, ere triflers half their wish obtain,
The toiling pleasure sickens into pain;
And, e'en while fashion's brightest arts decoy,
The heart distrusting asks if this be joy.

Ye friends to truth, ye statesmen who survey
The rich man's joys increase, the poor's decay,
'Tis yours to judge, how wide the limits stand
Between a splendid and a happy land.
Proud swells the tide with loads of freighted ore,
And shouting Folly hails them from her shore;
Hoards, e'en beyond the miser's wish abound,

And rich men flock from all the world around.
Yet count our gains. This wealth is but a name
That leaves our useful products still the same.
Not so the loss. The man of wealth and pride
Takes up a space that many poor supplied;
Space for his lake, his park's extended bounds,
Space for his horses, equipage, and hounds;
The robe that wraps his limbs in silken sloth
Has robbed the neighbouring fields of half their growth,
His seat, where solitary sports are seen,
Indignant spurns the cottage from the green;
Around the world each needful product flies,
For all the luxuries the world supplies;
While thus the land adorned for pleasure, all
In barren splendour feebly waits the fall.

As some fair female unadorned and plain,
Secure to please while youth confirms her reign,
Slights every borrowed charm that dress supplies,
Nor shares with art the triumph of her eyes;
But when those charms are past, for charms are frail,
When time advances, and when lovers fail,
She then shines forth, solicitous to bless,
In all the glaring impotence of dress.
Thus fares the land by luxury betrayed,
In nature's simplest charms at first arrayed,
But verging to decline, its splendours rise,
Its vistas strike, its palaces surprise;
While, scourged by famine from the smiling land,
The mournful peasant leads his humble band,
And while he sinks, without one arm to save,
The country blooms—a garden, and a grave.

Where then, ah! where, shall poverty reside,
To 'scape the pressure of contiguous pride?
If to some common's fenceless limits strayed
He drives his flock to pick the scanty blade,
Those fenceless fields the sons of wealth divide,
And e'en the bare-worn common is denied.

If to the city sped—What waits him there?

To see profusion that he must not share;
To see ten thousand baneful arts combined
To pamper luxury, and thin mankind;
To see those joys the sons of pleasure know
Extorted from his fellow-creature's woe.
Here, while the courtier glitters in brocade,
There the pale artist plies the sickly trade;
Here while the proud their long-drawn pomps display,
There the black gibbet glooms beside the way.
The dome where pleasure holds her midnight reign
Here, richly decked, admits the gorgeous train:
Tumultuous grandeur crowds the blazing square,
The rattling chariots clash, the torches glare.
Sure scenes like these no troubles e'er annoy!
Sure these denote one universal joy!
Are these thy serious thoughts?—Ah, turn thine eyes
Where the poor houseless shivering female lies.
She once, perhaps, in village plenty blest,
Has wept at tales of innocence distrest;
Her modest looks the cottage might adorn,
Sweet as the primrose peeps beneath the thorn;
Now lost to all; her friends, her virtue fled,
Near her betrayer's door she lays her head,
And, pinched with cold, and shrinking from the shower,
With heavy heart deplores that luckless hour,
When idly first, ambitious of the town,
She left her wheel and robes of country brown.

Do thine, sweet Auburn, thine, the loveliest train,
Do thy fair tribes participate her pain?
E'en now, perhaps, by cold and hunger led,
At proud men's doors they ask a little bread!

Ah, no! To distant climes, a dreary scene,
Where half the convex world intrudes between,
Through torrid tracts with fainting steps they go,
Where wild Altama murmurs to their woe.
Far different there from all that charmed before,
The various terrors of that horrid shore;
Those blazing suns that dart a downward ray,
And fiercely shed intolerable day;
Those matted woods where birds forget to sing

But silent bats in drowsy clusters cling;
Those pois'nous fields with rank luxuriance crowned,
Where the dark scorpion gathers death around;
Where at each step the stranger fears to wake
The rattling terrors of the vengeful snake;
Where crouching tigers wait their hapless prey,
And savage men more murd'rous still than they;
While oft in whirls the mad tornado flies,
Mingling the ravaged landscape with the skies.
Far different these from every former scene,
The cooling brook, the grassy-vested green,
The breezy covert of the warbling grove,
That only sheltered thefts of harmless love.

Good heaven! what sorrows gloomed that parting day,
That called them from their native walks away;
When the poor exiles, every pleasure past,
Hung round their bowers, and fondly looked their last,
And took a long farewell, and wished in vain
For seats like these beyond the western main,
And shuddering still to face the distant deep,
Returned and wept, and still returned to weep.
The good old sire, the first prepared to go
To new-found worlds, and wept for others' woe;
But for himself, in conscious virtue brave,
He only wished for worlds beyond the grave.
His lovely daughter, lovelier in her tears,
The fond companion of his helpless years,
Silent went next, neglectful of her charms,
And left a lover's for a father's arms.
With louder plaints the mother spoke her woes,
And blessed the cot where every pleasure rose,
And kissed her thoughtless babes with many a tear,
And clasped them close, in sorrow doubly dear,
Whilst her fond husband strove to lend relief
In all the silent manliness of grief.

O Luxury! thou curst by Heaven's decree,
How ill exchanged are things like these for thee!
How do thy potions, with insidious joy,
Diffuse their pleasures only to destroy!
Kingdoms, by thee, to sickly greatness grown,

Boast of a florid vigour not their own.
At every draught more large and large they grow,
A bloated mass of rank unwieldy woe;
Till sapped their strength, and every part unsound,
Down, down they sink, and spread a ruin round.

E'en now the devastation is begun,
And half the business of destruction done;
E'en now, methinks, as pondering here I stand,
I see the rural virtues leave the land.
Down where yon anchoring vessel spreads the sail,
That idly waiting flaps with every gale,
Downward they move, a melancholy band,
Pass from the shore, and darken all the strand.
Contented toil, and hospitable care,
And kind connubial tenderness, are there;
And piety, with wishes placed above,
And steady loyalty, and faithful love.
And thou, sweet Poetry, thou loveliest maid,
Still first to fly where sensual joys invade;
Unfit in these degenerate times of shame
To catch the heart, or strike for honest fame;
Dear charming nymph, neglected and decried,
My shame in crowds, my solitary pride;
Thou source of all my bliss, and all my woe,
That found'st me poor at first, and keep'st me so;
Thou guide by which the nobler arts excel,
Thou nurse of every virtue, fare thee well!
Farewell, and oh! where'er thy voice be tried,
On Torno's cliffs, or Pambamarca's side,
Whether where equinoctial fervours glow,
Or winter wraps the polar world in snow,
Still let thy voice, prevailing over time,
Redress the rigours of th' inclement clime;
Aid slighted truth; with thy persuasive strain
Teach erring man to spurn the rage of gain;
Teach him that states of native strength possest,
Though very poor, may still be very blest;
That trade's proud empire hastes to swift decay,
As ocean sweeps the laboured mole away;
While self-dependent power can time defy,
As rocks resist the billows and the sky.

from 'The Vicar of Wakefield'

Song

When lovely woman stoops to folly,
  And finds too late that men betray,
What charms can soothe her melancholy,
  What art can wash her guilt away?

The only art her guilt to cover,
  To hide her shame from every eye,
To give repentance to her lover,
  And wring his bosom, is – to die.

HARRY GRAHAM (1874–1936)

Tender-Heartedness

Billy, in one of his nice new sashes,
Fell in the fire and was burnt to ashes;
Now, although the room grows chilly,
I haven't the heart to poke poor Billy.

The Englishman's Home

I was playing golf the day
That the Germans landed;
All our troops had run away,
All our ships were stranded;
And the thought of England's shame
Altogether spoilt my game.

Lord Gorbals

Once, as old Lord Gorbals motored
Round his moors near John o' Groats,
He collided with a goatherd
And a herd of forty goats.
By the time his car got through
They were all defunct but two.

Roughly he addressed the goatherd:
  'Dash my whiskers and my corns!
Can't you teach your goats, you dotard,
  That they ought to sound their horns?
Look, my A.A. badge is bent!
I've a mind to raise your rent!'

ROBERT GRAVES (1895–1985)

'She tells her love while half asleep'

She tells her love while half asleep,
In the dark hours,
  With half-words whispered low:
As Earth stirs in her winter sleep
  And puts out grass and flowers
    Despite the snow,
    Despite the falling snow.

A Slice of Wedding Cake

Why have such scores of lovely, gifted girls
  Married impossible men?
Simple self-sacrifice may be ruled out,
  And missionary endeavour, nine times out of ten.

Repeat 'impossible men': not merely rustic,
  Foul-tempered or depraved
(Dramatic foils chosen to show the world
  How well women behave, and always have behaved).

Impossible men: idle, illiterate,
  Self-pitying, dirty, sly,
For whose appearance even in City parks
  Excuses must be made to casual passers-by.

Has God's supply of tolerable husbands
  Fallen, in fact, so low?
Or do I always over-value woman
  At the expense of man?
    Do I?
      It might be so.

THOMAS GRAY (1716–1771)

Elegy Written in a Country Churchyard

The curfew tolls the knell of parting day,
    The lowing herd wind slowly o'er the lea,
The ploughman homeward plods his weary way,
    And leaves the world to darkness and to me.

Now fades the glimmering landscape on the sight,
    And all the air a solemn stillness holds,
Save where the beetle wheels his droning flight,
    And drowsy tinklings lull the distant folds:

Save where from yonder ivy-mantled tower
    The moping owl does to the moon complain
Of such as, wandering near her secret bower,
    Molest her ancient solitary reign.

Beneath those rugged elms, that yew-tree's shade
    Where heaves the turf in many a mouldering heap,
Each in his narrow cell for ever laid,
    The rude forefathers of the hamlet sleep.

The breezy call of incense-breathing morn,
    The swallow twittering from the straw-built shed,
The cock's shrill clarion, or the echoing horn,
    No more shall rouse them from their lowly bed.

For them no more the blazing hearth shall burn
    Or busy housewife ply her evening care:
No children run to lisp their sire's return,
    Or climb his knees the envied kiss to share.

Oft did the harvest to their sickle yield,
    Their furrow oft the stubborn glebe has broke;
How jocund did they drive their team afield!
    How bowed the woods beneath their sturdy stroke!

Let not Ambition mock their useful toil,
    Their homely joys, and destiny obscure;

Nor Grandeur hear with a disdainful smile
  The short and simple annals of the poor.

The boast of heraldry, the pomp of power,
  And all that beauty, all that wealth e'er gave,
Awaits alike th' inevitable hour:
  The paths of glory lead but to the grave.

Nor you, ye proud, impute to these the fault
  If Memory o'er their tomb no trophies raise,
Where through the long-drawn aisle and fretted vault
  The pealing anthem swells the note of praise.

Can storied urn or animated bust
  Back to its mansion call the fleeting breath?
Can Honour's voice provoke the silent dust,
  Or Flattery soothe the dull cold ear of death?

Perhaps in this neglected spot is laid
  Some heart once pregnant with celestial fire;
Hands, that the rod of empire might have swayed,
  Or waked to ecstasy the living lyre:

But Knowledge to their eyes her ample page
  Rich with the spoils of time did ne'er unroll;
Chill Penury repressed their noble rage,
  And froze the genial current of the soul.

Full many a gem of purest ray serene
  The dark unfathomed caves of ocean bear:
Full many a flower is born to blush unseen,
  And waste its sweetness on the desert air.

Some village Hampden, that with dauntless breast
  The little tyrant of his fields withstood,
Some mute inglorious Milton here may rest,
  Some Cromwell, guiltless of his country's blood.

Th' applause of listening senates to command,
  The threats of pain and ruin to despise,
To scatter plenty o'er a smiling land,
  And read their history in a nation's eyes

Their lot forbade: nor circumscribed alone
    Their glowing virtues, but their crimes confined;
Forbade to wade through slaughter to a throne,
    And shut the gates of mercy on mankind;

The struggling pangs of conscious truth to hide,
    To quench the blushes of ingenuous shame,
Or heap the shrine of Luxury and Pride
    With incense kindled at the Muse's flame.

Far from the madding crowd's ignoble strife
    Their sober wishes never learned to stray;
Along the cool sequestered vale of life
    They kept the noiseless tenor of their way.

Yet e'en these bones from insult to protect
    Some frail memorial still erected nigh,
With uncouth rhymes and shapeless sculpture decked,
    Implores the passing tribute of a sigh.

Their name, their years, spelt by th' unlettered Muse,
    The place of fame and elegy supply:
And many a holy text around she strews,
    That teach the rustic moralist to die.

For who, to dumb Forgetfulness a prey,
    This pleasing anxious being e'er resigned,
Left the warm precincts of the cheerful day,
    Nor cast one longing lingering look behind?

On some fond breast the parting soul relies,
    Some pious drops the closing eye requires;
E'en from the tomb the voice of Nature cries,
    E'en in our Ashes live their wonted fires.

For thee, who, mindful of th' unhonoured dead,
    Dost in these lines their artless tale relate;
If chance, by lonely contemplation led,
    Some kindred spirit shall inquire thy fate,

Haply some hoary-headed Swain may say,
    'Oft have we seen him at the peep of dawn
Brushing with hasty steps the dews away,
    To meet the sun upon the upland lawn;

'There at the foot of yonder nodding beech
    That wreathes its old fantastic roots so high,
His listless length at noontide would he stretch,
    And pore upon the brook that babbles by.

'Hard by yon wood, now smiling as in scorn,
    Muttering his wayward fancies he would rove;
Now drooping, woeful-wan, like one forlorn,
    Or crazed with care, or crossed in hopeless love.

'One morn I missed him on the 'customed hill,
    Along the heath, and near his favourite tree;
Another came; nor yet beside the rill,
    Nor up the lawn, nor at the wood was he;

'The next with dirges due in sad array
    Slow through the church-way path we saw him borne.
Approach and read (for thou canst read) the lay
    Graved on the stone beneath yon aged thorn:'

The Epitaph

Here rests his head upon the lap of Earth
    A Youth, to Fortune and to Fame unknown;
Fair Science frowned not on his humble birth,
    And Melancholy marked him for her own.

Large was his bounty, and his soul sincere;
    Heaven did a recompense as largely send.
He gave to Misery all he had, a tear;
    He gained from Heaven ('twas all he wished) a friend.

No farther seek his merits to disclose,
    Or draw his frailties from their dread abode,
(There they alike in trembling hope repose)
    The bosom of his Father and his God.

THOMAS HARDY (1840–1928)

The Ruined Maid

'O 'Melia, my dear, this does everything crown!
Who could have supposed I should meet you in Town?
And whence such fair garments, such prosperi-ty?'—
'O didn't you know I'd been ruined?' said she.

—'You left us in tatters, without shoes or socks,
Tired of digging potatoes, and spudding up docks;
And now you've gay bracelets and bright feathers three!'—
'Yes: that's how we dress when we're ruined,' said she.

—'At home in the barton you said "thee" and "thou",
And "thik oon", and "theas oon", and "t'other"; but now
Your talking quite fits 'ee for high compa-ny!'—
'Some polish is gained with one's ruin,' said she.

—'Your hands were like paws then, your face blue and bleak,
But now I'm bewitched by your delicate cheek,
And your little gloves fit as on any la-dy!'—
'We never do work when we're ruined,' said she.

—'You used to call home-life a hag-ridden dream,
And you'd sigh, and you'd sock; but at present you seem
To know not of megrims or melancho-ly!'—
'True. There's an advantage in ruin,' said she.

—'I wish I had feathers, a fine sweeping gown,
And a delicate face, and could strut about Town!'—
'My dear—a raw country girl, such as you be,
Isn't equal to that. You ain't ruined,' said she.

The Self-Unseeing

Here is the ancient floor,
Footworn and hollowed and thin,
Here was the former door
Where the dead feet walked in.

She sat here in her chair,
Smiling into the fire;
He who played stood there,
Bowing it higher and higher.

Childlike, I danced in a dream;
Blessings emblazoned that day
 Everything glowed with a gleam;
Yet we were looking away!

Before Life and After

A time there was—as one may guess
And as, indeed, earth's testimonies tell—
Before the birth of consciousness,
 When all went well.

None suffered sickness, love, or loss,
None knew regret, starved hope, or heart-burnings;
None cared whatever crash or cross
 Brought wrack to things.

If something ceased, no tongue bewailed,
If something winced and waned, no heart was wrung;
If brightness dimmed, and dark prevailed,
 No sense was stung.

But the disease of feeling germed,
And primal rightness took the tinct of wrong;
Ere nescience shall be reaffirmed
 How long, how long?

Channel Firing

That night your great guns, unawares,
Shook all our coffins as we lay,
And broke the chancel window-squares,
We thought it was the Judgment-day

And sat upright. While drearisome
Arose the howl of wakened hounds:
The mouse let fall the altar-crumb,
The worms drew back into the mounds,

The glebe cow drooled. Till God called, 'No;
It's gunnery practice out at sea
Just as before you went below;
The world is as it used to be:

'All nations striving strong to make
Red war yet redder. Mad as hatters
They do no more for Christés sake
Than you who are helpless in such matters.

'That this is not the judgment-hour
For some of them's a blessed thing,
For if it were they'd have to scour
Hell's floor for so much threatening. . . .

'Ha, ha. It will be warmer when
I blow the trumpet (if indeed
I ever do; for you are men,
And rest eternal sorely need).'

So down we lay again. 'I wonder,
Will the world ever saner be,'
Said one, 'than when He sent us under
In our indifferent century!'

And many a skeleton shook his head.
'Instead of preaching forty year,'
My neighbour Parson Thirdly said,
'I wish I had stuck to pipes and beer.'

Again the guns disturbed the hour,
Roaring their readiness to avenge,
As far inland as Stourton Tower,
And Camelot, and starlit Stonehenge.

Afterwards

When the Present has latched its postern behind my tremulous stay,
    And the May month flaps its glad green leaves like wings,
Delicate-filmed as new-spun silk, will the neighbours say,
    'He was a man who used to notice such things'?

If it be in the dusk when, like an eyelid's soundless blink,
    The dewfall-hawk comes crossing the shades to alight
Upon the wind-warped upland thorn, a gazer may think,
    'To him this must have been a familiar sight.'

If I pass during some nocturnal blackness, mothy and warm,
    When the hedgehog travels furtively over the lawn,
One may say, 'He strove that such innocent creatures should come to no
        harm,
    But he could do little for them; and now he is gone.'

If, when hearing that I have been stilled at last, they stand at the door,
    Watching the full-starred heavens that winter sees,
Will this thought rise on those who will meet my face nomore,
    'He was one who had an eye for such mysteries'?

And will any say when my bell of quittance is heard in the gloom,
    And a crossing breeze cuts a pause in its outrollings,
Till they rise again, as they were a new bell's bloom,
    'He hears it not now, but used to notice such things'?

The Darkling Thrush

I leaned upon a coppice gate
    When Frost was spectre-grey,
And Winter's dregs made desolate
    The weakening eye of day.
The tangled bine-stems scored the sky
    Like strings from broken lyres,
And all mankind that haunted nigh
    Had sought their household fires.

The land's sharp features seemed to be
    The Century's corpse outleant,
His crypt the cloudy canopy,
    The wind his death-lament.
The ancient pulse of germ and birth
    Was shrunken hard and dry,
And every spirit upon earth
    Seemed fervourless as I.

At once a voice burst forth among
    The bleak twigs overhead
In a full-hearted evensong
    Of joy unlimited;
An aged thrush, frail, gaunt and small,
    In blast-beruffled plume,
Had chosen thus to fling his soul
    Upon the growing gloom.

So little cause for carollings
    Of such ecstatic sound
Was written on terrestrial things
    Afar or nigh around,
That I could think there trembled through
    His happy good-night air
Some blessed hope, whereof he knew
    And I was unaware.

The Oxen

Christmas Eve, and twelve of the clock,
    'Now they are all on their knees,'
An elder said as we sat in a flock
    By the embers in hearthside ease.

We pictured the meek mild creatures where
    They dwelt in their strawy pen,
Nor did it occur to one of us there
    To doubt they were kneeling then.

So fair a fancy few would weave
    In these years! Yet, I feel

If someone said on Christmas Eve,
   'Come; see the oxen kneel

'In the lonely barton by younder coomb[1]
   Our childhood used to know,'
I should go with him in the gloom,
   Hoping it might be so.

Weathers

This is the weather the cuckoo likes,
   And so do I;
When showers betumble the chestnut spikes,
   And nestlings fly;
And the little brown nightingale bills his best,
And they sit outside the 'Traveller's Rest,'
And maids come forth sprig-muslin drest,
And citizens dream of the South and West,
   And so do I.

This is the weather the shepherd shuns,
   And so do I;
When beeches drip in browns and duns,
   And thresh, and ply;
And hill-hid tides throb, throe on throe,
And meadow rivulets overflow,
And drops on gate-bars hang in a row,
And rooks in families homeward go,
   And so do I.

Christmas: 1924

'Peace upon earth!' was said. We sing it,
And pay a million priests to bring it.
After two thousand years of mass
We've got as far as poison-gas.

[1] coomb = farmyard in the hollow

STEPHEN HAWES (?–1523?)

Epitaph

O mortal folk, you may behold and see
How I lie here, sometime a mighty knight.
The end of joy and all prosperity
Is death at last—thorough his course and might:
After the day there cometh the dark night:
For though the day be never so long,
At last the bell ringeth to evensong.

SEAMUS HEANEY (1939–   )

A Call

'Hold on,' she said, 'I'll just run out and get him.
'The weather here's so good, he took the chance
To do a bit of weeding.'
So I saw him
Down on his hands and knees beside the leek rig,
Touching, inspecting, separating one
Stalk from the other, gently pulling up
Everything not tapered, frail and leafless,
Pleased to feel each little weed-root break,
But rueful also . .

Then found myself listening to
The amplified grave ticking of hall clocks
Where the phone lay unattended in a calm
Of mirror glass and sunstruck pendulums. . .

And found myself then thinking: if it were nowadays,
This is how Death would summon Everyman.

Next thing he spoke and I nearly said I loved him.

WILLIAM ERNEST HENLEY (1849–1903)

Invictus

Out of the night that covers me,
    Black as the Pit from pole to pole,
I thank whatever gods may be
    For my unconquerable soul.

In the fell clutch of circumstance
    I have not winced nor cried aloud.
Under the bludgeonings of chance
    My head is bloody, but unbowed.

Beyond this place of wrath and tears
    Looms but the horror of the shade,
And yet the menace of the years
    Finds, and shall find, me unafraid.

It matters not how strait the gate,
    How charged with punishments the scroll,
I am the master of my fate:
    I am the captain of my soul.

To W. R.

Madam Life's a piece in bloom
    Death goes dogging everywhere:
She's the tenant of the room,
    He's the ruffian on the stair.

You shall see her as a friend,
    You shall bilk him once and twice;
But he'll trap you in the end,
    And he'll stick you for her price.

With his kneebones at your chest,
    And his knuckles in your throat,
You would reason—plead—protest!
    Clutching at her petticoat;

But she's heard it all before,
    Well she knows you've had your fun,

Gingerly she gains the door,
And your little job is done.

Margaritae Sorori

A late lark twitters from the quiet skies;
And from the west,
Where the sun, his day's work ended,
Lingers as in content,
There falls on the old, grey city
An influence luminous and serene,
A shining peace.

The smoke ascends
In a rosy-and-golden haze. The spires
Shine, and are changed. In the valley
Shadows rise. The lark sings on. The sun,
Closing his benediction,
Sinks, and the darkening air
Thrills with a sense of the triumphing night—
Night with her train of stars
And her great gift of sleep.

So be my passing!
My task accomplished and the long day done,
My wages taken, and in my heart
Some late lark singing,
Let me be gathered to the quiet west,
The sundown splendid and serene,
Death.

GEORGE HERBERT (1593–1633)

The Collar

I struck the board, and cried, 'No more!
I will abroad.
What! shall I ever sigh and pine?
My lines and life are free; free as the road,
Loose as the wind, as large as store.
Shall I be still in suit?
Have I no harvest but a thorn

To let me blood, and not restore
What I have lost with cordial fruit?
    Sure there was wine
Before my sighs did dry it; there was corn
  Before my tears did drown it.
Is the year only lost to me?
  Have I no bays to crown it?
No flowers, no garlands gay? all blasted?
    All wasted?
  Not so, my heart; but there is fruit,
    And thou hast hands.
  Recover all thy sigh-blown age
On double pleasures; leave thy cold dispute
Of what is fit and not; forsake thy cage,
    Thy rope of sands,
  Which petty thoughts have made, and made to thee
    Good cable, to enforce and draw,
      And be thy law,
    While thou didst wink and wouldst not see.
      Away! take heed;
      I will abroad.
Call in thy death's-head there; tie up thy fears;
    He that forbears
  To suit and serve his need
    Deserves his load.'
But as I raved, and grew more fierce and wild
    At every word,
  Methought I heard one calling, 'Child';
    And I replied, 'My Lord.'

Prayer

Prayer the church's banquet, angel's age,
  God's breath in man returning to his birth,
  The soul in paraphrase, heart in pilgrimage,
The Christian plummet sounding heaven and earth;
Engine against th' Almighty, sinner's tower,
  Reversèd thunder, Christ-side-piercing spear,
  The six-days' world transposing in an hour,
A kind of tune, which all things hear and fear;
Softness, and peace, and joy, and love, and bliss,

Exalted Manna, gladness of the best,
Heaven in ordinary, man well drest,
The milky way, the bird of Paradise;
Church-bells beyond the stars heard, the soul's blood,
The land of spices; something understood.

Love (III)

Love bade me welcome, yet my soul drew back,
Guilty of dust and sin.
But quick-eyed Love, observing me grow slack
From my first entrance in,
Drew nearer to me, sweetly questioning
If I lacked anything.

'A guest,' I answered, 'worthy to be here.'
Love said, 'You shall be he.'
'I, the unkind, the ungrateful? Ah my dear,
I cannot look on Thee.'
Love took my hand, and smiling, did reply,
'Who made the eyes but I?'

'Truth, Lord, but I have marred them; let my shame
Go where it doth deserve.'
'And know you not,' says Love, 'who bore the blame?'
'My dear, then I will serve.'
'You must sit down,' says Love, 'and taste my meat.'
So I did sit and eat.

ROBERT HERRICK (1591–1674)

The Argument of His Book

I sing of Brooks, of Blossoms, Birds, and Bowers,
Of April, May, of June, and July-Flowers.
I sing of May-poles, Hock-carts, Wassails, Wakes,
Of Bride-grooms, Brides, and of their Bridal-cakes.
I write of Youth, of Love, and have access
By these, to sing of cleanly wantonness.
I sing of Dews, of Rains, and piece by piece
Of Balm, of Oil, of Spice, and Amber-Greece.

I sing of Times trans-shifting; and I write
How Roses first came red, and Lilies white.
I write of Groves, of Twilights, and I sing
The Court of Mab, and of the Fairy King.
I write of Hell; I sing (and ever shall)
Of Heaven, and hope to have it after all.

To the Virgins, To Make Much of Time

Gather ye rosebuds while ye may,
    Old Time is still a-flying:
And this same flower that smiles today,
    Tomorrow will be dying.

The glorious lamp of heaven, the Sun,
    The higher he's a-getting,
The sooner will his race be run,
    And nearer he's to setting.

That age is best, which is the first,
    When youth and blood are warmer;
But being spent, the worse, and worst
    Times, still succeed the former.

Then be not coy, but use your time,
    And while ye may, go marry:
For having lost but once your prime,
    You may for ever tarry.

To Daffodils

Fair daffodils, we weep to see
    You haste away so soon;
As yet the early-rising Sun
    Has not attain'd his noon.
      Stay, stay,
    Until the hasting day
      Has run
    But to the evensong;
And, having prayed together, we
    Will go with you along.

We have short time to stay, as you;
　　We have as short a Spring!
As quick a growth to meet decay
　　As you, or any thing.
　　　　We die
　　As your hours do, and dry
　　　　Away,
　　Like to the summer's rain;
Or as the pearls of morning's dew,
　　Ne'er to be found again.

Upon Love

Love brought me to a silent grove,
　　And showed me there a tree,
Where some had hanged themselves for love,
　　And gave a twist to me.

The halter was of silk and gold,
　　That he reached forth unto me:
No otherwise, than if he would
　　By dainty things undo me.

He bade me then that necklace use;
　　And told me too, he maketh
A glorious end by such a noose,
　　His death for love that taketh.

'Twas but a dream. But had I been
　　There rèally alone,
My desperate fears, in love, had seen
　　Mine executiòn.

His Prayer to Ben Jonson

When I a verse shall make,
Know I have pray'd thee,
For old religion's sake,
Saint Ben, to aid me.

Make the way smooth for me,
When I, thy Herrick,
Honouring thee, on my knee
Offer my lyric.

Candles I'll give to thee,
And a new altar;
And thou, Saint Ben, shalt be
Writ in my psalter.

To Anthea, Who may Command Him Anything

Bid me to live, and I will live
  Thy Protestant to be;
Or bid me love, and I will give
  A loving heart to thee.

A heart as soft, a heart as kind,
  A heart as sound and free
As in the whole world thou canst find,
  That heart I'll give to thee.

Bid that heart stay, and it will stay
  To honour thy decree:
Or bid it languish quite away,
  And 't shall do so for thee.

Bid me to weep, and I will weep
  While I have eyes to see:
And having none, yet I will keep
  A heart to weep for thee.

Bid me despair, and I'll despair,
  Under that cypress tree:
Or bid me die, and I will dare
  E'en Death, to die for thee.

Thou art my life, my love, my heart,
  The very eyes of me,

And hast command of every part,
To live and die for thee.

Delight in Disorder

A sweet disorder in the dress
Kindles in clothes a wantonness:
A lawn about the shoulders thrown
Into a fine distractiòn.
An erring lace, which here and there
Enthrals the crimson stomacher,
A cuff neglectful, and thereby
Ribands to flow confusedly,
A winning wave (deserving note)
In the tempestuous petticoat,
A careless shoestring, in whose tie
I see a wild civility,
Do more bewitch me, than when art
Is too precise in every part.

Upon Julia's Clothes

Whenas in silks my Julia goes
Then, then (methinks) how sweetly flows
That liquefaction of her clothes.

Next, when I cast mine eyes, and see
That brave vibration each way free;
O how that glittering taketh me!

GEOFFREY HILL (1932–)

September Song

born 19.6.32—deported 24.9.42

Undesirable you may have been, untouchable
you were not. Not forgotten
or passed over at the proper time.

As estimated, you died. Things marched,
sufficient, to that end.
Just so much Zyklon and leather patented
terror, so many routine cries.

(I have made
an elegy for myself
it is true)

September fattens on vines. Roses
flake from the wall. The smoke
of harmless fires drifts to my eyes.

This is plenty. This is more than enough.

OLIVER WENDELL HOLMES (1809–1894)

The Last Leaf

I saw him once before,
As he passed by the door,
   And again
The pavement stones resound,
As he totters o'er the ground
   With his cane.

They say that in his prime,
Ere the pruning-knife of Time
   Cut him down,
Not a better man was found
By the Crier on his round
   Through the town.

But now he walks the streets,
And looks at all he meets
   Sad and wan,
And he shakes his feeble head,
That it seems as if he said,
   'They are gone.'

The mossy marbles rest
On the lips that he has prest
   In their bloom,

And the names he loved to hear
Have been carved for many a year
 On the tomb.

My grandmamma has said—
Poor old lady, she is dead
 Long ago—
That he had a Roman nose,
And his cheek was like a rose
 In the snow;

But now his nose is thin,
And it rests upon his chin
 Like a staff,
And a crook is in his back,
And a melancholy crack
 In his laugh.

I know it is a sin
For me to sit and grin
 At him here;
But the old three-cornered hat,
And the breeches, and all that,
 Are so queer!

And if I should live to be
The last leaf upon the tree
 In the spring,
Let them smile, as I do now,
At the old forsaken bough
 Where I cling.

THOMAS HOOD (1799–1845)

Past and Present

I remember, I remember
 The house where I was born,
The little window where the sun
 Came peeping in at morn:
He never came a wink too soon
 Nor brought too long a day;

But now, I often wish the night
    Had borne my breath away.

I remember, I remember
    The roses, red and white,
The violets, and the lily-cups—
    Those flowers made of light!
The lilacs where the robin built,
    And where my brother set
The laburnum on his birth day,—
    The tree is living yet!

I remember, I remember
    Where I was used to swing,
And thought the air must rush as fresh
    To swallows on the wing;
My spirit flew in feathers then
    That is so heavy now,
And summer pools could hardly cool
    The fever on my brow.

I remember, I remember
    The fir trees dark and high;
I used to think their slender tops
    Were close against the sky:
It was a childish ignorance,
    But now 'tis little joy
To know I'm farther off from Heaven
    Than when I was a boy.

GERARD MANLEY HOPKINS (1844–1889)

Pied Beauty

Glory be to God for dappled things—
    For skies of couple-coloured as a brindled cow;
      For rose-moles all in stipple upon trout that swim;
Fresh-firecoal chestnut-falls; finches' wings;
    Landscapes plotted and pieced—fold, fallow and plough;
      And all trades, their gear and tackle and trim.

All things counter, original, spare, strange;
　　Whatever is fickle, freckled, (who knows how?)
　　　　With swift, slow; sweet, sour; adazzle, dim;
He fathers-forth whose beauty is past change:
　　Praise him.

God's Grandeur

The world is charged with the grandeur of God.
　　It will flame out, like shining from shook foil;
　　It gathers to a greatness, like the ooze of oil
Crushed. Why do men then now not reck his rod?
Generations have trod, have trod, have trod;
　　And all is seared with trade; bleared, smeared with toil;
　　And wears man's smudge and shares man's smell: the soil
Is bare now, nor can foot feel, being shod.

And for all this, nature is never spent;
　　There lives the dearest freshness deep down things;
And though the last lights off the black West went
　　Oh, morning, at the brown brink eastward, springs—
Because the Holy Ghost over the bent
　　World broods with warm breast and with ah! bright wings.

The Windhover:
To Christ our Lord

I caught this morning morning's minion, king-
　　dom of daylight's dauphin, dapple-dawn-drawn Falcon, in his riding
　　Of the rolling level underneath him steady air, and striding
High there, how he rung upon the rein of a wimpling wing
In his ecstasy! then off, off forth on swing.
　　As a skate's heel sweeps smooth on a bow-bend: the hurl and gliding
　　Rebuffed the big wind. My heart in hiding
Stirred for a bird,—the achieve of, the mastery of the thing!

Brute beauty and valour and act, oh, air, pride, plume, here
　　Buckle! and the fire that breaks from thee then, a billion
Times told lovelier, more dangerous, O my chevalier!

No wonder of it: shéer plód makes plough down sillion
Shine, and blue-bleak embers, ah my dear,
　　Fall, gall themselves, and gash gold-vermilion.

A. E. HOUSMAN (1859–1936)

'Loveliest of trees'

Loveliest of trees, the cherry now
Is hung with bloom along the bough,
And stands about the woodland ride
Wearing white for Eastertide.

Now, of my threescore years and ten,
Twenty will not come again,
And take from seventy springs a score,
It only leaves me fifty more.

And since to look at things in bloom
Fifty springs are little room,
About the woodlands I will go
To see the cherry hung with snow.

'On Wenlock Edge'

On Wenlock Edge the wood's in trouble;
　　His forest fleece the Wrekin heaves;
The gale, it plies the saplings double,
　　And thick on Severn snow the leaves.

'Twould blow like this through holt and hanger
　　When Uricon the city stood:
'Tis the old wind in the old anger,
　　But then it threshed another wood.

Then, 'twas before my time, the Roman
　　At yonder heaving hill would stare:
The blood that warms an English yeoman,
　　The thoughts that hurt him, they were there.

There, like the wind through woods in riot,
　　Through him the gale of life blew high;

The tree of man was never quiet:
　　Then 'twas the Roman, now 'tis I.

The gale, it plies the saplings double,
　　It blows so hard, 'twill soon be gone:
Today the Roman and his trouble
　　Are ashes under Uricon.

'Into my heart an air that kills'

Into my heart an air that kills
　　From yon far country blows:
What are those blue remembered hills,
　　What spires, what farms are those?

That is the land of lost content,
　　I see it shining plain,
The happy highways where I went
　　And cannot come again.

'The Sigh that Heaves the Grasses'

The sigh that heaves the grasses
　　Whence thou wilt never rise
Is of the air that passes
　　And knows not if it sighs.

The diamond tears adorning
　　Thy low mound on the lea,
Those are the tears of morning,
　　That weeps, but not for thee.

TED HUGHES (1930–1998)

Esther's Tomcat

Daylong this tomcat lies stretched flat
As an old rough mat, no mouth and no eyes,
Continual wives and wars are what
Have tattered his ears and battered his head.

Like a bundle of old rope and iron
Sleeps till blue dusk. Then reappear
His eyes, green as ringstones: he yawns wide red,
Fangs fine as a lady's needle and bright.

A tomcat sprang at a mounted knight,
Locked round his neck like a trap of hooks
While the knight rode fighting its clawing and bite.
After hundreds of years the stain's there

On the stone where he fell, dead of the torn:
That was at Barnborough. The tomcat still
Grallochs odd dogs on the quiet,
Will take the head clean off your simple pullet,

Is unkillable. From the dog's fury,
From gunshot fired point-blank he brings
His skin whole, and whole
From owlish moons of bekittenings

Among ashcans. He leaps and lightly
Walks upon sleep, his mind on the moon.
Nightly over the round world of men,
Over the roofs go his eyes and outcry.

LEIGH HUNT (1784–1859)

'Abou Ben Adhem'

Abou Ben Adhem (may his tribe increase!)
Awoke one night from a deep dream of peace,
And saw, within the moonlight in his room,
Making it rich, and like a lily in bloom,
An angel writing in a book of gold:—
Exceeding peace had made Ben Adhem bold,
And to the presence in the room he said,
    'What writest thou?'—The vision raised its head,
And with a look made of all sweet accord,
Answered, 'The names of those that love the Lord.'
    'And is mine one?' said Abou. 'Nay, not so,'
Replied the angel. Abou spoke more low,
But cheerly still; and said, 'I pray thee, then,

Write me as one that loves his fellow men.'
    The angel wrote, and vanished. The next night
It came again with a great wakening light,
And showed the names whom love of God had blessed,
And lo! Ben Adhem's name led all the rest.

'Jenny kissed me'

Jenny kissed me when we met,
    Jumping from the chair she sat in;
Time, you thief, who love to get
    Sweets into your list, put that in!

Say I'm weary, say I'm sad,
    Say that health and wealth have missed me,
Say I'm growing old, but add,
    Jenny kissed me.

SAMUEL JOHNSON (1709–1784)

from 'The Vanity of Human Wishes'

Let observation with extensive view,
Survey mankind, from China to Peru;
Remark each anxious toil, each eager strife,
And watch the busy scenes of crowded life;
Then say how hope and fear, desire and hate,
O'erspread with snares the clouded maze of fate,
Where wavering man, betrayed by venturous pride,
To tread the dreary paths without a guide,
As treacherous phantoms in the mist delude,
Shuns fancied ills, or chases airy good;
How rarely reason guides the stubborn choice.
Rules the bold hand, or prompts the suppliant voice;
How nations sink, by darling schemes oppressed,
When vengeance listens to the fool's request.
Fate wings with every wish the afflictive dart,
Each gift of nature, and each grace of art,
With fatal heat impetuous courage glows,
With fatal sweetness elocution flows,
Impeachment stops the speaker's powerful breath,

And restless fire precipitates on death.
　　But scarce observed, the knowing and the bold
Fall in the general massacre of gold;
Wide-wasting pest! that rages unconfined,
And crowds with crimes the records of mankind;
For gold his sword the hireling ruffian draws,
For gold the hireling judge distorts the laws;
Wealth heaped on wealth, nor truth nor safety buys,
The dangers gather as the treasures rise.
　　Let history tell where rival kings command,
And dubious title shakes the madded land,
When statutes glean the refuse of the sword,
How much more safe the vassal than the lord;
Low skulks the hind beneath the rage of power,
And leaves the wealthy traitor in the Tower,
Untouched his cottage, and his slumbers sound,
Tho' confiscation's vultures hover round.
　　The needy traveller, serene and gay,
Walks the wild heath, and sings his toil away.
Does envy seize thee? crush th' upbraiding joy,
Increase his riches and his peace destroy;
Now fears in dire vicissitude invade,
The rustling brake alarms, and quivering shade,
Nor light nor darkness bring his pain relief,
One shews the plunder, and one hides the thief.
　　Yet still one general cry the skies assails,
And gain and grandeur load the tainted gales;
Few know the toiling statesman's fear or care,
Th' insidious rival and the gaping heir.
　　Once more, Democritus, arise on earth,
With chearful wisdom and instructive mirth,
See motley life in modern trappings dressed,
And feed with varied fools the eternal jest:
Thou who couldst laugh where want enchained caprice,
Toil crushed conceit, and man was of a piece;
Where wealth unloved without a mourner died
And scarce a sycophant was fed by pride;
Where ne'er was known the form of mock debate,
Or seen a new-made mayor's unwieldy state;
Where change of favourites made no change of laws,
And senates heard before they judged a cause;
How wouldst thou shake at Britain's modish tribe,

Dart the quick taunt, and edge the piercing gibe?
Attentive truth and nature to descry,
And pierce each scene with philosophic eye.
To thee were solemn toys or empty show,
The robes of pleasure and the veils of woe:
All aid the farce, and all thy mirth maintain,
Whose joys are causeless, or whose griefs are vain.

Such was the scorn that filled the sage's mind,
Renewed at every glance on humankind;
How just that scorn ere yet thy voice declare,
Search every state, and canvass every prayer.

Unnumbered suppliants crowd Preferment's gate,
Athirst for wealth, and burning to be great;
Delusive Fortune hears th' incessant call,
They mount, they shine, evaporate, and fall.
On every stage the foes of peace attend,
Hate dogs their flight, and insult mocks their end.
Love ends with hope, the sinking statesman's door
Pours in the morning worshiper no more;
For growing names the weekly scribbler lies,
To growing wealth the dedicator flies,
From every room descends the painted face,
That hung the bright Palladium of the place,
And smoked in kitchens, or in auctions sold,
To better features yields the frame of gold;
For now no more we trace in every line
Heroic worth, benevolence divine:
The form distorted justifies the fall,
And detestation rids th' indignant wall.

But will not Britain hear the last appeal,
Sign her foe's doom, or guard her favourite's zeal?
Through Freedom's sons no more remonstrance rings,
Degrading nobles and controuling kings;
Our supple tribes repress their patriot throats,
And ask no questions but the price of votes;
With weekly libels and septennial ale,
Their wish is full to riot and to rail.

In full-blown dignity, see Wolsey stand,
Law in his voice, and fortune in his hand:
To him the church, the realm, their powers consign,
Thro' him the rays of regal bounty shine,
Turned by his nod the stream of honour flows,

His smile alone security bestows:
Still to new heights his restless wishes tower,
Claim leads to claim, and power advances power;
Till conquest unresisted ceased to please,
And rights submitted, left him none to seize.
At length his sovereign frowns—the train of state
Mark the keen glance, and watch the sign to hate.
Where'er he turns he meets a stranger's eye,
His suppliants scorn him, and his followers fly;
At once is lost the pride of aweful state,
The golden canopy, the glittering plate,
The regal palace, the luxurious board,
The liveried army, and the menial lord.
With age, with cares, with maladies oppressed,
He seeks the refuge of monastic rest.
Grief aids disease, remembered folly stings,
And his last sighs reproach the faith of kings.

    Speak thou, whose thoughts at humble peace repine,
Shall Wolsey's wealth, with Wolsey's end be thine?
Or liv'st thou now, with safer pride content,
The wisest justice on the banks of Trent?
For why did Wolsey near the steeps of fate,
On weak foundations raise th' enormous weight?
Why but to sink beneath misfortune's blow,
With louder ruin to the gulfs below?

    What gave great Villiers to th' assassin's knife,
And fixed disease on Harley's closing life?
What murdered Wentworth, and what exiled Hyde,
By kings protected, and to kings ally'd?
What but their wish indulged in courts to shine,
And power too great to keep, or to resign?

    When first the college rolls receive his name,
The young enthusiast quits his ease for fame;
Through all his veins the fever of renown
Burns from the strong contagion of the gown;
O'er Bodley's dome his future labours spread,
And Bacon's mansion trembles o'er his head.
Are these thy views? proceed, illustrious youth,
And virtue guard thee to the throne of Truth!
Yet should thy soul indulge the generous heat,
Till captive Science yields her last retreat;
Should Reason guide thee with her brightest ray,

And pour on misty Doubt resistless day,
Should no false Kindness lure to loose delight,
Nor Praise relax, nor Difficulty fright;
Should tempting Novelty thy cell refrain,
And Sloth effuse her opiate fumes in vain;
Should Beauty blunt on fops her fatal dart,
Nor claim the triumph of a lettered heart;
Should no Disease thy torpid veins invade,
Nor Melancholy's phantoms haunt thy shade;
Yet hope not life from grief or danger free,
Nor think the doom of man reversed for thee:
Deign on the passing world to turn thine eyes,
And pause awhile from letters, to be wise;
There mark what ills the scholar's life assail,
Toil, envy, want, the patron, and the jail.
See nations slowly wise, and meanly just,
To buried merit raise the tardy bust.
If dreams yet flatter, once again attend,
Hear Lydiat's life, and Galileo's end.

    Nor deem, when learning her last prize bestows,
The glittering eminence exempt from foes;
See when the vulgar 'scape, despised or awed,
Rebellion's vengeful talons seize on Laud.
From meaner minds, tho' smaller fines content,
The plundered palace or sequestered rent;
Marked out by dangerous parts he meets the shock,
And fatal Learning leads him to the block:
Around his tomb let Art and Genius weep,
But hear his death, ye blockheads, hear and sleep.

    The festal blazes, the triumphal show,
The ravished standard, and the captive foe,
The senate's thanks, the gazette's pompous tale,
With force resistless o'er the brave prevail.
Such bribes the rapid Greek o'er Asia whirled,
For such the steady Romans shook the world;
For such in distant lands the Britons shine,
And stain with blood the Danube or the Rhine;
This power has praise, that virtue scarce can warm
Till fame supplies the universal charm.
Yet Reason frowns on War's unequal game,
Where wasted nations raise a single name,
And mortgaged states their grandsires wreaths regret,

From age to age in everlasting debt;
Wreaths which at last the dear-bought right convey
To rust on medals, or on stones decay.
        On what foundation stands the warrior's pride,
How just his hopes let Swedish Charles decide;
A frame of adamant, a soul of fire,
No dangers fright him, and no labours tire;
O'er love, o'er fear, extends his wide domain,
Unconquered lord of pleasure and of pain;
No joys to him pacific scepters yield,
War sounds the trump, he rushes to the field:
Behold surrounding kings their power combine,
And one capitulate, and one resign;
Peace courts his hand, but spreads her charms in vain;
'Think nothing gained,' he cries, 'till nought remain,
On Moscow's walls till Gothic standards fly,
And all be mine beneath the polar sky.'
The march begins in military state,
And nations on his eye suspended wait;
Stern Famine guards the solitary coast,
And Winter barricades the realms of Frost;
He comes, not want and cold his course delay;—
Hide, blushing Glory, hide Pultowa's day:
The vanquished hero leaves his broken bands,
And shows his miseries in distant lands;
Condemned a needy supplicant to wait,
While ladies interpose, and slaves debate.
But did not Chance at length her error mend?
Did no subverted empire mark his end?
Did rival monarchs give the fatal wound?
Or hostile millions press him to the ground?
His fall was destined to a barren strand,
A petty fortress, and a dubious hand;
He left the name, at which the world grew pale,
To point a moral, or adorn a tale. . . .

On the Death of Dr Robert Levet

Condemned to hope's delusive mine,
    As on we toil from day to day,

By sudden blasts, or slow decline,
　　Our social comforts drop away.

Well tried through many a varying year,
　　See Levet to the grave descend;
Officious, innocent, sincere,
　　Of every friendless name the friend.

Yet still he fills affection's eye,
　　Obscurely wise, and coarsely kind;
Nor, lettered arrogance, deny
　　Thy praise to merit unrefined.

When fainting nature called for aid,
　　And hovering death prepared the blow,
His vigorous remedy displayed
　　The power of art without the show.

In misery's darkest caverns known,
　　His useful care was ever nigh,
Where hopeless anguish poured his groan,
　　And lonely want retired to die.

No summons mocked by chill delay,
　　No petty gain disdained by pride,
The modest wants of every day
　　The toil of every day supplied.

His virtues walked their narrow round,
　　Nor made a pause, nor left a void;
And sure th' Eternal Master found
　　The single talent well employed.

The busy day, the peaceful night,
　　Unfelt, uncounted, glided by;
His frame was firm, his powers were bright,
　　Tho' now his eightieth year was nigh.

Then with no throbbing fiery pain,
　　No cold gradations of decay,
Death broke at once the vital chain,
　　And freed his soul the nearest way.

<u>Ben</u> <u>Jonson</u> (1572–1637)

Short Measures
from 'An Ode'

It is not growing like a tree
In bulk, doth make man better be;
Or standing long an oak, three hundred year,
To fall a log at last, dry, bald, and sere:
    A lily of a day
    Is fairer far in May,
Although it fall and die that night—
It was the plant and flower of light.
In small proportions we just beauties see;
And in short measures life may perfect be.

To Celia

Drink to me only with thine eyes,
    And I will pledge with mine;
Or leave a kiss but in the cup
    And I'll not look for wine.
The thirst that from the soul doth rise
    Doth ask a drink divine;
But might I of Jove's nectar sup,
    I would not change for thine.

I sent thee late a rosy wreath,
    Not so much honouring thee
As giving it a hope that there
    It could not withered be;
But thou thereon didst only breathe
    And sent'st it back to me;
Since when it grows, and smells, I swear,
    Not of itself but thee!

Sweet Neglect

Still to be neat, still to be drest,
As you were going to a feast:

Still to be powdered, still perfumed:
Lady, it is to be presumed.
Though art's hid causes are not found,
All is not sweet, all is not sound.

Give me a look, give me a face
That makes simplicity a grace;
Robes loosely flowing, hair as free:
Such sweet neglect more taketh me,
Than all th' adulteries of art,
That strike mine eyes, but not my heart.

On My First Son

Farewell, thou child of my right hand, and joy;
My sin was too much hope of thee, loved boy.
Seven years thou wert lent to me, and I thee pay,
Exacted by thy fate, on the just day.
O, could I lose all father now! For why
Will man lament the state he should envy?

To have so soon 'scaped world's and flesh's rage,
And if no other misery, yet age?
Rest in soft peace, and, asked, say, 'Here doth lie
BEN JONSON his best piece of poetry.'
For whose sake henceforth all his vows be such,
As what he loves may never like too much.

'Fools, they are the only nation'
(from 'Volpone', Act 1, Scene 2)

Fools, they are the only nation
Worth men's envy or admiration;
Free from care or sorrow-taking,
Selves and others merry making:
All they speak or do is sterling.
Your fool, he is your great man's darling,
And your ladies' sport and pleasure;
Tongue and bauble are his treasure.
Ev'n his face begetteth laughter,
And he speaks truth free from slaughter

He's the grace of every feast,
And sometimes the chiefest guest;
Hath his trencher and his stool,
When wit waits upon the fool.
O, who would not be
He, he, he?

Hymn to Diana
(from 'Cynthia's Revels' Act 6, Scene 3)

Queen and Huntress, chaste and fair,
Now the sun is laid to sleep,
Seated in thy silver chair
State in wonted manner keep:
Hesperus entreats thy light,
Goddess excellently bright.

Earth, let not thy envious shade
Dare itself to interpose;
Cynthia's shining orb was made
Heaven to clear when day did close:
Bless us then with wishèd sight,
Goddess excellently bright.

JOHN KEATS (1795–1821)

On First Looking into Chapman's Homer

Much have I travelled in the realms of gold,
And many goodly states and kingdoms seen;
Round many western islands have I been
Which bards in fealty to Apollo hold.
Oft of one wide expanse had I been told
That deep-browed Homer ruled as his demesne;
Yet did I never breathe its pure serene
Till I heard Chapman speak out loud and bold:
Then felt I like some watcher of the skies
When a new planet swims into his ken;
Or like stout Cortez when with eagle eyes
He stared at the Pacific—and all his men

Looked at each other with a wild surmise—
Silent, upon a peak in Darien.

A Thing of Beauty
(from 'Endymion')

A thing of beauty is a joy for ever;
Its loveliness increases; it will never
Pass into nothingness; but still will keep
A bower quiet for us, and a sleep
Full of sweet dreams, and health, and quiet breathing.
Therefore, on every morrow, are we wreathing
A flowery band to bind us to the earth,
Spite of despondence, of the inhuman dearth
Of noble natures, of the gloomy days,
Of all the unhealthy and o'er-darkened ways
Made for our searching: yes, in spite of all,
Some shape of beauty moves away the pall
From our dark spirits. Such the sun, the moon,
Trees old and young, sprouting a shady boon
For simple sheep; and such are daffodils
With the green world they live in; and clear rills
That for themselves a cooling covert make
'Gainst the hot season; the mid-forest brake,
Rich with a sprinkling of fair musk-rose blooms:
And such too is the grandeur of the dooms
We have imagined for the mighty dead;
All lovely tales that we have heard or read:
An endless fountain of immortal drink,
Pouring unto us from the heaven's brink.

Ode on a Grecian Urn

Thou still unravished bride of quietness,
    Thou foster-child of silence and slow Time,
Sylvan historian, who canst thus express
    A flowery tale more sweetly than our rhyme:
What leaf-fringed legend haunts about thy shape
    Of deities or mortals, or of both,
        In Tempe or the dales of Arcady?
    What men or gods are these? What maidens loath?

What mad pursuit? What struggle to escape?
　　What pipes and timbrels? What wild ecstasy?

Heard melodies are sweet, but those unheard
　　Are sweeter; therefore, ye soft pipes, play on;
Not to the sensual ear, but, more endeared,
　　Pipe to the spirit ditties of no tone:
Fair youth, beneath the trees, thou canst not leave
　　Thy song, nor ever can those trees be bare;
　　　　Bold Lover, never, never canst thou kiss,
Though winning near the goal—yet, do not grieve;
　　She cannot fade, though thou hast not thy bliss,
　　For ever wilt thou love, and she be fair!

Ah, happy, happy boughs! that cannot shed
　　Your leaves, nor ever bid the Spring adieu;
And, happy melodist, unwearièd,
　　For ever piping songs for ever new;
More happy love! more happy, happy love!
　　For ever warm and still to be enjoyed,
　　　　For ever panting, and for ever young;
All breathing human passion far above,
　　That leaves a heart high-sorrowful and cloyed,
　　　　A burning forehead, and a parching tongue.

Who are these coming to the sacrifice?
　　To what green altar, O mysterious priest,
Lead'st thou that heifer lowing at the skies,
　　And all her silken flanks with garlands drest?
What little town by river or seashore,
　　Or mountain-built with peaceful citadel,
　　　　Is emptied of its folk, this pious morn?
And, little town, thy streets for evermore
　　Will silent be; and not a soul to tell
　　　　Why thou art desolate, can e'er return.

O Attic shape! Fair attitude! with brede
　　Of marble men and maidens overwrought,
With forest branches and the trodden weed;
　　Thou, silent form, dost tease us out of thought
As doth eternity: Cold Pastoral!
　　When old age shall this generation waste,
　　　　Thou shalt remain, in midst of other woe
　　　　Than ours, a friend to man, to whom thou say'st,

'Beauty is truth, truth beauty,—that is all
Ye know on earth, and all ye need to know.'

On the Sea

It keeps eternal whisperings around
   Desolate shores, and with its mighty swell
      Gluts twice ten thousand caverns, till the spell
Of Hecate leaves them their old shadowy sound.
Often 'tis in such gentle temper found,
   That scarcely will the very smallest shell
      Be moved for days from whence it sometime fell,
When last the winds of heaven were unbound.
   Oh ye! whose ears are dinned with uproar rude,
      Or fed too much with cloying melody,—
   Sit ye near some old cavern's mouth, and brood
Until ye start, as if the sea-nymphs quired!

Ode to a Nightingale

My heart aches, and a drowsy numbness pains
   My sense, as though of hemlock I had drunk,
Or emptied some dull opiate to the drains
   One minute past, and Lethe-wards had sunk:
'Tis not through envy of thy happy lot,
   But being too happy in thine happiness,—
      That thou, light-wingèd Dryad of the trees
      In some melodious plot
   Of beechen green, and shadows numberless,
      Singest of summer in full-throated ease.

O for a draught of vintage, that hath been
   Cooled a long age in the deep-delvèd earth,
Tasting of Flora and the country green,
Dance, and Provençal song, and sunburnt mirth!
O for a beaker full of the warm South,
   Full of the true, the blushful Hippocrene,
      With beaded bubbles winking at the brim,
      And purple-stainèd mouth;
   That I might drink, and leave the world unseen,
      And with thee fade away into the forest dim:

Fade far away, dissolve, and quite forget
    What thou among the leaves hast never known,
The weariness, the fever, and the fret
    Here, where men sit and hear each other groan;
Where palsy shakes a few, sad, last grey hairs,
      Where youth grows pale, and spectre-thin, and dies;
        Where but to think is to be full of sorrow
          And leaden-eyed despairs,
      Where beauty cannot keep her lustrous eyes,
        Or new love pine at them beyond tomorrow.

Away! away! for I will fly to thee,
    Not charioted by Bacchus and his pards,
But on the viewless wings of Poesy,
    Though the dull brain perplexes and retards:
Already with thee! tender is the night,
      And haply the Queen-Moon is on her throne,
        Clustered around by all her starry fays;
          But here there is no light,
    Save what from heaven is with the breezes blown
      Through verdurous glooms and winding mossy ways.

I cannot see what flowers are at my feet,
    Nor what soft incense hangs upon the boughs,
But, in embalmèd darkness, guess each sweet
    Wherewith the seasonable month endows
The grass, the thicket, and the fruit-tree wild;
      White hawthorn, and the pastoral eglantine;
        Fast-fading violets covered up in leaves;
          And mid-May's eldest child,
    The coming musk-rose, full of dewy wine,
      The murmurous haunt of flies on summer eves.

Darkling I listen; and for many a time
    I have been half in love with easeful Death,
Called him soft names in many a musèd rhyme,
    To take into the air my quiet breath;
Now more than ever seems it rich to die,
    To cease upon the midnight with no pain,
      While thou art pouring forth thy soul abroad
        In such an ecstasy!
    Still wouldst thou sing, and I have ears in vain—
      To thy high requiem become a sod.

Thou wast not born for death, immortal Bird!
　No hungry generations tread thee down;
The voice I hear this passing night was heard
　In ancient days by emperor and clown:
Perhaps the self-same song that found a path
　　Through the sad heart of Ruth, when, sick for home,
　　　She stood in tears amid the alien corn;
　　　　The same that oft-times hath
　　Charmed magic casements, opening on the foam
　　Of perilous seas, in faery lands forlorn.

Forlorn! the very word is like a bell
　To toll me back from thee to my sole self.
Adieu! the fancy cannot cheat so well
　As she is famed to do, deceiving elf.
Adieu! adieu! thy plaintive anthem fades
　　Past the near meadows, over the still stream,
　　　Up the hill-side; and now 'tis buried deep
　　　　In the next valley-glades:
　　Was it a vision, or a waking dream?
　　　Fled is that music:—do I wake or sleep?

Ode to Autumn

Season of mists and mellow fruitfulness!
　Close bosom-friend of the maturing sun;
Conspiring with him how to load and bless
　With fruit the vines that round the thatch-eves run;
To bend with apples the mossed cottage-trees,
　And fill all fruit with ripeness to the core;
　　To swell the gourd, and plump the hazel shells
　　With a sweet kernel; to set budding more,
And still more, later flowers for the bees,
Until they think warm days will never cease,
　For summer has o'er-brimmed their clammy cells.

Who hath not seen thee oft amid thy store?
　Sometimes whoever seeks abroad may find
Thee sitting careless on a granary floor,
　Thy hair soft-lifted by the winnowing wind;
Or on a half-reaped furrow sound asleep,
　Drowsed with the fume of poppies, while thy hook

Spares the next swath and all its twinèd flowers;
And sometimes like a gleaner thou dost keep
    Steady thy laden head across a brook;
    Or by a cider-press, with patient look,
        Thou watchest the last oozings, hours by hours.

Where are the songs of Spring? Ay, where are they?
    Think not of them, thou hast thy music too,
While barrèd clouds bloom the soft-dying day,
    And touch the stubble-plains with rosy hue;
Then in a wailful choir, the small gnats mourn
    Among the river sallows, borne aloft
        Or sinking as the light wind lives or dies;
And full-grown lambs loud bleat from hilly bourn;
    Hedge-crickets sing; and now with treble soft
    The redbreast whistles from a garden-croft,
        And gathering swallows twitter in the skies.

La Belle Dame sans Merci

1

Oh, what can ail thee, knight-at-arms,
    Alone and palely loitering?
The sedge has withered from the lake,
    And no birds sing.

2

Oh, what can ail thee, knight-at-arms,
    So haggard and so woebegone?
The squirrel's granary is full,
    And the harvest's done.

3

I see a lily on thy brow,
    With anguish moist and fever dew;
And on thy cheek a fading rose
    Fast withereth too.

4

I met a lady in the meads
    Full beautiful, a faery's child;
Her hair was long, her foot was light,
    And her eyes were wild.

5

I made a garland for her head,
  And bracelets too, and fragrant zone;
She looked at me as she did love,
  And made sweet moan.

6

I set her on my pacing steed,
  And nothing else saw all day long,
For sidelong would she bend, and sing
  A faery's song.

7

She found me roots of relish sweet,
  And honey wild, and manna dew;
And sure in language strange she said
  'I love thee true.'

8

She took me to her elfin grot,
  And there she wept and sighed full sore,
And there I shut her wild sad eyes
  With kisses four.

9

And there she lullèd me asleep,
  And there I dreamed—Ah woe betide!—
The latest dream I ever dreamed
  On the cold hill side.

10

I saw pale kings, and princes too,
  Pale warriors, death-pale were they all;
They cried—'La Belle Dame sans Merci
  Hath thee in thrall!'

11

I saw their starved lips in the gloom
  With horrid warning gapèd wide,
And I awoke, and found me here
  On the cold hill's side.

12

And this is why I sojourn here
    Alone and palely loitering,
Though the sedge is withered from the lake,
    And no birds sing.

'When I have fears'

When I have fears that I may cease to be
    Before my pen has gleaned my teeming brain,
Before high piled books, in charactry,
    Hold like rich garners the full ripened grain;
When I behold, upon the night's starred face,
    Huge cloudy symbols of a high romance,
And think that I may never live to trace
    Their shadows, with the magic hand of chance;
And when I feel, fair creature of an hour
    That I shall never look upon thee more,
Never have relish in the fairy power
    Of unreflecting love;—then on the shore
Of the wide world I stand alone, and think
Till love and fame to nothingness do sink.

RUDYARD KIPLING (1865–1936)

The Conundrum of the Workshops

When the flush of a new-born sun fell first on Eden's green and gold,
Our father Adam sat under the Tree and scratched with a stick in the mould;
And the first rude sketch that the world had seen was joy to his mighty
    heart,
Till the Devil whispered behind the leaves, 'It's pretty, but is it Art?'

Wherefore he called to his wife, and fled to fashion his work anew—
The first of his race who cared a fig for the first, most dread review;
And he left his lore to the use of his sons—and that was a glorious gain
When the Devil chuckled 'Is it Art?' in the ear of the branded Cain.

They fought and they talked in the North and the South, they talked
    and they fought in the West,
Till the waters rose on the pitiful land, and the poor Red Clay had rest—

Had rest till that dank blank-canvas dawn when the dove was preened to
    start,
And the Devil bubbled below the keel: 'It's human, but is it Art?'

They builded a tower to shiver the sky and wrench the stars apart,
Till the Devil grunted behind the bricks: 'It's striking, but is it Art?'
The stone was dropped at the quarry-side and the idle derrick swung,
While each man talked of the aims of Art, and each in an alien tongue.

The tale is as old as the Eden Tree—and new as the new-cut tooth—
For each man knows ere his lip-thatch grows he is master of Art and Truth;
And each man hears as the twilight nears, to the beat of his dying heart,
The Devil drum on the darkened pane: 'You did it, but was it Art?'

We have learned to whittle the Eden Tree to the shape of a surplice-peg,
We have learned to bottle our parents twain in the yolk of an addled egg,
We know that the tail must wag the dog, for the horse is drawn by the cart;
But the Devil whoops, as he whooped of old: 'It's clever, but is it Art?'

When the flicker of London sun falls faint on the Club-room's green
    and gold,
The sons of Adam sit them down and scratch with their pens in the
    mould—
They scratch with their pens in the mould of their graves, and the ink
    and the anguish start,
For the Devil mutters behind the leaves: 'It's pretty, but is it Art?'

Now, if we could win to the Eden Tree where the Four Great Rivers flow,
And the Wreath of Eve is red on the turf as she left it long ago,
And if we could come when the sentry slept and softly scurry through,
By the favour of God we might know as much—as our father Adam knew!

If ——

If you can keep your head when all about you
    Are losing theirs and blaming it on you,
If you can trust yourself when all men doubt you,
    But make allowance for their doubting too;
If you can wait and not be tired by waiting,
    Or being lied about, don't deal in lies,
Or being hated, don't give way to hating,
    And yet don't look too good, nor talk too wise:

If you can dream—and not make dreams your master;
    If you can think—and not make thoughts your aim;
If you can meet with Triumph and Disaster
    And treat those two imposters just the same;
If you can bear to hear the truth you've spoken
    Twisted by knaves to make a trap for fools,
Or watch the things you gave your life to, broken,
    And stoop and build 'em up with worn-out tools:

If you can make one heap of all your winnings
    And risk it on one turn of pitch-and-toss,
And lose, and start again at your beginnings
    And never breathe a word about your loss;
If you can force your heart and nerve and sinew
    To serve your turn long after they are gone,
And so hold on when there is nothing in you
    Except the Will which says to them: 'Hold on!'

If you can talk with crowds and keep your virtue,
    Or walk with Kings—nor lose the common touch,
If neither foes nor loving friends can hurt you,
    If all men count with you, but none too much;
If you can fill the unforgiving minute
    With sixty seconds' worth of distance run,
Yours is the Earth and everything that's in it,
    And—which is more—you'll be a Man, my son!

The Way through the Woods

They shut the road through the woods
Seventy years ago.
Weather and rain have undone it again,
And now you would never know
There was once a road through the woods
Before they planted the trees.
It is underneath the coppice and heath
And the thin anemones.
Only the keeper sees
That, where the ring-dove broods,
And the badgers roll at ease,
There was once a road through the woods.

Yet, if you enter the woods
Of a summer evening late,
When the night-air cools on the trout-ringed pools
Where the otter whistles his mate,
(They fear not men in the woods,
Because they see so few.)
You will hear the beat of a horse's feet,
And the swish of a skirt in the dew,
Steadily cantering through
The misty solitudes,
As though they perfectly knew
The old lost road through the woods . . .
But there is no road through the woods.

The Rabbi's Song

If thought can reach to Heaven,
On Heaven let it dwell,
For fear that Thought be given
Like power to reach to Hell.

For fear the desolation
And darkness of thy mind,
Perplex an habitation
Which thou hast left behind.

Let nothing linger after—
No whispering ghost remain,
In wall, or beam, or rafter,
Of any hate or pain:

Cleanse and call home thy spirit,
Deny her leave to cast,
On aught thy heirs inherit,
The shadow of her past.

For think, in all thy sadness,
What road our griefs may take;
Whose brain reflect our madness,
Or whom our terrors shake.

For think, lest any languish
By cause of thy distress
The arrows of our anguish
Fly farther than we guess.

Our lives, our tears, as water,
Are spilled upon the ground;
God giveth no man quarter,
Yet God a means hath found;

Though faith and hope have vanished,
And even love grows dim;
A means whereby His banished
Be not expelled from Him!

CHARLES LAMB (1775–1834)

The Old Familiar Faces

I have had playmates, I have had companions
In my days of childhood, in my joyful schooldays;
    All, all are gone, the old familiar faces.

I have been laughing, I have been carousing,
Drinking late, sitting late, with my bosom cronies;
    All, all are gone, the old familiar faces.

I loved a love once, fairest among women:
Closed are her doors on me, I must not see her—
    All, all are gone, the old familiar faces.

I have a friend, a kinder friend has no man;
Like an ingrate, I left my friend abruptly;
    Left him, to muse on the old familiar faces.

Ghost-like I paced round the haunts of my childhood;
Earth seemed a desert I was bound to traverse,
    Seeking to find the old familiar faces.

Friend of my bosom, thou more than a brother,
Why wert not thou born in my father's dwelling!
    So might we talk of the old familiar faces,

How some they have died, and some they have left me,
And some are taken from me; all are departed;
    All, all are gone, the old familiar faces.

WALTER SAVAGE LANDOR (1775–1864)

'Mother, I cannot mind my wheel'

Mother, I cannot mind my wheel;
    My fingers ache, my lips are dry;
O, if you felt the pain I feel!
    But O, who ever felt as I!

No longer could I doubt him true—
    All other men may use deceit.
He always said my eyes were blue,
    And often swore my lips were sweet.

Rose Aylmer

Ah, what avails the sceptred race,
    Ah, what the form divine!
What every virtue, every grace!
    Rose Aylmer, all were thine.

Rose Aylmer, whom these wakeful eyes
    May weep, but never see,
A night of memories and of sighs
    I consecrate to thee.

Dirce

Stand close around, ye Stygian set,
    With Dirce in one boat conveyed,
Or Charon, seeing, may forget
    That he is old and she a shade.

To Robert Browning

There is delight in singing, though none hear
Beside the singer; and there is delight
In praising, though the praiser sits alone
And see the praised far off him, far above.
Shakespeare is not our poet, but the world's,
Therefore on him no speech! and brief for thee,
Browning! Since Chaucer was alive and hale
No man hath walked along our roads with step
So active, so inquiring eye, or tongue
So varied in discourse. But warmer climes
Give brighter plumage, stronger wing; the breeze
Of Alpine heights thou playest with, borne on
Beyond Sorrento and Amalfi, where
The Siren waits thee, singing song for song.

PHILIP LARKIN (1922–1985)

Faith Healing

Slowly the women file to where he stands
Upright in rimless glasses, silver hair,
Dark suit, white collar. Stewards tirelessly
Persuade them onwards to his voice and hands,
Within whose warm spring rain of loving care
Each dwells some twenty seconds. Now, dear child,
What's wrong, the deep American voice demands,
And, scarcely pausing, goes into a prayer
Directing God about this eye, that knee.
Their heads are clasped abruptly; then, exiled
Like losing thoughts, they go in silence; some
Sheepishly stray, not back into their lives
Just yet; but some stay stiff, twitching and loud
With deep hoarse tears, as if a kind of dumb
And idiot child within them still survives
To re-awake at kindness, thinking a voice
At last calls them alone, that hands have come
To lift and lighten; and such joy arrives
Their thick tongues blort, their eyes squeeze grief, a crowd
Of huge unheard answers jam and rejoice—

What's wrong! Moustached in flowered frocks they shake:
By now, all's wrong. In everyone there sleeps
A sense of life lived according to love.
To some it means the difference they could make
By loving others, but across most it sweeps
As all they might have done had they been loved.
That nothing cures. An immense slackening ache,
As when, thawing, the rigid landscape weeps,
Spreads slowly through them—that, and the voice above
Saying *Dear child*, and all time has disproved.

Annus Mirabilis

Sexual intercourse began
In nineteen sixty-three
(Which was rather late for me)—
Between the end of
the Chatterly ban
And the Beatles' first LP.

Up till then there'd only been
A sort of bargaining,
A wrangle for a ring,
A shame that started at sixteen
And spread to everything.

Then all at once the quarrel sank:
Everyone felt the same,
And every life became
A brilliant breaking of the bank,
A quite unlosable game.

So life was never better than
In nineteen sixty-three
(Though just too late for me)—
Between the end of the
Chatterley ban
And the Beatles' first LP
16 June 1967

D. H. LAWRENCE (1885–1930)

Snake

A snake came to my water-trough
On a hot, hot day, and I in pyjamas for the heat,
To drink there.

In the deep, strange-scented shade of the great dark carob-tree
I came down the steps with my pitcher
And must wait, must stand and wait, for there he was at the trough
    before me.

He reached down from a fissure in the earth-wall in the gloom
And trailed his yellow-brown slackness soft-bellied down, over the edge
    of the stone trough
And rested his throat upon the stone bottom,
And where the water had dripped from the tap, in a small clearness,
He sipped with his straight mouth,
Softly drank through his straight gums, into his slack long body,
Silently.

Someone was before me at my water-trough,
And I, like a second comer, waiting.

He lifted his head from his drinking, as cattle do,
And looked at me vaguely, as drinking cattle do,
And flickered his two-forked tongue from his lips, and mused a moment,
And stooped and drank a little more,
Being earth-brown, earth-golden from the burning bowels of the earth
On the day of Sicilian July, with Etna smoking.

The voice of my education said to me
He must be killed,
For in Sicily the black, black snakes are innocent, the gold are venomous.

And voices in me said, If you were a man
You would take a stick and break him now; and finish him off.

But must I confess how I liked him,
How glad I was he had come like a guest in quiet, to drink at my water-
    trough

And depart peaceful, pacified, and thankless,
Into the burning bowels of this earth?

Was it cowardice, that I dared not kill him?
Was it perversity, that I longed to talk to him?
Was it humility, to feel so honoured?
I felt so honoured.

And yet those voices:
If you were not afraid you would kill him!

And truly I was afraid, I was most afraid,
But even so, honoured still more
That he should seek my hospitality
From out the dark door of the secret earth.

He drank enough
And lifted his head, dreamily, as one who has drunk
And flickered his tongue like a forked night on the air, so black;
Seeming to lick his lips,
And looked around like a god, unseeing, into the air,
And slowly turned his head,
And slowly, very slowly, as if thrice adream,
Proceeded to draw his slow length curving round
And climb again the broken bank of my wall-face.

And as he put his head into that dreadful hole,
And as he slowly drew up, snake-easing his shoulders, and entered farther,
A sort of horror, a sort of protest against his withdrawing into that
    horrid black hole,
Deliberately going into the blackness, and slowly drawing himself after,
Overcame me now his back was turned.

I looked round, I put down my pitcher,
I picked up a clumsy log
And threw it at the water-trough with a clatter.

I think it did not hit him,
But suddenly that part of him that was left behind convulsed in undigni-
    fied haste,
Writhed like lightning, and was gone
Into the black hole, the earth-lipped fissure in the wall-front,
At which, in the intense still noon, I stared with fascination.

And immediately I regretted it.
I thought how paltry, how vulgar, what a mean act!
I despised myself and the voices of my accursed human education.

And I thought of the albatross,
And I wished he would come back, my snake.

For he seemed to me again like a king,
Like a king in exile, uncrowned in the underworld,
Now due to be crowned again.

And so, I missed my chance with one of the lords
Of life.
And I have something to expiate;
A pettiness.

Bavarian Gentians

Not every man has gentians in his house
in Soft September, at slow, sad Michaelmas.

Bavarian gentians, big and dark, only dark
darkening the day-time, torch-like with the smoking blueness of Pluto's
    gloom,
ribbed and torch-like, with their blaze of darkness spread blue
down flattening into points, flattened under the sweep of white day
torch-flower of the blue-smoking darkness, Pluto's dark-blue daze,
black lamps from the halls of Dis, burning dark blue,
giving off darkness, blue darkness, as Demeter's pale lamps give off light,
lead me then, lead the way.

Reach me a gentian, give me a torch!
let me guide myself with the blue, forked torch of this flower
down the darker and darker stairs, where blue is darkened on blueness
even where Persephone goes, just now, from the frosted September
to the sightless realm where darkness is awake upon the dark
and Persephone herself is but a voice
or a darkness invisible enfolded in the deeper dark
of the arms Plutonic, and pierced with the passion of dense gloom,
among the splendour of torches of darkness, shedding darkness on the
    lost bride and her groom.

Mountain Lion

Climbing through the January snow, into the Lobo canyon
Dark grow the spruce-trees, blue is the balsam, water sounds still unfrozen,
  and the trail is still evident.

Men!
Two men!
Men! The only animal in the world to fear!

They hesitate.
We hesitate.
They have a gun.
We have no gun.

Then we all advance, to meet.

Two Mexicans, strangers, emerging out of the dark and snow and
inwardness of the Lobo valley.
What are they doing here on this vanishing trail?

What is he carrying?
Something yellow.
A deer?

Qué tiene, amigo?
Leon—

He smiles, foolishly, as if he were caught doing wrong.
And we smile, foolishly, as if we didn't know.
He is quite gentle and dark-faced.

It is a mountain lion,
A long, long slim cat, yellow like a lioness.
Dead.

He trapped her this morning, he says, smiling foolishly.

Lift up her face,
Her round, bright face, bright as frost.
Her round, fine-fashioned head, with two dead ears;
And stripes in the brilliant frost of her face, sharp, fine dark rays,
Dark, keen, fine rays in the brilliant frost of her face.
Beautiful dead eyes.

Hermeso es!

They go out towards the open;
We go on into the gloom of Lobo.
And above the trees I found her lair,
A hole in the blood-orange brilliant rocks that stick up, little cave.
And bones, and twigs, and a perilous ascent.

So, she will never leap up that way again, with the yellow flash of a
    mountain lion's long shoot!
And her bright striped frost-face will never watch any more,
    out of the shadow of the cave in the blood-orange rock,
Above the trees of the Lobo dark valley-mouth!

Instead, I look out.
And out to the dim of the desert, like a dream, never real,
To the snow of the Sangre de Cristo mountains, the ice of the
    mountains of Picoris,
And near across at the opposite steep of snow, green trees motionless
    standing in snow, like a Christmas toy.

And I think in this empty world there was room for me and a mountain
    lion.
And I think in the world beyond, how easily we might spare a million or
    two of humans
And never miss them.
Yet what a gap in the world, the missing white frost-face of that slim
    yellow mountain lion!

EDWARD LEAR (1812–1888)

'How pleasant to know Mr Lear'

    'How pleasant to know Mr Lear!'
        Who has written such volumes of stuff!
    Some think him ill-tempered and queer,
        But a few think him pleasant enough.

    His mind is concrete and fastidious,
        His nose is remarkably big;
    His visage is more or less hideous,
        His beard it resembles a wig.

He has ears, and two eyes, and ten fingers,
    Leastways if you reckon two thumbs;
Long ago he was one of the singers,
    But now he is one of the dumbs.

He sits in a beautiful parlour,
    With hundreds of books on the wall:
He drinks a great deal of Marsala,
    But he never gets tipsy at all.

He has many friends, laymen and clerical,
    Old Foss is the name of his cat:
His body is perfectly spherical,
    He weareth a runcible hat.

When he walks in a waterproof white,
    The children run after him so!
Calling out, 'He's come out in his night-
    gown, that crazy old Englishman, oh!'

He weeps by the side of the ocean,
    He weeps on the top of the hill,
He purchases pancakes and lotion,
    And chocolate shrimps from the mill.

He reads but he cannot speak Spanish,
    He cannot abide ginger-beer:
Ere the days of his pilgrimable vanish,
    How pleasant to know Mr Lear!

The Owl and the Pussy-Cat

The Owl and the Pussy-Cat went to sea
    In a beautiful pea-green boat:
They took some honey, and plenty of money
    Wrapped up in a five-pound note.
The Owl looked up to the stars above,
    And sang to a small guitar,
'O lovely Pussy, O Pussy, my love,
    What a beautiful Pussy you are,
        You are,
        You are!
What a beautiful Pussy you are!'

Pussy said to the Owl, 'You elegant fowl,
    How charmingly sweet you sing!
Oh! let us be married; too long we have tarried:
    But what shall we do for a ring?'
They sailed away, for a year and a day,
    To the land where the bong-tree grows;
And there in a wood a Piggy-wig stood,
        With a ring at the end of his nose,
            His nose,
            His nose,
        With a ring at the end of his nose.

'Dear Pig, are you willing to sell for one shilling
    Your ring?' Said the Piggy, 'I will.'
So they took it away, and were married next day
    By the Turkey who lives on the hill.
They dined on mince and slices of quince,
    Which they ate with a runcible spoon;
And hand in hand, on the edge of the sand,
        They danced by the light of the moon,
            The moon,
            The moon,
        They danced by the light of the moon.

ALUN LEWIS (1915–1944)

'All day it has rained'

All day it has rained, and we on the edge of the moors
Have sprawled in our bell-tents, moody and dull as boors,
Groundsheets and blankets spread on the muddy ground
And from the first grey wakening we have found
No refuge from the skirmishing fine rain
And the wind that made the canvas heave and flap
And the taut wet guy-ropes ravel out and snap.
All day the rain has glided, wave and mist and dream,
Drenching the gorse and heather, a gossamer stream
Too light to stir the acorns that suddenly
Snatched from their cups by the wild south-westerly
Pattered against the tent and our upturned dreaming faces.
And we stretched out, unbuttoning our braces,

Smoking a Woodbine, darning dirty socks,
Reading the Sunday papers—I saw a fox
And mentioned it in the note I scribbled home;—
And we talked of girls, and dropping bombs on Rome
And thought of the quiet dead and the loud celebrities
Exhorting us to slaughter, and the herded refugees:
—Yet thought softly, morosely of them, and as indifferently
As of ourselves or those whom we
For years have loved, and will again
Tomorrow maybe love; but now it is the rain
Possesses us entirely, the twilight and the rain.

And I can remember nothing dearer or more to my heart
Than the children I watched in the woods on Saturday
Shaking down burning chestnuts for the schoolyard's merry play,
Or the shaggy patient dog who followed me
By Sheet and Steep and up the wooded scree
To the Shoulder o' Mutton where Edward Thomas brooded long
On death and beauty—till a bullet stopped his song.

HENRY WADSWORTH LONGFELLOW (1807–1882)

My Lost Youth

Often I think of the beautiful town
    That is seated by the sea;
Often in thought go up and down
The pleasant streets of that dear old town,
    And my youth comes back to me.
        And a verse of a Lapland song
        Is haunting my memory still:
        'A boy's will is the wind's will,
And the thoughts of youth are long, long thoughts.'

I can see the shadowy lines of its trees,
    And catch, in sudden gleams,
The sheen of the far-surrounding seas,
And islands that were the Hesperides
    Of all my boyish dreams.
        And the burden of that old song,

It murmurs and whispers still:
'A boy's will is the wind's will,
And the thoughts of youth are long, long thoughts.'

I remember the black wharves and the slips,
    And the sea-tides tossing free;
And Spanish sailors with bearded lips,
And the beauty and mystery of the ships,
    And the magic of the sea.
        And the voice of that wayward song
        Is singing and saying still:
        'A boy's will is the wind's will,
And the thoughts of youth are long, long thoughts.'

I remember the bulwarks by the shore,
    And the fort upon the hill;
The sunrise gun, with its hollow roar,
The drum-beat repeated o'er and o'er,
    And the bugle wild and shrill.
        And the music of that old song
        Throbs in my memory still:
        'A boy's will is the wind's will,
And the thoughts of youth are long, long thoughts.'

I remember the sea-fight far away,
    How it thundered o'er the tide!
And the dead captains, as they lay
In their graves, o'erlooking the tranquil bay,
    Where they in battle died.
        And the sound of that mournful song
        Goes through me with a thrill:
        'A boy's will is the wind's will,
And the thoughts of youth are long, long thoughts.'

I can see the breezy dome of groves,
    The shadows of Deering's Woods;
And the friendships old and the early loves
Come back with a Sabbath sound, as of doves
    In quiet neighbourhoods.
        And the verse of that sweet old song,
        It flutters and murmurs still:

'A boy's will is the wind's will,
And the thoughts of youth are long, long thoughts.'

I remember the gleams and glooms that dart
   Across the schoolboys brain;
The song and the silence in the heart,
That in part are prophecies, and in part
    Are longings wild and vain.
      And the voice of that fitful song
      Sings on, and is never still:
      'A boy's will is the wind's will,
And the thoughts of youth are long, long thoughts.'

There are things of which I may not speak;
   There are dreams that cannot die;
There are thoughts that make the strong heart weak,
And bring a pallor into the cheek,
    And a mist before the eye.
      And the words of that fatal song
      Come over me like a chill:
      'A boy's will is the wind's will,
And the thoughts of youth are long, long thoughts.'

Strange to me now are the forms I meet
   When I visit the dear old town;
But the native air is pure and sweet,
And the trees that o'er-shadow each well-known street,
    As they balance up and down,
      Are singing the beautiful song,
      Are sighing and whispering still:
      'A boy's will is the wind's will,
And the thoughts of youth are long, long thoughts.'

And Deering's Woods are fresh and fair,
   And with joy that is almost pain
My heart goes back to wander there,
And among the dreams of the days that were,
    I find my lost youth again.
      And the strange and beautiful song,
      The groves are repeating it still:
      'A boy's will is the wind's will,
And the thoughts of youth are long, long thoughts.'

The Jewish Cemetery at Newport

How strange it seems! These Hebrews in their graves,
    Close by the street of this fair seaport town,
Silent beside the never-silent waves,
    At rest in all this moving up and down!

The trees are white with dust, that o'er their sleep
    Wave their broad curtains in the south-wind's breath,
While underneath these leafy tents they keep
    The long, mysterious Exodus of Death.

And these sepulchral stones, so old and brown,
    That pave with level flags their burial-place,
Seem like the tablets of the Law, thrown down
    And broken by Moses at the mountain's base.

The very names recorded here are strange,
    Of foreign accent, and of different climes;
Alvares and Rivera interchange
    With Abraham and Jacob of old times.

'Blessed be God! for he created Death!'
    The mourners said, 'and Death is rest and peace;'
Then added, in the certainty of faith,
    'And giveth Life that nevermore shall cease.'

Closed are the portals of their Synagogue,
    No Psalms of David now the silence break,
No Rabbi reads the ancient Decalogue
    In the grand dialect the Prophets spake.

Gone are the living, but the dead remain,
    And not neglected; for a hand unseen,
Scattering its bounty, like a summer rain,
    Still keeps their graves and their remembrance green.

How came they here? What burst of Christian hate,
    What persecution, merciless and blind,
Drove o'er the sea—that desert desolate—
    These Ishmaels and Hagars of mankind?

They lived in narrow streets and lanes obscure,
    Ghetto and Judenstrass, in mirk and mire;

Taught in the school of patience to endure
　　The life of anguish and the death of fire.

All their lives long, with the unleavened bread
　　And bitter herbs of exile and its fears,
The wasting famine of the heart they fed,
　　And slaked its thirst with marah of their tears.

Anathema maranatha! was the cry
　　That rang from town to town, from street to street;
At every gate the accursed Mordecai
　　Was mocked and jeered, and spurned by Christian feet.

Pride and humiliation hand in hand
　　Walked with them through the world where'er they went;
Trampled and beaten were they as the sand,
　　And yet unshaken as the continent.

For in the background figures vague and vast
　　Of patriarchs and of prophets rose sublime,
And all the great traditions of the Past
　　They saw reflected in the coming time.

And thus forever with reverted look
　　The mystic volume of the world they read,
Spelling it backward, like a Hebrew book,
　　Till life became a Legend of the Dead.

But ah! what once has been shall be no more!
　　The groaning earth in travail and in pain
Brings forth its races, but does not restore,
　　And the dead nations never rise again.

RICHARD LOVELACE (1618–1658)

To Althea from Prison

When Love with unconfinèd wings
　　Hovers within my gates,
And my divine Althea brings
　　To whisper at the grates;
When I lie tangled in her hair
　　And fettered to her eye,
The birds that wanton in the air
　　Know no such liberty.

When flowing cups run swiftly round
    With no allaying Thames,
Our careless heads with roses crowned,
    Our hearts with loyal flames;
When thirsty grief in wine we steep,
    When healths and draughts go free,
Fishes that tipple in the deep
    Know no such liberty.

When, like committed linnets,
    With shriller throat shall sing
The sweetness, mercy, majesty,
    And glories of my King;
When I shall voice aloud how good
    He is, how great should be,
Enlargèd winds, that curl the flood
    Know no such liberty.

Stone walls do not a prison make,
    Nor iron bars a cage;
Minds innocent and quiet take
    That for an hermitage;
If I have freedom in my love
    And in my soul am free,
Angels alone, that soar above,
    Enjoy such liberty.

Norman McCaig (1910–1996)

Power Dive

He spent a fortune on architects and builders.
He signed tickertapes of cheques for furniture,
carpets, paintings, filmstar beds. He surrounded the house
with plantations and parterres, hahas and gazebos.
And in the right place, the properest place
at last he saw completed a swimming pool
that glittered like ancient Rome.

It was just before he hit the water
in his first dive that he glimpsed
the triangular fin cutting the surface.

HUGH MACDIARMID (1892–1978)

Of John Davidson

I remember one death in my boyhood
That next to my father's, and darker, endures;
Not Queen Victoria's, but Davidson, yours,
And something in me has always stood
Since then looking down the sandslope
On your small black shape by the edge of the sea,
—A bullet-hole through a great scene's beauty,
God through the wrong end of a telescope.

LOUIS MACNEICE (1907–1963)

Bagpipe Music

It's no go the merrygoround, it's no go the rickshaw,
All we want is a limousine and a ticket for the peep-show.
Their knickers are made of crépe-de-chine, their shoes are made of python,
Their halls are lined with tiger rugs and their walls with heads of bison.

John MacDonald found a corpse, put it under the sofa,
Waited till it came to life and hit it with a poker,
Sold its eyes for souvenirs, sold its blood for whisky,
Kept its bones for dumb-bells to use when he was fifty.

It's no go the Yogi-man, it's no go Blavatsky,
All we want is a bank balance and a bit of skirt in a taxi.

Annie MacDougall went to milk, caught her foot in the heather,
Woke to hear a dance record playing of Old Vienna.
It's no go your maidenheads, it's no go your culture,
All we want is a Dunlop tyre and the devil mend the puncture.

The Laird o' Phelps spent Hogmanay declaring he was sober,
Counted his feet to prove the fact and found he had one foot over.
Mrs Carmichael had her fifth, looked at the job with repulsion,
Said to the midwife 'Take it away; I'm through with over-production'.

It's no go the gossip column, it's no go the ceilidh,
All we want is a mother's help and a sugar-stick for the baby.

Willie Murray cut his thumb, couldn't count the damage,
Took the hide of an Ayrshire cow and used it for a bandage.
His brother caught three hundred cran when the seas were lavish,
Threw the bleeders back in the sea and went upon the parish.

It's no go the Herring Board, it's no go the Bible,
All we want is a packet of fags when our hands are idle.

It's no go the picture palace, it's no go the stadium,
It's no go the country cot with a pot of pink geraniums,
It's no go the Government grants, it's no go the elections,
Sit on your arse for fifty years and hang your hat on a pension.

It's no go my honey love, it's no go my poppet;
Work your hands from day to day, the winds will blow the profit.
The glass is falling hour by hour, the glass will fall for ever,
But if you break the bloody glass you won't hold up the weather.

John Gillespie Magee, Jr (1922–1941)

High Flight

Oh! I have slipped the surly bonds of earth
And danced the skies on laughter-silvered wings;
Sunward I've climbed, and joined the tumbling mirth
Of sun-split clouds—and done a hundred things
You have not dreamed of—wheeled and soared and swung
High in the sunlit silence. Hov'ring there,
I've chased the shouting wind along, and flung
My eager craft through footless halls of air.
Up, up the long, delirious, burning blue
I've topped the wind-swept heights with easy grace
Where never lark, or even eagle flew—
And, while with silent lifting mind I've trod
The high untrespassed sanctity of space,
Put out my hand and touched the face of God.

LEO MARKS (1921–2001)

The Life That I Have

The life that I have is all that I have
And the life that I have is yours.
The love that I have of the life that I have
Is yours and yours and yours.

A sleep I shall have
A rest I shall have,
Yet death will be but a pause,
For the peace of my years in the long green grass
Will be yours and yours and yours.

CHRISTOPHER MARLOWE (1564–1593)

from 'Hero and Leander'

It lies not in our power to love, or hate,
For will in us is overruled by fate.
When two are stripped, long ere the course begin
We wish that one should lose, the other win;
And one especially do we affect,
Of two gold ingots like in each respect.
The reason no man knows, let it suffice,
What we behold is censured by our eyes.
Where both deliberate, the love is slight;
Who ever loved, that loved not at first sight?

The Passionate Shepherd to His Love

Come live with me and be my Love,
And we will all the pleasures prove
That hills and valleys, dale and field,
And all the craggy mountains yield.

There will we sit upon the rocks
And see the shepherds feed their flocks,
By shallow rivers, to whose falls
Melodious birds sing madrigals.

There will I make thee beds of roses
And a thousand fragrant posies,
A cap of flowers, and a kirtle
Embroider'd all with leaves of myrtle.

A gown made of the finest wool
Which from our pretty lambs we pull,
Fair linèd slippers for the cold,
With buckles of the purest gold.

A belt of straw and ivy buds
With coral clasps and amber studs:
And if these pleasures may thee move,
Come live with me and be my Love.

Thy silver dishes for thy meat
As precious as the gods do eat,
Shall on an ivory table be
Prepared each day for thee and me.

The shepherd swains shall dance and sing
For thy delight each May morning:
If these delights thy mind may move,
Then live with me and be my Love.

DON MARQUIS (1878–1937)

the song of mehitabel

this is the song of mehitabel
of mehitabel the alley cat
as i wrote you before boss
mehitabel is a believer
in the pythagorean
theory of the transmigration
of the soul and she claims
that formerly her spirit
was incarnated in the body
of cleopatra
that was a long time ago
and one must not be
surprised if mehitabel

has forgotten some of her
more regal manners

i have had my ups and downs
but wotthehell wotthehell
yesterday sceptres and crowns
fried oysters and velvet gowns
and today i herd with bums
but wotthehell wotthehell
i wake the world from sleep
as i caper and sing and leap
when i sing my wild free tune
wotthehell wotthehell
under the blear eyed moon
i am pelted with cast off shoon
but wotthehell wotthehell

do you think that i would change
my present freedom to range
for a castle or moated grange
wotthehell wotthehell
cage me and i d go frantic
my life is so romantic
capricious and corybantic
and i m toujours gai toujours gai

i know that i am bound
for a journey down the sound
in the midst of a refuse mound
but wotthehell wotthehell
oh i should worry and fret
death and i will coquette
there s a dance in the old dame yet
toujours gai toujours gai

i once was an innocent kit
wotthehell wotthehell
with a ribbon my neck to fit
and bells tied onto it
o wotthehell wotthehell
but a maltese cat came by
with a come hither look in his eye

and a song that soared to the sky
and wotthehell wotthehell
and i followed adown the street
the pad of his rhythmical feet
o permit me again to repeat
wotthehell wotthehell

my youth i shall never forget
but there s nothing i really regret
wotthehell wotthehell
there s a dance in the old dame yet
toujours gai toujours gai

the things that i had not ought to
i do because i ve gotto
wotthehell wotthehell
and i end with my favorite motto
toujours gai toujours gai

boss sometimes i think
that our friend mehitabel
is a trifle too gay

the cockroach who had been to hell

listen to me i have
been mobbed almost
theres an old simp cockroach
here who thinks he has
been to hell and all
the young cockroaches make a
hero out of him and admire
him he sits and runs his front
feet through his long white
beard and tells the story one
day he says he crawled into a yawning
cavern and suddenly came on a
vast abyss full of whirling
smoke there was a light
at the bottom billows
and billows of yellow smoke
swirled up at him and

through the horrid gloom he
saw things with wings flying
and dropping and dying they veered
and fluttered like damned
spirits through that sulphurous mist

listen i says to him
old man youve never been to hell
at all there isnt any hell
transmigration is the game i
used to be a human vers libre
poet and i died and went
into a cockroach s body if
there was a hell id know
it wouldnt i youre
irreligious says the old simp
combing his whiskers excitedly
ancient one i says to him
while all those other
cockroaches gathered into a
ring around us what you
beheld was not hell all that
was natural some one was fumigating
a room and you blundered
into it through a crack
in the wall atheist he cries
and all those young
cockroaches cried atheist
and made for me if it
had not been for freddy
the rat i would now be
on my way once more i mean
killed as a cockroach and transmigrating
into something else well
that old whitebearded devil is
laying for me with his
gang he is jealous
because i took his glory away
from him dont ever tell me
insects are any more liberal
than humans
archy

<u>ANDREW MARVELL</u> (1621–1678)

To His Coy Mistress

Had we but world enough, and time.
This coyness, lady, were no crime.
We would sit down, and think which way
To walk, and pass our long love's day.
Thou by the Indian Ganges' side
Should'st rubies find: I by the tide
Of Humber would complain. I would
Love you ten years before the Flood,
And you should, if you please, refuse
Till the conversion of the Jews.
My vegetable love should grow
Vaster than empires, and more slow.
An hundred years should go to praise
Thine eyes, and on thy forehead gaze:
Two hundred to adore each breast;
But thirty thousand to the rest;
An age at least to every part,
And the last age should show your heart.
For, lady, you deserve this state,
Nor would I love at lower rate.
But at my back I always hear
Time's wingèd chariot hurrying near:
And yonder all before us lie
Deserts of vast eternity.
Thy beauty shall no more be found;
Nor, in thy marble vault, shall sound
My echoing song: then worms shall try
That long-preserved virginity,
And your quaint honour turn to dust,
And into ashes all my lust.
The grave's a fine and private place,
But none, I think, do there embrace.
Now, therefore, while the youthful hue
Sits on thy skin like morning dew,
And while thy willing soul transpires
At every pore with instant fires,
Now let us sport us while we may;

And now, like amorous birds of prey,
Rather at once our Time devour,
Than languish in his slow-chapt power.
Let us roll all our strength and all
Our sweetness up into one ball,
And tear our pleasures with rough strife
Thorough the iron gates of life.
Thus, though we cannot make our Sun
Stand still, yet we will make him run.

The Garden

How vainly men themselves amaze
To win the palm, the oak, or bays;
And their uncessant labours see
Crowned from some single herb or tree,
Whose short and narrow-vergèd shade
Does prudently their toils upbraid;
While all the flowers and trees do close
To weave the garlands of repose!

Fair Quiet, have I found thee here,
And Innocence thy sister dear?
Mistaken long, I sought you then
In busy companies of men.
Your sacred plants, if here below,
Only among the plants will grow;
Society is all but rude
To this delicious solitude.

No white nor red was ever seen
So amorous as this lovely green.
Fond lovers, cruel as their flame,
Cut in these trees their mistress' name:
Little, alas! they know or heed
How far these beauties hers exceed!
Fair trees! wheres'e'er your barks I wound,
No name shall but your own be found.

When we have run our passion's heat,
Love hither makes his best retreat.

The gods, that mortal beauty chase,
Still in a tree did end their race;
Apollo hunted Daphne so,
Only that she might laurel grow;
And Pan did after Syrinx speed,
Not as a nymph, but for a reed.

What wondrous life is this I lead!
Ripe apples drop about my head;
The luscious clusters of the vine
Upon my mouth do crush their wine;
The nectarine and curious peach,
Into my hands themselves do reach;
Stumbling on melons, as I pass,
Ensnared with flowers, I fall on grass.

Meanwhile the mind from pleasure less
Withdraws into its happiness;
The mind, that ocean where each kind
Does straight its own resemblance find;
Yet it creates, transcending these,
Far other worlds, and other seas;
Annihilating all that's made
To a green thought in a green shade.

Here at the fountain's sliding foot,
Or at some fruit-tree's mossy root,
Casting the body's vest aside,
My soul into the boughs does glide;
There, like a bird, it sits and sings,
Then whets and combs its silver wings;
And, till prepared for longer flight,
Waves in its plumes the various light.

Such was that happy garden-state
While man there walked without a mate:
After a place so pure and sweet,
What other help could yet be meet!
But 'twas beyond a mortal's share
To wander solitary there:
Two paradises 'twere in one,
To live in Paradise alone.

How well the skilful gardener drew
Of flowers, and herbs, this dial new;
Where, from above, the milder sun
Does through a fragrant zodiac run;
And, as it works, th' industrious bee
Computes its time as well as we.
How could such sweet and wholesome hours
Be reckoned, but with herbs and flowers!

An Horatian Ode upon Cromwell's Return from Ireland

The forward youth that would appear
Must now forsake his Muses dear,
    Nor in the shadows sing
    His numbers languishing.
'Tis time to leave the books in dust,
And oil the unusèd armour's rust,
    Removing from the wall
    The corslet of the hall.
So restless Cromwell could not cease
In the inglorious arts of peace,
    But through adventurous war
    Urgèd his active star.
And, like the three-forked lightning, first
Breaking the clouds where it was nurst,
    Did thorough his own side
    His fiery way divide.
For 'tis all one to courage high
The emulous or enemy;
    And with such to enclose
    Is more than to oppose.
Then burning through the air he went
And palaces and temples rent:
    And Caesar's head at last
    Did through his laurels blast.
'Tis madness to resist or blame
The face of angry Heaven's flame:
    And, if we would speak true,
    Much to the man is due,

Who, from his private gardens, where
He lived reservèd and austere,
    As if his highest plot
    To plant the bergamot,
Could by industrious valour climb
To ruin the great work of Time,
    And cast the Kingdoms old
    Into another mould.
Though Justice against Fate complain,
And plead the ancient rights in vain:
    But those do hold or break
    As men are strong or weak.
Nature that hateth emptiness,
Allows of penetration less:
    And therefore must make room
    Where greater spirits come.
What field of all the Civil Wars
Where his were not the deepest scars?
    And Hampton shows what part
    He had of wiser art,
Where, twining subtle fears with hope,
He wove a net of such a scope,
    That Charles himself might chase
    To Carisbrooke's narrow case:
That thence the Royal actor borne
The tragic scaffold might adorn:
    While round the armèd bands
    Did clap their bloody hands.
He nothing common did or mean
Upon that memorable scene:
    But with his keener eye
    The axe's edge did try.
Nor called the gods with vulgar spite
To vindicate his helpless right,
    But bowed his comely head,
    Down, as upon a bed.
This was that memorable hour
Which first assured the forcèd power.
    So when they did design
    The Capitol's first line,
A bleeding head, where they begun,
Did fright the architects to run;

And yet in that the State
Foresaw its happy fate.
And now the Irish are ashamed
To see themselves in one year tamed:
So much one man can do,
That does both act and know.
They can affirm his praises best,
And have, though overcome, confest
How good he is, how just,
And fit for highest trust:
Nor yet grown stiffer with command,
But still in the Republic's hand:
How fit he is to sway
That can so well obey.
He to the Commons' feet presents
A kingdom for his first year's rents;
And, what he may, forbears
His fame, to make it theirs:
And has his sword and spoils ungirt,
To lay them at the public's skirt.
So when the falcon high
Falls heavy from the sky,
She, having killed, no more does search,
But on the next green bough to perch;
Where, when he first does lure,
The falconer has her sure.
What may not then our isle presume
While victory his crest does plume!
What may not others fear
If thus he crowns each year!
As Caesar he ere long to Gaul,
To Italy an Hannibal,
And to all states not free
Shall climacteric be.
The Pict no shelter now shall find
Within his particoloured mind;
But from this valour sad
Shrink underneath the plaid:
Happy if in the tufted brake
The English hunter him mistake;
Nor lay his hounds in near
The Caledonian deer.

But thou, the war's and fortune's son,
March indefatigably on;
    And for the last effect
    Still keep the sword erect:
Besides the force it has to fright
The spirits of the shady night,
    The same arts that did gain
    A power must it maintain.

JOHN MASEFIELD (1878–1967)

Sea Fever

I must go down to the sea again, to the lonely sea and the sky,
And all I ask is a tall ship and a star to steer her by,
And the wheel's kick and the wind's song and the white sails shaking,
And a grey mist on the sea's face and a grey dawn breaking.

I must go down to the sea again, for the call of the running tide
Is a wild call and a clear call that may not be denied;
And all I ask is a windy day with the white clouds flying,
And the flung spray and the blown spume, and the seagulls crying.

I must go down to the sea again to the vagrant gypsy life,
To the gull's way and the whale's way where the wind's like a whetted knife;
And all I ask is a merry yarn from a laughing fellow-rover,
And quiet sleep and a sweet dream when the long trick's over.

Cargoes

Quinquireme of Nineveh from distant Ophir
Rowing home to haven in sunny Palestine,
With a cargo of ivory,
And apes and peacocks,
Sandalwod, cedarwood, and sweet white wine.

Stately Spanish galleon coming from the Isthmus,
Dipping through the Tropics by the palm-green shores,
With a cargo of diamonds,
Emeralds, amethysts,
Topazes, and cinnamon, and gold moidores.

Dirty British coaster with a salt-caked smoke stack
Butting through the Channel in the mad March days,
With a cargo of Tyne coal,
Road-rail, pig-lead,
Firewood, iron-ware, and cheap tin trays.

GEORGE MEREDITH (1828–1909)

Lucifer in Starlight

On a starred night Prince Lucifer uprose.
Tired of his dark dominion swung the fiend
Above the rolling ball in cloud part screened,
Where sinners hugged their spectre of repose.
Poor prey to his hot fit of pride were those.
And now upon his western wing he leaned,
Now his huge bulk o'er Afric's sands careened,
Now the black planet shadowed Arctic snows.
Soaring through wider zones that pricked his scars
With memory of the old revolt from Awe,
He reached a middle height, and at the stars,
Which are the brain of heaven, he looked, and sank.
Around the ancient track marched, rank on rank,
The army of unalterable law.

CHARLOTTE MEW (1869–1928)

Sea Love

Tide be runnin' the great world over:
    'Twas only last June month I mind that we
Was thinkin' the toss and the call in the breast of the lover
    So everlastin' as the sea.

Here's the same little fishes that sputter and swim,
    Wi' the moon's old glim on the gray, wet sand;
An' him no more to me nor me to him
    Than the wind goin' over my hand.

EDNA ST VINCENT MILLAY (1892–1950)

Dirge without Music

I am not resigned to the shutting away of loving hearts in the hard ground.
So it is, and so it will be, for so it has been, time out of mind:
Into the darkness they go, the wise and the lovely. Crowned
With lilies and with laurel they go; but I am not resigned.

Lovers and thinkers, into the earth with you.
Be one with the dull, the indiscriminate dust.
A fragment of what you felt, of what you knew,
A formula, a phrase remains,—but the best is lost.

The answers quick and keen, the honest look, the laughter, the love,—
They are gone. They have gone to feed the roses. Elegant and curled
Is the blossom. Fragrant is the blossom. I know. But I do not approve.
More precious was the light in your eyes than all the roses in the world.

Down, down, down into the darkness of the grave
Gently they go, the beautiful, the tender, the kind;
Quietly they go, the intelligent, the witty, the brave.
I know. But I do not approve. And I am not resigned.

JOHN MILTON (1608–1674)

On Shakespeare

What needs my Shakespeare for his honoured bones
The labour of an age in pilèd stones?
Or that his hallowed reliques should be hid
Under a starry-pointing pyramid?
Dear son of memory, great heir of fame,
What need'st thou such weak witness of thy name?
Thou in our wonder and astonishment
Hast built thyself a livelong monument.
For whilst, to the shame of slow-endeavouring art,
Thy easy numbers flow, and that each heart
Hath from the leaves of thy unvalued book
Those Delphic lines with deep impression took,

Then thou, our fancy of itself bereaving,
Dost make us marble with too much conceiving,
And so sepùlchred in such pomp dost lie
That kings for such a tomb would wish to die.

On His Blindness

When I consider how my light is spent
Ere half my days in this dark world and wide,
And that one talent which is death to hide
Lodged with me useless, though my soul more bent
To serve therewith my Maker, and present
My true account, lest He returning chide,
'Doth God exact day-labour, light denied?'
I fondly ask. But Patience, to prevent
That murmur, soon replies, 'God doth not need
Either man's work or his own gifts. Who best
Bear his mild yoke, they serve him best. His state
Is kingly: thousands at his bidding speed,
And post o'er land and ocean without rest;
They also serve who only stand and wait.'

Song on May Morning

Now the bright morning star, Day's harbinger,
Comes dancing from the east, and leads with her
The flowery May, who from her green lap throws
The yellow cowslip and the pale primrose.
    Hail, bounteous May, that does inspire
    Mirth, and youth, and warm desire!
    Woods and groves are of thy dressing;
    Hill and dale doth boast thy blessing.
    Thus we salute thee with our early song,
    And welcome thee, and wish thee long.

'Methought I saw my late espoused Saint'

Methought I saw my late espoused Saint
Brought to me like Alcestis from the grave,
Whom Jove's great Son to her glad Husband gave,

Rescued from death by force though pale and faint.
Mine as whom washt from spot of child-bed taint,
Purification in the old Law did save,
And such, as yet once more I trust to have
Full sight of her in Heaven without restraint,
Came vested all in white, pure as her mind:
Her face was vail'd, yet to my fancied sight,
Love, sweetness, goodness, in her person shined
So clear, as in no face with more delight.
But O as to embrace me she enclin'd
I wak'd, she fled, and day brought back my night.

L'Allegro

Hence, loathèd Melancholy,
   Of Cerberus and blackest Midnight born
In Stygian cave forlorn
   'Mongst horrid shapes, and shrieks, and sights unholy!
Find out some uncouth cell,
   Where brooding Darkness spreads his jealous wings
And the night-raven sings;
   There, under ebon shades, and low-browed rocks,
As ragged as thy locks,
   In dark Cimmerian desert ever dwell!

     But come, thou Goddess fair and free,
   In heaven yclept Euphrosyne,
   And by men, heart-easing Mirth,
   Whom lovely Venus, at a birth,
   With two sister Graces more,
   To ivy-crownèd Bacchus bore;
   Or whether (as some sages sing)
   The frolic wind that breathes the spring
   Zephyr, with Aurora playing,
   As he met her once a-Maying—
   There on beds of violets blue
   And fresh-blown roses washed in dew
   Filled her with thee, a daughter fair,
   So buxom, blithe, and debonair.
     Haste thee, Nymph, and bring with thee
   Jest, and youthful Jollity,

Quips, and cranks, and wanton wiles,
Nods, and becks, and wreathèd smiles
Such as hang on Hebe's cheek,
And love to live in dimple sleek;
Sport that wrinkled Care derides,
And Laughter holding both his sides:—
Come, and trip it, as you go,
On the light fantastic toe;
And in thy right hand lead with thee
The mountain-nymph, sweet Liberty;
And if I give thee honour due,
Mirth, admit me of thy crew,
To live with her, and live with thee
In unreprovèd pleasures free;
To hear the lark begin his flight,
And singing startle the dull night
From his watchtower in the skies,
Till the dappled dawn doth rise;
Then to come, in spite of sorrow,
And at my window bid good-morrow,
Through the sweet-brier, or the vine,
Or the twisted eglantine:
While the cock with lively din
Scatters the rear of darkness thin,
And to the stack, or the barn-door,
Stoutly struts his dames before:
Oft listening how the hounds and horn
Cheerly rouse the slumbering morn,
From the side of some hoar hill,
Through the high wood echoing shrill:
Sometime walking, not unseen,
By hedgerow elms, on hillocks green,
Right against the eastern gate
Where the great Sun begins his state
Robed in flames and amber light,
The clouds in thousand liveries dight;
While the ploughman, near at hand,
Whistles o'er the furrowed land,
And the milkmaid singeth blithe,
And the mower whets his scythe,
And every shepherd tells his tale
Under the hawthorn in the dale.

Straight mine eye hath caught new pleasures
Whilst the landscape round it measures;
Russet lawns, and fallows grey,
Where the nibbling flocks do stray;
Mountains, on whose barren breast
The labouring clouds do often rest;
Meadows trim with daisies pied,
Shallow brooks, and rivers wide;
Towers and battlements it sees
Bosomed high in tufted trees,
Where perhaps some Beauty lies,
The Cynosure of neighbouring eyes.
Hard by, a cottage chimney smokes
From betwixt two aged oaks,
Where Corydon and Thyrsis met,
Are at their savoury dinner set
Of herbs, and other country messes
Which the neat-handed Phillis dresses;
And then in haste her bower she leaves
With Thestylis to bind the sheaves;
Or, if the earlier season lead,
To the tanned haycock in the mead.
Sometimes, with secure delight
The upland hamlets will invite,
When the merry bells ring round,
And the jocund rebecks sound
To many a youth and many a maid,
Dancing in the chequered shade;
And young and old come forth to play
On a sunshine holy-day,
Till the livelong daylight fail.
Then to the spicy nut-brown ale,
With stories told of many a feat,
How Faery Mab the junkets eat:—
She was pinched and pulled, she said;
And he, by Friar's lantern led;
Tells how the drudging Goblin sweat
To earn his cream-bowl duly set,
When in one night, ere glimpse of morn,
His shadowy flail hath threshed the corn
That ten day-labourers could not end;
Then lies him down, the lubber fiend,

And, stretched out all the chimney's length
Basks at the fire his hairy strength;
And crop-full out of doors he flings,
Ere the first cock his matin rings.
Thus done the tales, to bed they creep,
By whispering winds soon lulled asleep.

    Towered cities please us then
And the busy hum of men,
Where throngs of knights and barons bold,
In weeds of peace, high triumphs hold.
With store of ladies, whose bright eyes
Rain influence, and judge the prize
Of wit or arms, while both contend
To win her grace whom all commend.
There let Hymen oft appear
In saffron robe, with taper clear,
And pomp, and feast, and revelry,
With mask, and antique pageantry;
Such sights as youthful poets dream
On summer eves by haunted stream.
Then to the well-trod stage anon,
If Jonson's learned sock be on,
Or sweetest Shakespeare, Fancy's child,
Warble his native wood-notes wild.

    And ever against eating cares
Lap me in soft Lydian airs
Married to immortal verse,
Such as the meeting soul may pierce
In notes, with many a winding bout
Of linkèd sweetness long drawn out,
With wanton heed and giddy cunning,
The melting voice through mazes running,
Untwisting all the chains that tie
The hidden soul of harmony;
That Orpheus' self may heave his head
From golden slumber on a bed
Of heaped Elysian flowers, and hear
Such strains as would have won the ear
Of Pluto, to have quite set free
His half-regained Eurydice.

    These delights if thou canst give,
Mirth, with thee I mean to live.

Il Penseroso

Hence, vain deluding Joys,
    The brood of Folly without father bred!
How little you bestead
    Or fill the fixèd mind with all your toys!
Dwell in some idle brain,
    And fancies fond with gaudy shapes possess
As thick and numberless
    As the gay motes that people the sunbeams,
Or likest hovering dreams,
    The fickle pensioners of Morpheus' train.

    But, hail, thou goddess sage and holy,
Hail, divinest Melancholy!
Whose saintly visage is too bright
To hit the sense of human sight,
And therefore to our weaker view
O'erlaid with black, staid Wisdom's hue;
Black, but such as in esteem
Prince Memnon's sister might beseem,
Or that starred Ethiop queen that strove
To set her beauty's praise above
The sea-nymphs, and their powers offended.
Yet thou art higher far descended:
Thee bright-haired Vesta long of yore,
To solitary Saturn bore;
His daughter she; in Saturn's reign
Such mixture was not held a stain:
Oft in glimmering bowers and glades
He met her, and in secret shades
Of woody Ida's inmost grove,
While yet there was no fear of Jove.
    Come, pensive Nun, devout and pure,
Sober, steadfast, and demure,
All in a robe of darkest grain,
Flowing with majestic train,
And sable stole of cypress lawn
Over thy decent shoulders drawn:
Come; but keep thy wonted state,
With even step, and musing gait,
And looks commercing with the skies,

Thy rapt soul sitting in thine eyes:
There, held in holy passion still,
Forget thyself to marble, till
With a sad leaden downward cast
Thou fix them on the earth as fast:
And join with thee calm Peace and Quiet,
Spare Fast, that oft with gods doth diet,
And hears the Muses in a ring
Aye round about Jove's altar sing:
And add to these retirèd Leisure,
That in trim gardens takes his pleasure:—
But first and chiefest, with thee bring
Him that yon soars on golden wing
Guiding the fiery-wheelèd throne,
The Cherub Contemplatión;
And the mute Silence hist along,
'Less Philomel will deign a song
In her sweetest saddest plight
Smoothing the rugged brow of Night,
While Cynthia checks her dragon yoke
Gently o'er the accustomed oak.
—Sweet bird, that shunn'st the noise of folly,
Most musical, most melancholy!
Thee, chauntress, oft the woods among
I woo, to hear thy even-song;
And missing thee, I walk unseen
On the dry smooth-shaven green,
To behold the wandering Moon,
Riding near her highest noon,
Like one that had been led astray
Through the heaven's wide pathless way,
And oft, as if her head she bowed,
Stooping through a fleecy cloud.
    Oft, on a plat of rising ground
I hear the far-off curfew sound
Over some wide-watered shore,
Swinging slow with sullen roar:
Or, if the air will not permit,
Some still removèd place will fit,
Where glowing embers through the room
Teach light to counterfeit a gloom;
Far from all resort of mirth,

Save the cricket on the hearth,
Or the bellman's drowsy charm
To bless the doors from nightly harm.
    Or let my lamp at midnight hour
Be seen in some high lonely tower,
Where I may oft outwatch the Bear
With thrice-great Hermes, or unsphere
The spirit of Plato, to unfold
What worlds or what vast regions hold
The immortal mind, that hath forsook
Her mansion in this fleshly nook:
And of those demons that are found
In fire, air, flood, or underground,
Whose power hath a true consent
With planet or with element.
Sometime let gorgeous Tragedy
In sceptred pall come sweeping by,
Presenting Thebes, or Pelops' line,
Or the tale of Troy divine;
Or what (though rare) of later age
Ennobled hath the buskined stage.
    But, O sad Virgin, that thy power
Might raise Musaeus from his bower,
Or bid the soul of Orpheus sing
Such notes as, warbled to the string,
Drew iron tears down Pluto's cheek
And made Hell grant what Love did seek!
Or call up him that left half-told
The story of Cambuscan bold,
Of Camball, and of Algarsife,
And who had Canacé to wife
That owned the virtuous ring and glass;
And of the wondrous horse of brass
On which the Tartar king did ride;
And if aught else great bards beside
In sage and solemn tunes have sung
Of tourneys, and of trophies hung,
Of forests, and enchantments drear,
Where more is meant than meets the ear.
    Thus, Night, oft see me in thy pale career,
Till civil-suited Morn appear,
Not tricked and frounced, as she was wont

With the Attic boy to hunt,
But kercheft in a comely cloud
While rocking winds are piping loud,
Or ushered with a shower still,
When the gust hath blown his fill,
Ending on the rustling leaves
With minute drops from off the eaves.
And when the sun begins to fling
His flaring beams, me, goddess, bring
To archèd walks of twilight groves,
And shadows brown, that Sylvan loves,
Of pine, or monumental oak,
Where the rude axe, with heavèd stroke,
Was never heard the nymphs to daunt
Or fright them from their hallowed haunt.
There in close covert by some brook
Where no profaner eye may look,
Hide me from day's garish eye,
While the bee with honeyed thigh
That at her flowery work doth sing,
And the waters murmuring,
With such consort as they keep
Entice the dewy-feathered Sleep;
And let some strange mysterious dream
Wave at his wings in airy stream
Of lively portraiture displayed,
Softly on my eyelids laid:
And, as I wake, sweet music breathe
Above, about, or underneath,
Sent by some Spirit to mortals good,
Or the unseen Genius of the wood.
　　But let my due feet never fail
To walk the studious cloister's pale,
And love the high embowèd roof,
With antique pillars massy proof,
And storied windows richly dight
Casting a dim religious light.
There let the pealing organ blow
To the full-voiced quire below
In service high and anthems clear,
As may with sweetness, through mine ear,
Dissolve me into ecstasies,

And bring all Heaven before mine eyes.
　And may at last my weary age
Find out the peaceful hermitage,
The hairy gown and mossy cell
Where I may sit, and rightly spell
Of every star that heaven doth show,
And every herb that sips the dew;
Till old experience do attain
To something like prophetic strain.
　These pleasures, Melancholy, give,
And I with thee will choose to live.

Lycidas

In this Monody the author bewails a learned friend unfortunately drowned in his passage from Chester on the Irish Seas, 1637; and, by occasion, foretells the ruin of the corrupted Clergy, then in their height.

Yet once more, O ye laurels, and once more,
Ye myrtles brown, with ivy never sere,
I come to pluck your berries harsh and crude,
And with forced fingers rude
Shatter your leaves before the mellowing year.
Bitter constraint and sad occasion dear
Compels me to disturb your season due:
For Lycidas is dead, dead ere his prime,
Young Lycidas, and hath not left his peer.
Who would not sing for Lycidas? he knew
Himself to sing, and build the lofty rhyme.
He must not float upon his watery bier
Unwept, and welter to the parching wind,
Without the meed of some melodious tear.

Begin, then, Sisters of the sacred well
That from beneath the seat of Jove doth spring;
Begin, and somewhat loudly sweep the string.
Hence with denial vain and coy excuse:
So may some gentle Muse
With lucky words favour my destined urn,
And as he passes, turn
And bid fair peace be to my sable shroud.

For we were nursed upon the selfsame hill,
Fed the same flock, by fountain, shade, and rill:
Together both, ere the high lawns appeared
Under the opening eyelids of the Morn,
We drove afield, and both together heard
What time the grey-fly winds her sultry horn,
Battening our flocks with the fresh dews of night,
Oft till the star that rose at evening bright
Toward heaven's descent had sloped his westering wheel.
Meanwhile the rural ditties were not mute,
Tempered to the oaten flute,
Rough Satyrs danced, and Fauns with cloven heel
From the glad sound would not be absent long;
And old Damoetas loved to hear our song.

But oh the heavy change, now thou art gone—
Now thou art gone, and never must return!
Thee, Shepherd, thee the woods and desert caves
With wild thyme and the gadding vine o'ergrown,
And all their echoes, mourn:
The willows and the hazel copses green
Shall now no more be seen
Fanning their joyous leaves to thy soft lays:—
As killing as the canker to the rose,
Or taint-worm to the weanling herds that graze,
Or frost to flowers, that their gay wardrobe wear
When first the white-thorn blows;
Such, Lycidas, thy loss to shepherd's ear.

Where were ye, Nymphs, when the remorseless deep
Closed o'er the head of your loved Lycidas?
For neither were ye playing on the steep
Where your old bards, the famous Druids, lie,
Nor on the shaggy top of Mona high,
Nor yet where Deva spreads her wizard stream:
Ay me! I fondly dream—
Had ye been there ... For what could that have done?
What could the Muse herself that Orpheus bore,
The Muse herself, for her enchanting son,
Whom universal nature did lament,
When by the rout that made the hideous roar
His gory visage down the stream was sent,
Down the swift Hebrus to the Lesbian shore?

Alas! what boots it with uncessant care
To tend the homely, slighted, shepherd's trade
And strictly meditate the thankless Muse?
Were it not better done, as others use,
To sport with Amaryllis in the shade,
Or with the tangles of Neaera's hair?
Fame is the spur that the clear spirit doth raise
(That last infirmity of noble mind)
To scorn delights and live laborious days;
But the fair guerdon when we hope to find,
And think to burst out into sudden blaze,
Comes the blind Fury with the abhorrèd shears,
And slits the thin-spun life. 'But not the praise,'
Phoebus replied, and touched my trembling ears;
'Fame is no plant that grows on mortal soil,
Nor in the glistering foil
Set off to the world, nor in broad rumour lies:
But lives and spreads aloft by those pure eyes
And perfect witness of all-judging Jove;
As he pronounces lastly on each deed,
Of so much fame in heaven expect thy meed.'

O fountain Arethuse, and thou honoured flood,
Smooth-sliding Mincius, crowned with vocal reeds,
That strain I heard was of a higher mood.
But now my oat proceeds,
And listens to the herald of the sea
That came in Neptune's plea;
He asked the waves, and asked the felon winds,
What hard mishap hath doomed this gentle swain?
And questioned every gust of rugged wings
That blows from off each beakèd promontory:
They knew not of his story;
And sage Hippotades their answer brings,
That not a blast was from his dungeon strayed;
The air was calm, and on the level brine
Sleek Panope with all her sisters played.
It was that fatal and perfidious bark,
Built in the eclipse, and rigged with curses dark,
That sunk so low that sacred head of thine.

Next Camus, reverend sire, went footing slow,
His mantle hairy, and his bonnet sedge

Inwrought with figures dim, and on the edge
Like to that sanguine flower inscribed with woe:
'Ah! who hath reft,' quoth he, 'my dearest pledge?'
Last came, and last did go
The Pilot of the Galilean lake;
Two massy keys he bore of metals twain
(The golden opes, the iron shuts amain);
He shook his mitred locks, and stern bespake:
'How well could I have spared for thee, young swain,
Enow of such, as for their bellies' sake
Creep and intrude and climb into the fold!
Of other care they little reckoning make
Than how to scramble at the shearers' feast,
And shove away the worthy bidden guest.
Blind mouths! that scarce themselves know how to hold
A sheep-hook, or have learned aught else the least
That to the faithful herdman's art belongs!
What recks it them? What need they? They are sped;
And when they list, their lean and flashy songs
Grate on their scrannel pipes of wretched straw:
The hungry sheep look up, and are not fed
But swoln with wind and the rank mist they draw
Rot inwardly, and foul contagion spread:
Besides what the grim wolf with privy paw
Daily devours apace, and nothing said:
—But that two-handed engine at the door
Stands ready to smite once, and smite no more.'
    Return, Alpheus; the dread voice is past
That shrunk thy streams; return, Sicilian Muse,
And call the vales, and bid them hither cast
Their bells and flowerets of a thousand hues.
Ye valleys low, where the mild whispers use
Of shades, and wanton winds, and gushing brooks,
On whose fresh lap the swart star sparely looks,
Throw hither all your quaint enamelled eyes,
That on the green turf suck the honeyed showers
And purple all the ground with vernal flowers.
Bring the rathe primrose that forsaken dies,
The tufted crow-toe, and pale jessamine,
The white pink, and the pansy freaked with jet,
The glowing violet,
The musk-rose, and the well-attirèd woodbine,

With cowslips wan that hang the pensive head,
And every flower that sad embroidery wears:
Bid amarantus all his beauty shed,
And daffadillies fill their cups with tears
To strew the laureat hearse where Lycid lies.
For so to interpose a little ease,
Let our frail thoughts dally with false surmise:—
Ay me! whilst thee the shores and sounding seas
Wash far away,—where'er thy bones are hurled;
Whether beyond the stormy Hebrides
Where thou perhaps, under the whelming tide,
Visitest the bottom of the monstrous world;
Or whether thou, to our moist vows denied,
Sleep'st by the fable of Bellerus old,
Where the great Vision of the guarded mount
Looks towards Namancos and Bayona's hold,
—Look homeward, Angel, now, and melt with ruth:
—And, O ye dolphins, waft the hapless youth!

Weep no more, woeful shepherds, weep no more,
For Lycidas, your sorrow, is not dead,
Sunk though he be beneath the watery floor:
So sinks the day-star in the ocean-bed,
And yet anon repairs his drooping head
And tricks his beams, and with new-spangled ore
Flames in the forehead of the morning sky:
So Lycidas sunk low, but mounted high
Through the dear might of Him that walked the waves;
Where, other groves and other streams along,
With nectar pure his oozy locks he laves,
And hears the unexpressive nuptial song
In the blest kingdoms meek of joy and love.
There entertain him all the Saints above
In solemn troops, and sweet societies,
That sing, and singing, in their glory move,
And wipe the tears for ever from his eyes.
Now, Lycidas, the shepherds weep no more;
Henceforth thou art the Genius of the shore
In thy large recompense, and shalt be good
To all that wander in that perilous flood.

Thus sang the uncouth swain to the oaks and rills,

While the still morn went out with sandals grey;
He touched the tender stops of various quills,
With eager thought warbling his Doric lay:
And now the sun had stretched out all the hills,
And now was dropt into the western bay.
At last he rose, and twitched his mantle blue:
Tomorrow to fresh woods, and pastures new.

from 'Paradise Lost'
(from Book 1)

          . . . His pride
Had cast him out from Heaven, with all his host
Of rebel Angels, by whose aid, aspiring
To set himself in glory above his peers,
He trusted to have equalled the Most High,
If he opposed, and with ambitious aim
Against the throne and monarchy of God,
Raised impious war in Heaven and battle proud,
With vain attempt. Him the Almighty Power
Hurled headlong flaming from th' ethereal sky,
With hideous ruin and combustion, down
To bottomless perdition, there to dwell
In adamantine chains and penal fire,
Who durst defy th' Omnipotent to arms.
    Nine times the space that measures day and night
To mortal men, he, with his horrid crew,
Lay vanquished, rolling in the fiery gulf,
Confounded, though immortal. But his doom
Reserved him to more wrath; for now the thought
Both of lost happiness and lasting pain
Torments him: round he throws his baleful eyes,
That witnessed huge affliction and dismay,
Mixed with obdurate pride and steadfast hate.
At once, as far as Angels ken, he views
The dismal situation waste and wild.
A dungeon horrible, on all sides round,
As one great furnace flamed; yet from those flames
No light; but rather darkness visible
Served only to discover sights of woe,

Regions of sorrow, doleful shades, where peace
And rest can never dwell, hope never comes
That comes to all, but torture without end
Still urges, and a fiery deluge, fed
With ever-burning sulphur unconsumed.
Such place Eternal Justice has prepared
For those rebellious; here their prison ordained
In utter darkness, and their portion set,
As far removed from God and light of Heaven
As from the centre thrice to th' utmost pole.
Oh how unlike the place from whence they fell!
There the companions of his fall, o'erwhelmed
With floods and whirlwinds of tempestuous fire,
He soon discerns; and, weltering by his side,
One next himself in power, and next in crime,
Long after known in Palestine, and named
Beelzebub. To whom th' Arch-Enemy,
And thence in Heaven called Satan, with bold words
Breaking the horrid silence, thus began:—
      'If thou beest he—but O how fallen! how changed
From him who, in the happy realms of light
Clothed with transcendent brightness, didst outshine
Myriads, though bright!—if he whom mutual league,
United thoughts and counsels, equal hope
And hazard in the glorious enterprise
Joined with me once, now misery hath joined
In equal ruin; into what pit thou seest
From what height fallen: so much the stronger proved
He with his thunder; and till then who knew
The force of those dire arms? Yet not for those,
Nor what the potent Victor in his rage
Can else inflict, do I repent, or change,
Though changed in outward lustre, that fixed mind,
And high disdain from sense of injured merit,
That with the Mightiest raised me to contend,
And to the fierce contentions brought along
Innumerable force of Spirits armed,
That durst dislike his reign, and, me preferring,
His utmost power with adverse power opposed
In dubious battle on the plains of Heaven,
And shook his throne. What though the field be lost?
All is not lost—the unconquerable will,

And study of revenge, immortal hate,
And courage never to submit or yield:
And what is else not to be overcome?
. . .

Thus Satan, talking to his nearest mate,
With head uplift above the wave, and eyes
That sparkling blazed; his other parts besides
Prone on the flood, extended long and large,
Lay floating many a rood, in bulk as huge
As whom the fables name of monstrous size,
Titanian or Earth-born, that warred on Jove,
Briareos or Typhon, whom the den
By ancient Tarsus held, or that sea-beast
Leviathan, which God of all his works
Created hugest that swim th' ocean-stream.
Him, haply slumbering on the Norway foam,
The pilot of some small night-foundered skiff,
Deeming some island, oft, as seamen tell,
With fixed anchor in his scaly rind,
Moors by his side under the lee, while night
Invests the sea, and wished morn delays.
So stretched out huge in length the Arch-fiend lay,
Chained on the burning lake; nor ever thence
Had risen, or heaved his head, but that the will
And high permission of all-ruling Heaven
Left him at large to his own dark designs. . . .

Forthwith upright he rears from off the pool
His mighty stature; on each hand the flames
Driven backward slope their pointing spires, and,rolled
In billows, leave i' th' midst a horrid vale.
Then with expanded wings he steers his flight
Aloft, incumbent on the dusky air,
That felt unusual weight; till on dry land
He lights—if it were land that ever burned
With solid, as the lake with liquid fire,
And such appeared in hue as when the force
Of subterranean wind transports a hill
Torn from Pelorus, or the shattered side
Of thundering Etna, whose combustible
And fuelled entrails, thence conceiving fire,
Sublimed with mineral fury, aid the winds,
And leave a singed bottom all involved

With stench and smoke.

. . .

He scarce had ceased when the superior Fiend
Was moving toward the shore; his ponderous shield,
Ethereal temper, massy, large, and round,
Behind him cast. The broad circumference
Hung on his shoulders like the moon, whose orb
Through optic glass the Tuscan artist views
At evening, from the top of Fesole,
Or in Valdarno, to descry new lands,
Rivers, or mountains, in her spotty globe.
His spear—to equal which the tallest pine
Hewn on Norwegian hills, to be the mast
Of some great ammiral, were but a wand—
He walked with, to support uneasy steps
Over the burning marl, not like those steps
On Heaven's azure; and the torrid clime
Smote on him sore besides, vaulted with fire.
Nathless he so endured, till on the beach
Of that inflamed sea he stood, and called
His legions—Angel Forms, who lay entranced
Thick as autumnal leaves that strow the brooks
In Vallombrosa, where th' Etrurian shades
High over-arched embower; or scattered sedge
Afloat, when with fierce winds Orion armed
Hath vexed the Red-Sea coast, whose waves o'erthrew
Busiris and his Memphian chivalry,
While with perfidious hatred they pursued
The sojourners of Goshen, who beheld
From the safe shore their floating carcases
And broken chariot-wheels. So thick bestrown,
Abject and lost, lay these, covering the flood,
Under amazement of their hideous change.
He called so loud that all the hollow deep
Of Hell resounded:—'Princes, Potentates,
Warriors, the Flower of Heaven—once yours; now lost,
If such astonishment as this can seize
Eternal Spirits! Or have ye chosen this place
After the toil of battle to repose
Your wearied virtue, for the ease you find
To slumber here, as in the vales of Heaven?
Or in this abject posture have ye sworn

To adore the Conqueror, who now beholds
Cherub and Seraph rolling in the flood
With scattered arms and ensigns, till anon
His swift pursuers from Heaven-gates discern
Th' advantage, and, descending, tread us down
Thus drooping, or with linked thunderbolts
Transfix us to the bottom of this gulf?
Awake, arise, or be for ever fallen!'
  They heard, and were abashed, and up they sprung
Upon the wing, as when men wont to watch
On duty, sleeping found by whom they dread,
Rouse and bestir themselves ere well awake.
Nor did they not perceive the evil plight
In which they were, or the fierce pains not feel;
Yet to their General's voice they soon obeyed
Innumerable. As when the potent rod
Of Amram's son, in Egypt's evil day,
Waved round the coast, up-called a pitchy cloud
Of locusts, warping on the eastern wind,
That o'er the realm of impious Pharaoh hung
Like Night, and darkened all the land of Nile;
So numberless were those bad Angels seen
Hovering on wing under the cope of Hell.
. . .

  All these and more came flocking; but with looks
Downcast and damp; yet such wherein appeared
Obscure some glimpse of joy to have found their Chief
Not in despair, to have found themselves not lost
In loss itself; which on his countenance cast
Like doubtful hue. But he, his wonted pride
Soon recollecting, with high words, that bore
Semblance of worth, not substance, gently raised
Their fainting courage, and dispelled their fears.
Then straight commands that, at the warlike sound
Of trumpets loud and clarions, be upreared
His mighty standard. That proud honour claimed
Azazel as his right, a Cherub tall:
Who forthwith from the glittering staff unfurled
Th' imperial ensign; which, full high advanced,
Shone like a meteor streaming to the wind,
With gems and golden lustre rich emblazed,
Seraphic arms and trophies; all the while

Sonorous metal blowing martial sounds:
At which the universal host up-sent
A shout that tore Hell's concave, and beyond
Frighted the reign of Chaos and old Night.

(from Book 9)

As one who, long in populous city pent,
Where houses thick and sewers annoy the air,
Forth issuing on a summer's morn, to breathe
Among the pleasant villages and farms
Adjoined, from each thing met conceives delight;
The smell of grain, or tedded grass, or kine,
Or dairy, each rural sight, each rural sound;
If chance, with nymph-like step, fair virgin pass,
What pleasing seemed, for her now pleases more;
She most, and in her look sums all delight:
Such pleasure took the Serpent to behold
This flowery plat, the sweet recess of Eve
Thus early, thus alone: Her heavenly form
Angelick, but more soft, and feminine,
Her graceful innocence, her every air
Of gesture, or least action, overawed
His malice, and with rapine sweet bereaved
His fierceness of the fierce intent it brought:
That space the Evil-one abstracted stood
From his own evil, and for the time remained
Stupidly good; of enmity disarmed,
Of guile, of hate, of envy, of revenge:
But the hot Hell that always in him burns,
Though in mid Heaven, soon ended his delight,
And tortures him now more, the more he sees
Of pleasure, not for him ordained: then soon
Fierce hate he recollects, and all his thoughts
Of mischief, gratulating, thus excites.
Thoughts, whither have ye led me! with what sweet
Compulsion thus transported, to forget
What hither brought us! hate, not love;nor hope
Of Paradise for Hell, hope here to taste
Of pleasure; but all pleasure to destroy,
Save what is in destroying; other joy
To me is lost. Then, let me not let pass

Occasion which now smiles; behold alone
The woman, opportune to all attempts,
Her husband, for I view far round, not nigh,
Whose higher intellectual more I shun,
And strength, of courage haughty, and of limb
Heroick built, though of terrestrial mould;
Foe not informidable! exempt from wound,
I not; so much hath Hell debased, and pain
Enfeebled me, to what I was in Heaven.
She fair, divinely fair, fit love for Gods!
Not terrible, though terrour be in love
And beauty, not approached by stronger hate,
Hate stronger, under show of love well feigned;
The way which to her ruin now I tend.
So spake the enemy of mankind, enclosed
In serpent, inmate bad! and toward Eve
Addressed his way: not with indented wave,
Prone on the ground, as since; but on his rear,
Circular base of rising folds, that towered
Fold above fold, a surging maze! his head
Crested aloft, and carbuncle his eyes;
With burnished neck of verdant gold, erect
Amidst his circling spires, that on the grass
Floated redundant: pleasing was his shape
And lovely; never since of serpent-kind
Lovelier, not those that in Illyria changed,
Hermione and Cadmus, or the god
In Epidaurus; nor to which transformed
Ammonian Jove, or Capitoline, was seen;
He with Olympias; this with her who bore
Scipio, the highth of Rome. With tract oblique
At first, as one who sought access, but feared
To interrupt, side-long he works his way.
As when a ship, by skilful steersmen wrought
Nigh river's mouth or foreland, where the wind
Veers oft, as oft so steers, and shifts her sail:
So varied he, and of his tortuous train
Curled many a wanton wreath in sight of Eve,
To lure her eye; she, busied, heard the sound
Of rusling leaves, but minded not, as used
To such disport before her through the field,
From every beast; more duteous at her call,

Than at Circean call the herd disguised.
He, bolder now, uncalled before her stood,
But as in gaze admiring: oft he bowed
His turret crest, and sleek enamelled neck,
Fawning; and licked the ground whereon she trod.

from 'Samson Agonistes'

Ask for this great Deliverer now, and find him
Eyeless in Gaza at the Mill with slaves,
Himself in bonds under Philistian yoke;
Yet stay, let me not rashly call in doubt
Divine Prediction; what if all foretold
Had been fulfilled but through mine own default,
Whom have I to complain of but myself?
Who this high gift of strength committed to me,
In what part lodged, how easily bereft me,
Under the Seal of silence could not keep,
But weakly to a woman must reveal it
O'recome with importunity and tears.
O impotence of mind, in body strong!
But what is strength without a double share
Of wisdom, vast, unwieldy, burdensome,
Proudly secure, yet liable to fall
By weakest subtleties, not made to rule,
But to subserve where wisdom bears command.
God, when he gave me strength, to shew withal
How slight the gift was, hung it in my Hair.
But peace, I must not quarrel with the will
Of highest dispensation, which herein
Haply had ends above my reach to know:
Suffices that to me strength is my bane,
And proves the source of all my miseries;
So many, and so huge, that each apart
Would ask a life to wail, but chief of all,
O loss of sight, of thee I most complain!
Blind among enemies, O worse than chains,
Dungeon, or beggery, or decrepit age!
Light the prime work of God to me is extinct,
And all her various objects of delight
Annulled, which might in part my grief have eased,

Inferior to the vilest now become
Of man or worm; the vilest here excel me,
They creep, yet see, I dark in light exposed
To daily fraud, contempt, abuse and wrong,
Within doors, or without, still as a fool,
In power of others, never in my own;
Scarce half I seem to live, dead more than half.
O dark, dark, dark, amid the blaze of noon,
Irrecoverably dark, total Eclipse
Without all hope of day!
O first created Beam, and thou great Word,
Let there be light, and light was over all;
Why am I thus bereaved thy prime decree?
The Sun to me is dark
And silent as the Moon,
When she deserts the night
Hid in her vacant interlunar cave.

THOMAS MOORE (1779–1852)

'Oft in the stilly night'

Oft in the stilly night,
    Ere slumber's chain has bound me,
Fond memory brings the light
    Of other days around me;
        The smiles, the tears,
        Of boyhood's years,
    The words of love then spoken;
        The eyes that shone,
        Now dimmed and gone,
    The cheerful hearts now broken!
Thus in the stilly night,
    Ere slumber's chain hath bound me,
Sad memory brings the light
    Of other days around me.

When I remember all
    The friends, so linked together,
I've seen around me fall,
    Like leaves in wintry weather,

I feel like one
Who treads alone
Some banquet-hall deserted,
Whose lights are fled,
Whose garlands dead,
And all but he departed!
Thus in the stilly night,
Ere slumber's chain has bound me,
Sad memory brings the light
Of other days around me.

WILLIAM MORRIS (1834–1896)

from 'Love is Enough'

Love is enough: though the world be a-waning
And the woods have no voice but the voice of complaining,
Though the skies be too dark for dim eyes to discover
The gold-cups and daisies fair blooming thereunder,
Though the hills be held shadows, and the sea a dark wonder,
And this day draw a veil over all deeds passed over,
Yet their hands shall not tremble, their feet shall not falter;
The void shall not weary, the fear shall not alter
These lips and these eyes of the loved and the lover.

OGDEN NASH (1902–1971)

The People Upstairs

The people upstairs all practice ballet.
Their living room is a bowling alley.
Their bedroom is full of conducted tours.
Their radio is louder than yours.
They celebrate weekends all the week.
When they take a shower, your ceilings leak.
They try to get their parties to mix
By supplying their guests with Pogo sticks,
And when their orgy at last abates,
They go to the bathroom on roller skates.
I might love the people upstairs wondrous
If instead of above us, they just lived under us.

THOMAS NASHE (1567–1601)

'Adieu, farewell earth's bliss'

Adieu, farewell earth's bliss,
This world uncertain is:
Fond are life's lustful joys,
Death proves them all but toys,
None from his darts can fly—
I am sick, I must die:
Lord, have mercy on us!

Rich men, trust not in wealth,
Gold cannot buy you health,
Physic himself must fade.
All things to end are made,
The plague full swift goes by—
I am sick, I must die:
Lord, have mercy on us!

Beauty is but a flower,
Which wrinkles will devour;
Brightness falls from the air,
Queens have died young and fair,
Dust hath closed Helen's eye—
I am sick, I must die:
Lord, have mercy on us!

Strength stoops unto the grave,
Worms feed on Hector brave;
Swords may not fight with fate,
Earth still holds ope her gate,
Come, come, the bells do cry—
I am sick, I must die:
Lord, have mercy on us!

Wit with his wantonness
Tasteth death's bitterness;
Hell's executioner
Hath no ears for to hear
What vain art can reply—

I am sick, I must die:
Lord, have mercy on us!

Haste therefore each degree
To welcome destiny:
Heaven is our heritage,
Earth but a player's stage;
Mount we unto the sky—
I am sick, I must die:
Lord, have mercy on us!

Spring

Spring, the sweet spring, is the year's pleasant king,
Then blooms each thing, then maids dance in a ring,
Cold doth not sting, the pretty birds do sing,
    Cuckoo, jug-jug, pu-we, to-witta-woo!

The palm and may make country houses gay,
Lambs frisk and play, the shepherds pipe all day,
And we hear aye birds tune this merry lay,
    Cuckoo, jug-jug, pu-we, to-witta-woo!

The fields breathe sweet, the daisies kiss our feet,
Young lovers meet, old wives a-sunning sit,
In every street these tunes our ears do greet,
    Cuckoo, jug-jug, pu-we, to witta-woo!

SIR HENRY NEWBOLT (1862–1938)

Vitaï Lampada

There's a breathless hush in the Close tonight—
    Ten to make and the match to win—
A bumping pitch and a blinding light,
    An hour to play and the last man in.
And it's not for the sake of a ribboned coat,
    Or the selfish hope of a season's fame,
But his Captain's hand on his shoulder smote—
    'Play up! play up! and play the game!'

The sand of the desert is sodden red,—
    Red with the wreck of a square that broke;—
The Gatling's jammed and the Colonel dead,
    And the regiment blind with dust and smoke.
The river of death has brimmed his banks,
    And England far, and Honour, a name,
But the voice of a schoolboy rallies the ranks:
    'Play up! play up! and play the game!'

This is the word that year by year,
    While in her place the School is set,
Every one of her sons must hear,
    And none that hears it dare forget.
This they all with a joyful mind
    Bear through life like a torch in flame,
And falling fling to the host behind—
    'Play up! play up! and play the game!'

GEORGE ORWELL (1903–1950)

A Happy Vicar I Might Have Been

A happy vicar I might have been
Two hundred years ago,
To preach upon eternal doom
And watch my walnuts grow;

But born, alas, in an evil time,
I missed that pleasant haven,
For the hair has grown on my upper lip
And the clergy are all clean-shaven.

And later still the times were good,
We were so easy to please,
We rocked our troubled thoughts to sleep
On the bosoms of the trees.

All ignorant we dared to own
The joys we now dissemble;
The greenfinch on the apple bough
Could make my enemies tremble.

But girls' bellies and apricots,
Roach in a shaded stream,
Horses, ducks in flight at dawn,
All these are a dream.

It is forbidden to dream again;
We maim our joys or hide them;
Horses are made of chromium steel
And little fat men shall ride them.

I am the worm who never turned,
The eunuch without a harem;
Between the priest and the commissar
I walk like Eugene Aram;

And the commissar is telling my fortune
While the radio plays,
But the priest has promised an Austin Seven,
For Duggie always pays.

I dreamed I dwelt in marble halls,
And woke to find it true;
I wasn't born for an age like this;
Was Smith? Was Jones? Were you?

Arthur O'Shaughnessy (1844–1881)

from 'Ode'

We are the music makers,
    And we are the dreamers of dreams,
Wandering by lone sea-breakers,
    And sitting by desolate streams;
World-losers and world-forsakers,
    On whom the pale moon gleams:
Yet we are the movers and shakers
    Of the world for ever, it seems.

With wonderful deathless ditties
    We build up the world's great cities,

And out of a fabulous story
   We fashion an empire's glory:
One man with a dream, at pleasure,
   Shall go forth and conquer a crown;
And three with a new song's measure
   Can trample a kingdom down.

We, in the ages lying,
   In the buried past of the earth,
Built Nineveh with our sighing,
   And Babel itself in our mirth;
And o'erthrew them with prophesying
   To the old of the new world's worth;
For each age is a dream that is dying,
   Or one that is coming to birth.

WILFRED OWEN (1893–1918)

Anthem for Doomed Youth

What passing-bells for these who die as cattle?
Only the monstrous anger of the guns.
Only the stuttering rifles' rapid rattle
Can patter out their hasty orisons.
No mockeries for them; no prayers nor bells,
Nor any voice of mourning save the choirs,—
The shrill, demented choirs of wailing shells;
And bugles calling for them from sad shires.

What candles may be held to speed them all?
Not in the hands of boys, but in their eyes
Shall shine the holy glimmers of goodbyes.
The pallor of girls' brows shall be their pall;
Their flowers the tenderness of silent minds,
And each slow dusk a drawing-down of blinds.

Strange Meeting

It seemed that out of the battle I escaped
Down some profound dull tunnel, long since scooped

Through granites which titanic wars had groined.
Yet also there encumbered sleepers groaned,
Too fast in thought or death to be bestirred.
Then, as I probed them, one sprang up, and stared
With piteous recognition in fixed eyes,
Lifting distressful hands as if to bless.
And by his smile, I knew that sullen hall;
By his dead smile I knew we stood in Hell.
With a thousand fears that vision's face was grained;
Yet no blood reached there from the upper ground,
And no guns thumped, or down the flues made moan.
'Strange, friend,' I said, 'here is no cause to mourn.'
'None,' said the other, 'save the undone years,
The hopelessness. Whatever hope is yours,
Was my life also; I went hunting wild
After the wildest beauty in the world,
Which lies not calm in eyes, or braided hair,
But mocks the steady running of the hour,
And if it grieves, grieves richlier than here.
For by my glee might many men have laughed,
And of my weeping something had been left,
Which must die now. I mean the truth untold,
The pity of war, the pity war distilled.
Now men will go content with what we spoiled.
Or, discontent, boil bloody, and be spilled.
They will be swift with swiftness of the tigress,
None will break ranks, though nations trek from progress.
Courage was mine, and I had mystery;
Wisdom was mine, and I had mastery;
To miss the march of this retreating world
Into vain citadels that are not walled.
Then, when much blood had clogged their chariot-wheels
I would go up and wash them from sweet wells,
Even with truths that lie too deep for taint.
I would have poured my spirit without stint
But not through wounds; not on the cess of war.
Foreheads of men have bled where no wounds were.
I am the enemy you killed, my friend.
I knew you in this dark; for so you frowned
Yesterday through me as you jabbed and killed.
I parried; but my hands were loath and cold.
Let us sleep now . . .'

Dulce et Decorum est

Bent double, like old beggars under sacks,
Knock-kneed, coughing like hags, we cursed through sludge,
Till on the haunting flares we turned our backs,
And towards our distant rest began to trudge.
Men marched asleep. Many had lost their boots,
But limped on, blood-shod. All went lame, all blind;
Drunk with fatigue; deaf even to the hoots
Of gas-shells dropping softly behind.

Gas! GAS! Quick, boys!—An ecstasy of fumbling
Fitting the clumsy helmets just in time,
But someone still was yelling out and stumbling
And flound'ring like a man in fire or lime.—
Dim through the misty panes and thick green light,
As under a green sea, I saw him drowning.

In all my dreams before my helpless sight
He plunges at me, guttering, choking, drowning.

If in some smothering dreams, you too could pace
Behind the wagon that we flung him in,
And watch the white eyes writhing in his face,
His hanging face, like a devil's sick of sin,
If you could hear, at every jolt, the blood
Come gargling from the froth-corrupted lungs
Obscene as cancer, bitter as the cud
Of vile, incurable sores on innocent tongues,—
My friend, you would not tell with such high zest
To children ardent for some desperate glory,
The old Lie: Dulce et decorum est
Pro patria mori.

Futility

Move him into the sun—
Gently its touch awoke him once,
At home, whispering of fields unsown.
Always it woke him, even in France,
Until this morning and this snow.

If anything might rouse him now
The kind old sun will know.

Think how it wakes the seeds—
Woke, once, the clays of a cold star.
Are limbs so dear-achieved, are sides
Full-nerved,—still warm,—too hard to stir?
Was it for this the clay grew tall?
—O what made fatuous sunbeams toil
To break earth's sleep at all?

Arms and the Boy

Let the boy try along this bayonet-blade
How cold steel is, and keen with hunger of blood;
Blue with all malice, like a madman's flash;
And thinly drawn with famishing for flesh.

Lend him to stroke these blind, blunt bullet leads
Which long to nuzzle in the hearts of lads,
Or give him cartridges of fine zinc teeth,
Sharp with the sharpness of grief and death.

For his teeth seem for laughing round an apple.
There lurk no claws behind his fingers supple;
And God will grow no talons at his heels,
Nor antlers through the thickness of his curls.

COVENTRY PATMORE (1823–1896)

The Toys

My little Son, who looked from thoughtful eyes
And moved and spoke in quiet grown-up wise,
Having my law the seventh time disobeyed,
I struck him, and dismissed
With hard words and unkissed,
—His Mother, who was patient, being dead.
Then, fearing lest his grief should hinder sleep,
I visited his bed,

But found him slumbering deep,
With darkened eyelids, and their lashes yet
From his late sobbing wet.
And I, with moan,
Kissing away his tears, left others of my own;
For, on a table drawn beside his head,
He had put, within his reach,
A box of counters and a red-veined stone,
A piece of glass abraded by the beach,
And six or seven shells,
A bottle with bluebells,
And two French copper coins, ranged there with careful art,
To comfort his sad heart.
So when that night I prayed
To God, I wept, and said:
'Ah, when at last we lie with trancèd breath,
Not vexing Thee in death,
And Thou rememberest of what toys
We made our joys,
How weakly understood
Thy great commanded good,
Then, fatherly not less
Than I whom Thou hast moulded from the clay,
Thou'lt leave Thy wrath, and say,
"I will be sorry for their childishness."'

THOMAS LOVE PEACOCK (1785–1866)

The War Song of Dinas Vawr

The mountain sheep are sweeter,
But the valley sheep are fatter;
We therefore deemed it meeter
To carry off the latter.
We made an expedition;
We met a host, and quelled it;
We forced a strong position,
And killed the men who held it.

On Dyfed's richest valley,
Where herds of kine were brousing,

We made a mighty sally,
To furnish our carousing.
Fierce warriors rushed to meet us;
We met them, and o'erthrew them:
They struggled hard to beat us;
But we conquered them, and slew them.

As we drove our prize at leisure,
The king marched forth to catch us:
His rage surpassed all measure,
But his people could not match us.
He fled to his hall-pillars;
And, ere our force we led off,
Some sacked his house and cellars,
While others cut his head off.

We there, in strife bewildering,
Spilt blood enough to swim in:
We orphaned many children,
And widowed many women.
The eagles and the ravens
We glutted with our foemen;
The heroes and the cravens,
The spearmen and the bowmen.

We brought away from battle,
And much their land bemoaned them,
Two thousand head of cattle,
And the head of him who owned them:
Ednyfed, king of Dyfed,
His head was borne before us;
His wine and beasts supplied our feasts,
And his overthrow, our chorus.

Rich and Poor, or *Saint and Sinner*

The poor man's sins are glaring;
In the face of ghostly warning
    He is caught in the fact
    Of an overt act—
Buying greens on Sunday morning.

The rich man's sins are hidden
In the pomp of wealth and station;
  And escape the sight
  Of the children of light,
Who are wise in their generation.

The rich man has a kitchen,
And cooks to dress his dinner;
  The poor who would roast
  To the baker's must post,
And thus becomes a sinner.

The rich man has a cellar,
And a ready butler by him;
  The poor man must steer
  For his pint of beer
Where the saint can't choose but spy him.

The rich man's painted windows
Hide the concerts of the quality;
  The poor can but share
  A crack'd fiddle in the air,
Which offends all sound morality.

The rich man is invisible
In the crowd of his gay society;
  But the poor man's delight
  Is a sore in the sight,
And a stench in the nose of piety.

The rich man has a carriage
Where no rude eye can flout him;
  The poor man's bane
  Is a third–class train,
With the daylight all about him.

The rich man goes out yachting,
Where sanctity can't pursue him,
  The poor goes afloat
  In a fourpenny boat,
Where the bishop groans to view him.

GEORGE PEELE (1556–1596)

Bethsabe's Song

Hot sun, cool fire, tempered with sweet air,
Black shade, fair nurse, shadow my white hair;
Shine, sun; burn, fire; breathe, air, and ease me;
Black shade, fair nurse, shroud me and please me:
Shadow, my sweet nurse, keep me from burning,
Make not my glad cause cause of mourning.
  Let not my beauty's fire
  Inflame unstaid desire,
  Nor pierce any bright eye
  That wandereth lightly.

'*When as the Rye*'

When as the Rye reach to the chin,
And chopcherry chopcherry ripe within,
Strawberries swimming in the cream,
And schoolboys playing in the stream:
Then O, then O, then O my true love said,
Till that time come again,
She could not live a maid.

EDGAR ALLAN POE (1809–1849)

To Helen

Helen, thy beauty is to me
 Like those Nicèan barks of yore,
That gently, o'er a perfumed sea,
 The weary way-worn wanderer bore
 To his own native shore.

On desperate seas long wont to roam,
 Thy hyacinth hair, thy classic face,
Thy Naiad airs have brought me home
 To the glory that was Greece,
 And the grandeur that was Rome.

Lo! in yon brilliant window-niche
How statue-like I see thee stand,
The agate lamp within thy hand!
Ah, Psyche, from the regions which
Are Holy-Land!

The City in the Sea

Lo! Death has reared himself a throne
In a strange city lying alone
Far down within the dim West,
Where the good and the bad and the worst and the best
Have gone to their eternal rest.
There shrines and palaces and towers
(Time-eaten towers that tremble not!)
Resemble nothing that is ours.
Around, by lifting winds forgot,
Resignedly beneath the sky
The melancholy waters lie.

No rays from the holy heaven come down
On the long night-time of that town;
But light from out the lurid sea
Streams up the turrets silently—
Gleams up the pinnacles far and free—
Up domes—up spires—up kingly halls—
Up fanes—up Babylon-like walls—
Up shadowy long-forgotten bowers
Of sculptured ivy and stone flowers—
Up many and many a marvellous shrine
Whose wreathèd friezes intertwine
The viol, the violet, and the vine.

Resignedly beneath the sky
The melancholy waters lie.
So blend the turrets and shadows there
That all seem pendulous in air,
While from a proud tower in the town
Death looks gigantically down.

There open fanes and gaping graves
Yawn level with the luminous waves;
But not the riches there that lie
In each idol's diamond eye—
Not the gaily-jewelled dead
Tempt the waters from their bed;
For no ripples curl, alas!
Along that wilderness of glass—
No swellings tell that winds may be
Upon some far-off happier sea—
No heavings hint that winds have been
On seas less hideously serene.

But lo, a stir is in the air!
The wave—there is a movement there!
As if the towers had thrown aside,
In slightly sinking, the dull tide—
As if their tops had feebly given
A void within the filmy Heaven.

The waves have now a redder glow—
The hours are breathing faint and low—
And when, amid no earthly moans,
Down, down that town shall settle hence,
Hell, rising from a thousand thrones,
Shall do it reverence.

ALEXANDER POPE (1688–1744)

Solitude: An Ode

Happy the man, whose wish and care
A few paternal acres bound,
Content to breathe his native air
   In his own ground.

Whose herds with milk, whose fields with bread,
Whose flocks supply him with attire;
Whose trees in summer yield him shade,
   In winter fire.

Blest, who can unconcernedly find
Hours, days, and years slide soft away
In health of body, peace of mind;
    Quiet by day,

Sound sleep by night; study and ease
Together mixed, sweet recreation,
And innocence, which most does please
    With meditation.

Thus let me live, unheard, unknown;
Thus unlamented let me dye;
Steal from the world, and not a stone
    Tell where I lie.

from 'An Essay on Criticism'

1

'Tis hard to say, if greater want of skill
Appear in writing or in judging ill;
But, of the two, less dangerous is the offence
To tire our patience, than mislead our sense.
Some few in that, but numbers err in this,
Ten censure wrong for one who writes amiss;
A fool might once himself alone expose,
Now one in verse makes many more in prose.
   'Tis with our judgments as our watches, none
Go just alike, yet each believes his own.
In poets as true genius is but rare,
True taste as seldom is the critic's share;
Both must alike from Heaven derive their light,
These born to judge, as well as those to write.
Let such teach others who themselves excel,
And censure freely who have written well.
Authors are partial to their wit, 'tis true,
But are not critics to their judgment too?
   Yet, if we look more closely, we shall find
Most have the seeds of judgment in their mind:
Nature affords at least a glimmering light;
The lines, though touched but faintly, are drawn right.
But as the slightest sketch, if justly traced,

Is by ill colouring but the more disgraced,
So by false learning is good sense defaced;
Some are bewildered in the maze of schools,
And some made coxcombs Nature meant but fools.
In search of wit these lose their common sense,
And then turn critics in their own defence:
Each burns alike, who can, or cannot write,
Or with a rival's, or an eunuch's spite.
All fools have still an itching to deride,
And fain would be upon the laughing side.
If Maevius scribble in Apollo's spite,
There are who judge still worse than he can write.

    Some have at first for wits, then poets passed,
Turned critics next, and proved plain fools at last.
Some neither can for wits nor critics pass,
As heavy mules are neither horse nor ass.

. . .

    But you who seek to give and merit fame,
And justly bear a critic's noble name,
Be sure yourself and your own reach to know,
How far your genius, taste, and learning go;
Launch not beyond your depth, but be discreet,
And mark that point where sense and dulness meet.
    Nature to all things fixed the limits fit,
And wisely curbed proud man's pretending wit:
As on the land while here the ocean gains,
In other parts it leaves wide sandy plains;
Thus in the soul while memory prevails,
The solid power of understanding fails;
Where beams of warm imagination play,
The memory's soft figures melt away.
One science only will one genius fit:
So vast is art, so narrow human wit:
Not only bounded to peculiar arts,
But oft in those, confined to single parts.
Like kings we lose the conquests gained before,
By vain ambition still to make them more:
Each might his several province well command,
Would all but stoop to what they understand.
    First follow Nature, and your judgment frame
By her just standard, which is still the same:
Unerring Nature, still divinely bright,

One clear, unchanged, and universal light,
Life, force, and beauty, must to all impart,
At once the source, and end, and test of Art.
Art from that fund each just supply provides,
Works without show, and without pomp presides:
In some fair body thus th' informing soul
With spirits feeds, with vigour fills the whole,
Each motion guides, and every nerve sustains;
Itself unseen, but in th' effects remains.
Some, to whom Heaven in wit has been profuse,
Want as much more, to turn it to its use;
For wit and judgment often are at strife,
Though meant each other's aid, like man and wife.
'Tis more to guide, than spur the Muse's steed;
Restrain his fury, than provoke his speed:
The wingèd courser, like a generous horse,
Shows most true mettle when you check his course.
. . .
Cavil you may, but never criticise.
Be Homer's works your study and delight,
Read them by day, and meditate by night;
Thence form your judgment, thence your maxims bring,
And trace the Muses upward to their spring.
Still with itself compared, his text peruse;
And let your comment be the Mantuan Muse.
. . .
Great wits sometimes may gloriously offend,
And rise to faults true critics dare not mend;
From vulgar bounds with brave disorder part,
And snatch a grace beyond the reach of art,
Which, without passing through the judgment, gains
The heart, and all its end at once attains.
. . .

2

. . .
A little learning is a dangerous thing;
Drink deep, or taste not the Pierian spring:
There shallow draughts intoxicate the brain,
And drinking largely sobers us again.
Fired at first sight with what the Muse imparts,
In fearless youth we tempt the heights of arts,
While from the bounded level of our mind,

Short views we take, nor see the lengths behind;
But more advanced, behold with strange surprise
New distant scenes of endless science rise!
. . .

    A perfect judge will read each work of wit
With the same spirit that its author writ:
Survey the WHOLE, nor seeks slight faults to find
Where Nature moves, and rapture warms the mind,
Nor lose, for that malignant dull delight,
The generous pleasure to be charmed with wit.
But in such lays as neither ebb, nor flow,
Correctly cold, and regularly low,
That shunning faults, one quiet tenour keep;
We cannot blame indeed—but we may sleep.
In wit, as Nature, what affects our hearts
Is not th' exactness of peculiar parts;
'Tis not a lip, or eye, we beauty call,
But the joint force and full result of all.
. . .

Poets, like painters, thus, unskilled to trace
The naked nature and the living grace,
With gold and jewels cover every part,
And hide with ornaments their want of art.
True wit is nature to advantage dressed,
What oft was thought, but ne'er so well expressed,
Something, whose truth convinced at sight we find,
That gives us back the image of our mind.
As shades more sweetly recommend the light,
So modest plainness sets off sprightly wit.
For works may have more wit than does 'em good,
As bodies perish through excess of blood.

    Others for language all their care express,
And value books, as women men, for dress:
Their praise is still—The style is excellent,
The sense, they humbly take upon content.
Words are like leaves; and where they most abound,
Much fruit of sense beneath is rarely found.
False eloquence, like the prismatic glass,
Its gaudy colours spreads on every place;
The face of Nature we no more survey,
All glares alike, without distinction gay:
But true expression, like th' unchanging sun,

Clears and improves whate'er it shines upon,
It gilds all objects, but it alters none.
Expression is the dress of thought, and still
Appears more decent, as more suitable;
A vile conceit in pompous words expressed
Is like a clown in regal purple dressed:
For different styles with different subjects sort,
As several garbs with country, town, and court.
Some by old words to fame have made pretence,
Ancients in phrase, mere moderns in their sense;
Such laboured nothings, in so strange a style,
Amaze the unlearned, and make the learnèd smile.
. . .

True ease in writing comes from art, not chance,
As those move easiest who have learned to dance.
'Tis not enough no harshness gives offence,
The sound must seem an echo to the sense:
Soft is the strain when Zephyr gently blows,
And the smooth stream in smoother numbers flows;
But when loud billows lash the sounding shore,
The hoarse, rough verse should like the torrent roar.
When Ajax strives some rock's vast weight to throw,
The line too labours, and the words move slow:
Not so, when swift Camilla scours the plain,
Flies o'er the unbending corn, and skims along the main.
. . .

    Avoid extremes, and shun the fault of such,
Who still are pleased too little or too much.
At every trifle scorn to take offence,
That always shows great pride, or little sense;
Those heads, as stomachs, are not sure the best,
Which nauseate all, and nothing can digest.
Yet let not each gay turn thy rapture move;
For fools admire, but men of sense approve:
As things seem large which we through mists descry,
Dulness is ever apt to magnify.
. . .

    But where's the man, who counsel can bestow,
Still pleased to teach, and yet not proud to know?
Unbiased, or by favour or by spite;
Not dully prepossessed, nor blindly right;
Though learned, well-bred; and though well-bred, sincere;

Modestly bold, and humanly severe:
Who to a friend his faults can freely show,
And gladly praise the merit of a foe?
Blest with a taste exact, yet unconfined;
A knowledge both of books and human kind;
Generous converse; a soul exempt from pride;
And love to praise, with reason on his side?
. . .

    Horace still charms with graceful negligence,
And without methods talks us into sense,
Will, like a friend, familiarly convey
The truest notions in the easiest way.
He, who supreme in judgment, as in wit,
Might boldly censure, as he boldly writ,
Yet judged with coolness, though he sung with fire;
His precepts teach but what his works inspire.
Our critics take a contrary extreme,
They judge with fury, but they write with phlegm:
Nor suffers Horace more in wrong translations
By wits, than critics in as wrong quotations.
    See Dionysius Homer's thoughts refine,
And call new beauties forth from every line!
    Fancy and art in gay Petronius please,
The scholar's learning with the courtier's ease.
. . .

from 'The Rape of the Lock'

Close by those meads, for ever crowned with flowers,
Where Thames with pride surveys his rising towers,
There stands a structure of majestic frame,
Which from the neighb'ring Hampton takes its name.
Here Britain's statesmen oft the fall foredoom
Of foreign tyrants and of nymphs at home;
Here thou, great Anna! whom three realms obey,
Dost sometimes counsel take—and sometimes tea.
    Hither the heroes and the nymphs resort,
To taste awhile the pleasures of a court;
In various talk the instructive hours they passed,
Who gave the ball, or paid the visit last;
One speaks the glory of the British queen,

And one describes a charming Indian screen;
A third interprets motions, looks, and eyes.
At every word a reputation dies.
Snuff, or the fan, supply each pause of chat,
With singing, laughing, ogling, and all that.
    Meanwhile, declining from the noon of day,
The sun obliquely shoots his burning ray;
The hungry judges soon the sentence sign,
And wretches hang that jury-men may dine;
The merchant from the Exchange returns in peace,
And the long labours of the toilet cease. . .

. . .

'To arms, to arms!' the fierce virago cries,
And swift as lightning to the combat flies.
All side in parties, and begin the attack;
Fans clap, silks rustle, and tough whalebones crack;
Heroes' and heroines' shouts confusedly rise,
And bass, and treble voices strike the skies.
No common weapons in their hands are found,
Like gods they fight, nor dread a mortal wound.

. . .

There broken vows and deathbed alms are found,
And lovers' hearts with ends of ribband bound,
The courtier's promises, and sick man's prayers,
The smiles of harlots, and the tears of heirs,
Cages for gnats, and chains to yoke a flea,
Dried butterflies, and tomes of casuistry.

. . .

from 'An Essay on Man'

    Know, then, thyself, presume not God to scan;
The proper study of mankind is man.
Placed on this isthmus of a middle state,
A being darkly wise, and rudely great:
With too much knowledge for the sceptic side,
With too much weakness for the stoic's pride,
He hangs between; in doubt to act, or rest;
In doubt to deem himself a god, or beast;
In doubt his mind or body to prefer;
Born but to die, and reasoning but to err;

Alike in ignorance, his reason such,
Whether he thinks too little, or too much:
Chaos of thought and passion, all confused;
Still by himself abused, or disabused;
Created half to rise, and half to fall;
Great lord of all things, yet a prey to all;
Sole judge of truth, in endless error hurled:
The glory, jest, and riddle of the world!
. . .

    Whate'er the passion, knowledge, fame, or pelf,
Not one will change his neighbour with himself.
The learned is happy nature to explore,
The fool is happy that he knows no more;
The rich is happy in the plenty given,
The poor contents him with the care of Heaven.
See the blind beggar dance, the cripple sing,
The sot a hero, lunatic a king;
The starving chemist in his golden views
Supremely blest, the poet in his muse.
    See some strange comfort every state attend,
And pride bestowed on all, a common friend;
See some fit passion every age supply,
Hope travels through, nor quits us when we die.
    Behold the child, by Nature's kindly law,
Pleased with a rattle, tickled with a straw:
Some livelier plaything gives his youth delight,
A little louder, but as empty quite:
Scarves, garters, gold, amuse his riper stage,
And beads and prayer-books are the toys of age:
Pleased with this bauble still, as that before;
Till tired he sleeps, and life's poor play is o'er.
. . .

    Honour and shame from no condition rise;
Act well your part, there all the honour lies.
Fortune in men has some small difference made,
One flaunts in rags, one flutters in brocade;
The cobbler aproned, and the parson gowned,
The friar hooded, and the monarch crowned,
'What differ more (you cry) than crown and cowl?'
I'll tell you, friend! a wise man and a fool.
You'll find, if once the monarch acts the monk,
Or, cobbler-like, the parson will be drunk,

Worth makes the man, and want of it, the fellow;
The rest is all but leather or prunella.

Epigram

*Engraved on the Collar of a Dog which I gave to his
Royal Highness*

I am his Highness' Dog at Kew;
Pray tell me, Sir, whose Dog are you?

F. T. PRINCE (1912–)

Soldiers Bathing

The sea at evening moves across the sand.
Under a reddening sky I watch the freedom of a band
Of soldiers who belong to me. Stripped bare
For bathing in the sea, they shout and run in the warm air;
Their flesh worn by the trade of war, revives
And my mind towards the meaning of it strives.

All's pathos now. The body that was gross,
Rank, ravenous, disgusting in the act or in repose,
All fever, filth and sweat, its bestial strength
And bestial decay, by pain and labour grows at length
Fragile and luminous. 'Poor bare forked animal,'
Conscious of his desires and needs and flesh that rise and fall,
Stands in the soft air, tasting after toil
The sweetness of his nakedness: letting the sea-waves coil
Their frothy tongues about his feet, forgets
His hatred of the war, its terrible pressure that begets
A machinery of death and slavery,
Each being a slave and making slaves of others: finds that he
Remembers his old freedom in a game
Mocking himself, and comically mimics fear and shame.

He plays with death and animality;
And reading in the shadows of his pallid flesh, I see
The idea of Michelangelo's cartoon
Of soldiers bathing, breaking off before they were half done

At some sortie of the enemy, an episode
Of the Pisan wars with Florence. I remember how he showed
Their muscular limbs that clamber from the water,
And heads that turn across the shoulder, eager for the slaughter,
Forgetful of their bodies that are bare,
And hot to buckle on and use the weapons lying there.
—And I think too of the theme another found
When, shadowing men's bodies on a sinister red ground,
Another Florentine, Pollaiuolo,
Painted a naked battle: warriors, straddled, hacked the foe,
Dug their bare toes into the ground and slew
The brother-naked man who lay between their feet and drew
His lips back from his teeth in a grimace.

They were Italians who knew war's sorrow and disgrace
And showed the thing suspended, stripped: a theme
Born out of the experience of war's horrible extreme
Beneath a sky where even the air flows
With *lacrimae Christi*. For that rage, that bitterness, those blows,
That hatred of the slain, what could they be
But indirectly or directly a commentary
On the Crucifixion? And the picture burns
With indignation and pity and despair by turns,
Because it is the obverse of the scene
Where Christ hangs murdered, stripped, upon the Cross. I mean,
That is the explanation of its rage.

And we too have our bitterness and pity that engage
Blood, spirit, in this war. But night begins,
Night of the mind: who nowadays is conscious of our sins?
Though every human need concerns our blood,
And even we must know, what nobody has understood,
That some great love is over all we do,
And that is what has driven us to this fury, for so few
Can suffer all the terror of that love:
The terror of that love has set us spinning in this groove
Greased with our blood.

These dry themselves and dress,
Combing their hair, forget the fear and shame of nakedness.
Because to love is frightening we prefer
The freedom of our crimes. Yet, as I drink the dusky air,

I feel a strange delight that fills me full,
Strange gratitude, as if evil itself were beautiful.
And kiss the wound in thought, while in the west
I watch a streak of red that might have issued
from Christ's breast.

Matthew Prior (1664–1721)

Song

The merchant, to secure his treasure,
    Conveys it in a borrowed name:
Euphelia serves to grace my measure,
    But Cloe is my real flame.

My softest verse, my darling lyre
    Upon Euphelia's toilet lay—
When Cloe noted her desire
    That I should sing, that I should play.

My lyre I tune, my voice I raise,
    But with my numbers mix my sighs;
And whilst I sing Euphelia's praise,
    I fix my soul on Cloe's eyes.

Fair Cloe blushed; Euphelia frowned:
    I sung, and gazed; I played, and trembled:
And Venus to the Loves around
    Remarked how ill we all dissembled.

A Reasonable Affliction

On his death-bed poor Lubin lies:
    His spouse is in despair;
With frequent cries, and mutual sighs,
    They both express their care.

'A different cause,' says Parson Sly,
    'The same effect may give:
Poor Lubin fears that he may die;
    His wife, that he may live.'

SIR WALTER RALEIGH (1552?–1618)

'As you came from the holy land'

As you came from the holy land
Of Walsinghame
Met you not with my true love
By the way as you came?

How shall I know your true love,
That have met many one,
As I went to the holy land,
That have come, that have gone?

She is neither white nor brown,
But as the heavens fair;
There is none hath a form so divine
In the earth or the air.

Such a one did I meet, good sir,
Such an angel-like face,
Who like a queen, like a nymph, did appear,
By her gait, by her grace.

She hath left me here all alone,
All alone, as unknown,
Who sometimes did me lead with herself,
And me loved as her own.

What's the cause that she leaves you alone,
And a new way doth take,
Who loved you once as her own,
And her joy did you make?

I have loved her all my youth,
But now old, as you see,
Love likes not the falling fruit
From the withered tree:

Know that love is a careless child,
And forgets promise past;
He is blind, he is deaf when he list,
And in faith never fast.

His desire is a dureless content,
And a trustless joy;
He is won with a world of despair,
And is lost with a joy:

Of womankind such indeed is the love
Or the word love abusèd,
Under which many childish desires
And conceits are excusèd.

But true love is a durable fire,
In the mind ever burning,
Never sick, never old, never dead,
From itself never turning.

The Nymph's Reply to the Shepherd

If all the world and love were young,
And truth in every shepherd's tongue,
These pretty pleasures might me move,
To live with thee and be thy love.

Time drives the flocks from field to fold,
When rivers rage, and rocks grow cold;
And Philomel becometh dumb;
The rest complains of cares to come.

The flowers do fade, and wanton fields
To wayward winter reckoning yields;
A honey tongue, a heart of gall,
Is fancy's spring, but sorrow's fall.

They gowns, thy shoes, thy beds of roses,
Thy cap, thy kirtle, and thy posies,
Soon break, soon wither, soon forgotten;
In folly ripe, in reason rotten.

Thy belt of straw and ivy buds,
Thy coral clasps and amber studs,
All these in me no means can move,
To come to thee and be thy love.

But could youth last, and love still breed,
Had joys no date, nor age no need,
Then these delights my mind might move
To live with thee and be thy love.

SIR WALTER RALEIGH (1861–1922)

Wishes of an Elderly Man at a Garden Party

I wish I loved the Human Race;
I wish I loved its silly face;
I wish I liked the way it walks;
I wish I liked the way it talks;
And when I'm introduced to one
I wish I thought What Jolly Fun!

HENRY REED (1914–1986)

Lessons of the War

Naming of Parts (I)

Today we have naming of parts. Yesterday,
We had daily cleaning. And tomorrow morning,
We shall have what to do after firing. But today,
Today we have naming of parts. Japonica
Glistens like coral in all of the neighbouring gardens,
　　And today we have naming of parts.

This is the lower sling swivel. And this
Is the upper sling swivel, whose use you will see,
When you are given your slings. And this is the piling swivel,
Which in your case you have not got. The branches

Hold in the gardens their silent, eloquent gestures,
    Which in our case we have not got.

This is the safety-catch, which is always released
With an easy flick of the thumb. And please do not let me
See anyone using his finger. You can do it quite easy
If you have any strength in your thumb. The blossoms
Are fragile and motionless, never letting anyone see
    Any of them using their finger.

And this you can see is the bolt. The purpose of this
Is to open the breech, as you see. We can slide it
Rapidly backwards and forwards: we call this
Easing the spring. And rapidly backwards and forwards
The early bees are assaulting and fumbling the flowers:
    They call it easing the Spring.

They call it easing the Spring: it is perfectly easy
If you have any strength in your thumb: like the bolt,
And the breech, and the cocking-piece, and the point of balance,
Which in our case we have not got; and the almond-blossom
Silent in all of the gardens and the bees going backwards and forwards,
For today we have naming of parts.

Judging Distances (II)

Not only how far away, but the way that you say it
Is very important. Perhaps you may never get
The knack of judging a distance, but at least you know
How to report on a landscape: the central sector,
The right of the arc and that, which we had last Tuesday,
    And at least you know

That maps are of time, not place, so far as the army
Happens to be concerned—the reason being,
Is one which need not delay us. Again, you know
There are three kinds of tree, three only, the fir and the poplar,
And those which have bushy tops to; and lastly
    That things only seem to be things.

A barn is not called a barn, to put it more plainly,
Or a field in the distance, where sheep may be safely grazing.

You must never be over-sure. You must say, when reporting:
At five o'clock in the central sector is a dozen
Of what appear to be animals; whatever you do,
  Don't call the bleeders *sheep*.

I am sure that's quite clear; and suppose, for the sake of example,
The one at the end, asleep, endeavours to tell us
What he sees over there to the west, and how far away,
After first having come to attention. There to the west,
Of the fields of the summer sun and the shadows bestow
  Vestments of purple and gold.

The white dwellings are like a mirage in the heat,
And under the swaying elms a man and a woman
Lie gently together. Which is, perhaps, only to say
That there is a row of houses to the left of the arc,
And that under some poplars a pair of what appear to be humans
  Appear to be loving.

Well that, for an answer, is what we rightly call
Moderately satisfactory only, the reason being,
Is that two things have been omitted, and those are very important.
The human beings, now: in what direction are they,
And how far away, would you say? And do not forget
  There may be dead ground in between.

There may be dead ground in between; and I may not have got
The knack of judging a distance; I will only venture
A guess that perhaps between me and the apparent lovers,
(Who, incidentally, appear by now to have finished,)
At seven o'clock from the houses, is roughly a distance
  Of about one year and a half.

Movement of Bodies (III)

Those of you that have got through the rest, I am going to rapidly
Devote a little time to showing you, those that can master it,
A few ideas about tactics, which must not be confused
With what we call strategy. Tactics is merely
The mechanical movement of bodies, and that is what we mean by it.
  Or perhaps I should say: by them.

Strategy, to be quite frank, you will have no hand in.
It is done by those up above, and it merely refers to,
The larger movements over which we have no control.
But tactics are also important, together or single.
You must never forget that, suddenly, in an engagement,
    You may find yourself alone.

This brown clay model is a characteristic terrain
Of a simple and typical kind. Its general character
Should be taken in at a glance, and its general character
You can, see at a glance it is somewhat hilly by nature,
With a fair amount of typical vegetation
    Disposed at certain parts.

Here at the top of the tray, which we might call the northwards,
Is a wooded headland, with a crown of bushy-topped trees on;
And proceeding downwards or south we take in at a glance
A variety of gorges and knolls and plateaus and basins and saddles,
Somewhat symmetrically put, for easy identification.
    And here is our point of attack.

But remember of course it will not be a tray you will fight on,
Nor always by daylight. After a hot day, think of the night
Cooling the desert down, and you still moving over it:
Past a ruined tank or a gun, perhaps, or a dead friend,
In the midst of war, at peace. It might quite well be that.
    It isn't always a tray.

And even this tray is different to what I had thought.
These models are somehow never always the same: for a reason
I do not know how to explain quite. Just as I do not know
Why there is always someone at this particular lesson
Who always starts crying. Now will you kindly
    Empty those blinking eyes?

I thank you. I have no wish to seem impatient.
I know it is all very hard, but you would not like,
To take a simple example, to take for example,
This place we have thought of here, you would not like
To find yourself face to face with it, and you not knowing
    What there might be inside?

Very well then: suppose this is what you must capture.
It will not be easy, not being very exposed,
Secluded away like it is, and somewhat protected
By a typical formation of what appear to be bushes,
So that you cannot see, as to what is concealed inside,
    As to whether it is friend or foe.

And so, a strong feint will be necessary in this connection.
It will not be a tray, remember. It may be a desert stretch
With nothing in sight, to speak of. I have no wish to be inconsiderate,
But I see there are two of you now, commencing to snivel.
I do not know where such emotional privates can come from.
    Try to behave like men.

I thank you. I was saying: a thoughtful deception
Is always somewhat essential in such a case. You can see
That if only the attacker can capture such an emplacement
The rest of the terrain is his: a key-position, and calling
For the most resourceful manoeuvres. But that is what tactics is.
    Or I should say rather: are.

Let us begin then and appreciate the situation.
I am thinking especially of the point we have been considering,
Though in a sense everything in the whole of the terrain,
Must be appreciated. I do not know what I have said
To upset so many of you. I know it is a difficult lesson.
    Yesterday a man was sick,

But I have never known as many as five in a single intake,
Unable to cope with this lesson. I think you had better
Fall out, all five, and sit at the back of the room,
Being careful not to talk. The rest will close up.
Perhaps it was me saying 'a dead friend', earlier on?
    Well, some of us live.

And I never know why, whenever we get to tactics,
Men either laugh or cry, though neither is strictly called for.
But perhaps I have started too early with a difficult task?
We will start again, further north, with a simpler problem.
Are you ready? Is everyone paying attention?
    Very well then. Here are two hills.

Unarmed Combat (IV)

In due course of course you will all be issued with
Your proper issue; but until tomorrow,
You can hardly be said to need it; and until that time,
We shall have unarmed combat. I shall teach you
The various holds and rolls and throws and breakfalls
    Which you may sometimes meet.

And the various holds and rolls and throws and breakfalls
Do not depend on any sort of weapon,
But only on what I might coin a phrase and call
The ever-important question of human balance,
And the ever-important need to be in a strong
    Position at the start.

There are many kinds of weakness about the body,
Where you would least expect, like the ball of the foot,
But the various holds and rolls and throws and breakfalls
Will always come in useful, and never be frightened
To tackle from behind: it may not be clean to do so,
    But this is global war.

So give them all you have, and always give them
As good as you get; it will always get you somewhere.
(You may not know it, but you can tie a Jerry
Up without a rope; it is one of the things I shall teach you.)
Nothing will matter if only you are ready for him.
    The readiness is all.

The readiness is all. How can I help but feel
I have been here before? But somehow then,
I was the tied-up one. How to get out
Was always my problem. And even if I had
A piece of rope I was always the sort of person
    Who threw the rope aside.

And in my time I have given them all I had,
Which was never as good as I got, and it got me nowhere.
And the various holds and rolls and throws and breakfalls

Somehow or other I always seemed to put
In the wrong place. And as for war, my wars
    Were global from the start.

Perhaps I was never in a strong position,
Or the ball of my foot got hurt, or I had some weakness
Where I had least expected. But I think I see your point.
While awaiting the proper issue, we must learn the lesson
Of the ever-important question of human balance.
    It is the courage that counts.

Things may be the same again; and we must fight
Not in the hope of winning but rather of keeping
Something alive: so that when we meet our end,
It may be said that we tackled wherever we could,
That battle-fit we lived, and though defeated,
    Not without glory fought.

JOHN WILMOT, EARL OF ROCHESTER (1647–1680)

Love and Life

All my past life is mine no more,
    The flying hours are gone,
Like transitory dreams given o'er,
Whose images are kept in store
    By memory alone.

The time that is to come is not;
    How can it then be mine?
The present moment's all my lot;
And that, as fast as it is got,
    Phillis, is only thine.

Then talk not of inconstancy,
    False hearts, and broken vows;
If I, by miracle, can be
This live-long minute true to thee,
    'Tis all that Heaven allows.

Constancy

I cannot change, as others do,
    Though you unjustly scorn;
Since that poor swain, that sights for you
    For you alone was born.
        No, Phillis, no, your heart to move
    A surer way I'll try:
    And to revenge my slighted love,
Will still love on, will still love on, and die.

    When, killed with grief, Amyntas lies;
    And you to mind shall call
The sights that now unpitied rise;
    The tears that vainly fall:
        The welcome hour that ends this smart,
    Will then begin your pain;
    For such a faithful, tender heart
Can never break, can never break in vain.

from 'A Satire Against Reason and Mankind'

Were I (who to my cost already am
One of those strange, prodigious creatures, man)
A spirit free to choose, for my own share,
What case of flesh and blood I pleased to wear,
I'd be a dog, a monkey, or a bear,
Or anything but that vain animal
Who is so proud of being rational.
The senses are too gross, and he'll contrive
A sixth, to contradict the other five,
And before certain instinct, will prefer
Reason, which fifty times for one does err;
Reason, an ignis fatuus in the mind,
Which, leaving light of nature, sense, behind,
Pathless and dangerous wandering ways it takes
Through error's fenny bogs and thorny brakes;
Whilst the misguided follower climbs with pain
Mountains of Whimseys, heaped in his own brain;

Stumbling from thought to thought, falls headlong down
Into doubt's boundless sea, where, like to drown,
Books bear him up awhile, and make him try
To swim with bladders of philosophy;
In hopes still o'ertake th' escaping light,
The vapour dances in his dazzling sight
Till, spent, it leaves him to eternal night.
The old age and experience, hand in hand,
Lead him to death, and make him understand,
After a search so painful and so long,
that all his life he has been in the wrong.
Huddled in dirt the reasoning engine lies,
who was so proud, so witty, and so wise.

Epitaph on Charles II

Here lies our Sovereign Lord the King,
    Whose word no man relies on,
Who never said a foolish thing,
    Nor ever did a wise one.

ISAAC ROSENBERG (1890-1918)

Break of Day in the Trenches

The darkness crumbles away—
It is the same old druid Time as ever.
Only a live thing leaps my hand—
A queer sardonic rat—
As I pull the parapet's poppy
To stick behind my ear.
Droll rat, they would shoot you if they knew
Your cosmopolitan sympathies.
Now you have touched this English hand
You will do the same to a German—
Soon, no doubt, if it be your pleasure
To cross the sleeping green between.
It seems you inwardly grin as you pass
Strong eyes, fine limbs, haughty athletes
Less chanced than you for life,
Bonds to the whims of murder,

Sprawled in the bowels of the earth,
The torn fields of France.
What do you see in our eves
At the shrieking iron and flame
Hurled through still heavens?
What quaver—what heart aghast?
Poppies whose roots are in man's veins
Drop, and are ever dropping;
But mine in my ear is safe,
Just a little white with the dust.

Returning, We Hear the Larks

Sombre the night is.
And though we have our lives, we know
What sinister threat lurks there.

Dragging these anguished limbs, we only know
This poison-blasted track opens on our camp—
On a little safe sleep.

But hark! joy—joy—strange joy.
Lo! heights of night ringing with unseen larks.
Music showering on our upturned list'ning faces.

Death could drop from the dark
As easily as song—
But song only dropped,
Like a blind man's dreams on the sand
By dangerous tides,
Like a girl's dark hair for she dreams no ruin lies there,
Or her kisses where a serpent hides.

CHRISTINA GEORGINA ROSSETTI (1830–1894)

'When I am dead, my dearest'

When I am dead, my dearest,
Sing no sad songs for me;
Plant thou no roses at my head,
Nor shady cypress tree:

Be the green grass above me
With showers and dewdrops wet:
And if thou wilt, remember,
And if thou wilt, forget.

I shall not see the shadows,
I shall not feel the rain;
I shall not hear the nightingale
Sing on as if in pain:
And dreaming through the twilight
That doth not rise nor set,
Haply I may remember,
And haply may forget.

'Remember'

Remember me when I am gone away,
Gone far away into the silent land;
When you can no more hold me by the hand,
Nor I half turn to go, yet turning stay.
Remember me when no more, day by day,
You tell me of our future that you planned;
Only remember me; you understand
It will be late to counsel then or pray.
Yet if you should forget me for a while
And afterwards remember, do not grieve;
For if the darkness and corruption leave
A vestige of the thoughts that once I had,
Better by far you should forget and smile
Than that you should remember and be sad.

A Birthday

My heart is like a singing bird
    Whose nest is in a watered shoot;
My heart is like an apple-tree
    Whose bough is bent with thick-set fruit;
My heart is like a rainbow shell
    That paddles in a halcyon sea;
My heart is gladder than all these
    Because my love is come to me.

Raise me a dais of silk and down;
    Hang it with vair and purple dyes;
Carve it in doves and pomegranates,
    And peacocks with a hundred eyes;
Work it in gold and silver grapes,
    In leaves and silver fleur-de-lys;
Because the birthday of my life
    Is come, my love is come to me.

DANTE GABRIEL ROSSETTI (1828–1882)

The Blessèd Damozel

The blessèd damozel leaned out
    From the gold bar of Heaven;
Her eyes were deeper than the depth
    Of waters stilled at even;
She had three lilies in her hand,
    And the stars in her hair were seven.

Her robe, ungirt from clasp to hem,
    No wrought flowers did adorn,
But a white rose of Mary's gift,
    For service meetly worn;
Her hair that lay along her back
    Was yellow like ripe corn.

Her seemed she scarce had been a day
    One of God's choristers;
The wonder was not yet quite gone
    From that still look of hers;
Albeit, to them she left, her day
    Had counted as ten years.

(To one, it is ten years of years.
    . . . Yet now, and in this place,
Surely she leaned o'er me—her hair
    Fell all about my face. . . .
Nothing: the autumn fall of leaves.
    The whole year sets apace.)

It was the rampart of God's house
    That she was standing on;
By God built over the sheer depth
    The which is Space begun;
So high, that looking downward thence
    She scarce could see the sun.

It lies in Heaven, across the flood
    Of ether, as a bridge.
Beneath, the tides of day and night
    With flame and darkness ridge
The void, as low as where this earth
    Spins like a fretful midge.

Around her, lovers, newly met
    'Mid deathless love's acclaims,
Spoke evermore among themselves
    Their heart-remembered names;
And the souls mounting up to God
    Went by her like thin flames.

And still she bowed herself and stooped
    Out of the circling charm;
Until her bosom must have made
    The bar she leaned on warm,
And the lilies lay as if asleep
    Along her bended arm.

From the fixed place of Heaven she saw
    Time like a pulse shake fierce
Through all the worlds. Her gaze still strove
    Within the gulf to pierce
Its path; and now she spoke as when
    The stars sang in their spheres.

The sun was gone now; the curled moon
    Was like a little feather
Fluttering far down the gulf; and now
    She spoke through the still weather.
Her voice was like the voice the stars
    Had when they sang together.

(Ah sweet! Even now, in that bird's song,
    Strove not her accents there,
Fain to be hearkened? When those bells
    Possessed the mid-day air,
Strove not her steps to reach my side
    Down all the echoing stair?)

'I wish that he were come to me,
    For he will come,' she said.
'Have I not prayed in Heaven?—on earth,
    Lord, Lord, has he not prayed?
Are not two prayers a perfect strength?
    And shall I feel afraid?

'When round his head the aureole clings,
    And he is clothed in white,
I'll take his hand and go with him
    To the deep wells of light;
As unto a stream we will step down,
    And bathe there in God's sight.

'We two will stand beside that shrine,
    Occult, withheld, untrod,
Whose lamps are stirred continually
    With prayer sent up to God;
And see our old prayers, granted, melt
    Each like a little cloud.

'We two will lie i' the shadow of
    That living mystic tree
Within whose secret growth the Dove
    Is sometimes felt to be,
While every leaf that His plumes touch
    Saith His Name audibly.

'And I myself will teach to him,
    I myself, lying so,
The songs I sing here; which his voice
    Shall pause in, hushed and slow,
And find some knowledge at each pause,
    Or some new thing to know.'

(Alas! We two, we two, thou say'st!
    Yea, one wast thou with me
That once of old. But shall God lift
    To endless unity
The soul whose likeness with thy soul
    Was but its love for thee?)

'We two,' she said, 'will seek the groves
    Where the lady Mary is,
With her five handmaidens, whose names
    Are five sweet symphonies,
Cecily, Gertrude, Magdalen,
    Margaret and Rosalys.

'Circlewise sit they, with bound locks
    And foreheads garlanded;
Into the fine cloth white like flame
    Weaving the golden thread,
To fashion the birth-robes for them
    Who are just born, being dead.

'He shall fear, haply, and be dumb:
    Then will I lay my cheek
To his, and tell about our love,
    Not once abashed or weak:
And the dear Mother will approve
    My pride, and let me speak.

'Herself shall bring us, hand in hand,
    To Him round whom all souls
Kneel, the clear-ranged unnumbered heads
    Bowed with their aureoles:
And angels meeting us shall sing
    To their citherns and citoles.

'There will I ask of Christ the Lord
    Thus much for him and me:—
Only to live as once on earth
    With Love, only to be,

As then awhile, for ever now
        Together, I and he.'

She gazed and listened and then said,
        Less sad of speech than mild:—
'All this is when he comes.' She ceased.
        Then light thrilled towards her, filled
With angels in strong level flight.
        Her eyes prayed, and she smiled.

(I saw her smile.) But soon their path
        Was vague in distant spheres:
And then she cast her arms along
        The golden barriers,
And laid her face between her hands,
        And wept. (I heard her tears.)

The Woodspurge

The wind flapped loose, the wind was still,
Shaken out dead from tree and hill:
I had walked on at the wind's will,—
I sat now, for the wind was still.

Between my knees my forehead was,—
My lips, drawn in, said not Alas!
My hair was over in the grass,
My naked ears heard the day pass.

My eyes, wide open, had the run
Of some ten weeds to fix upon;
Among those few, out of the sun,
The woodspurge flowered, three cups in one.

From perfect grief there need not be
Wisdom or even memory:
One thing then learnt remains to me,—
The woodspurge has a cup of three.

SIEGFRIED SASSOON (1886–1967)

The Rearguard

Groping along the tunnel, step by step,
He winked his prying torch with patching glare
From side to side, and sniffed the unwholesome air.

Tins, boxes, bottles, shapes too vague to know,
A mirror smashed, the mattress from a bed:
And he, exploring fifty feet below
The rosy gloom of battle overhead.
Tripping, he grabbed the wall; saw someone lie
Humped at his feet, half-hidden by a rug,
And stooped to give the sleeper's arm a tug.
'I'm looking for headquarters.' No reply.
'God blast your neck!' (For days he'd had no sleep.)
'Get up and guide me through this stinking place.'
Savage, he kicked a soft, unanswering heap,
And flashed his beam across the livid face
Terribly glaring up, whose eyes yet wore
Agony dying hard ten days before;
And fists of fingers clutched a blackening wound.
Alone he staggered on until he found
Dawn's ghost that filtered down a shafted stair
To the dazed, muttering creatures underground
Who hear the boom of shells in muffled sound.
At last, with sweat of horror in his hair,
He climbed through darkness to the twilight air,
Unloading hell behind him step by step.

The General

'Good-morning; good-morning!' the General said
When we met him last week on our way to the line.
Now the soldiers he smiled at are most of 'em dead,
And we're cursing his staff for incompetent swine.
'He's a cheery old card,' grunted Harry to Jack
As they slogged up to Arras with rifle and pack.

.   .   .

But he did for them both by his plan of attack.

SIR WALTER SCOTT (1771–1832)

from 'The Lay of the Last Minstrel'

1

Breathes there the man, with soul so dead,
Who never to himself hath said,
    This is my own, my native land!
Whose heart hath ne'er within him burned,
As home his footsteps he hath turned,
    From wandering on a foreign strand!
If such there breathe, go, mark him well;
For him no Minstrel raptures swell;
High though his titles, proud his name,
Boundless his wealth as wish can claim;
Despite those titles, power, and pelf,
The wretch, concentrated all in self,
Living, shall forfeit fair renown,
And, doubly dying, shall go down
To the vile dust, from whence he sprung,
Unwept, unhonoured, and unsung.

2

O Caledonia! stern and wild,
Meet nurse for a poetic child!
Land of brown heath and shaggy wood,
Land of the mountain and the flood,
Land of my sires! what mortal hand
Can e'er untie the filial band,
That knits me to thy rugged strand!
Still as I view each well-known scene,
Think what is now, and what hath been,
Seems as, to me, of all bereft,
Sole friends thy woods and streams were left;
And thus I love them better still,
Even in extremity of ill.
By Yarrow's stream still let me stray,
Though none should guide my feeble way;
Still feel the breeze down Ettrick break,
Although it chill my withered cheek;
Still lay my head by Teviot Stone,

Though there, forgotten and alone,
The Bard may draw his parting groan.

from 'The Lady of the Lake'

Boon nature scattered, free and wild,
Each plant or flower, the mountain's child.
Here eglantine embalmed the air,
Hawthorn and hazel mingled there;
The primrose pale, and violet flower,
Found in such cliff a narrow bower;
Foxglove and nightshade, side by side,
Emblems of punishment and pride,
Grouped their dark hues with every stain
The weather-beaten crags retain.
With boughs that quaked at every breath,
Grey birch and aspen wept beneath;
Aloft, the ash and warrior oak
Cast anchor in the rifted rock;
And, higher yet, the pine tree hung
His shattered trunk, and frequent flung,
Where seemed the cliffs to meet on high,
His boughs athwart the narrowed sky.
Highest of all, where white peaks glanced,
Where glistening streamers waved and danced,
The wanderer's eye could barely view
The summer heaven's delicious blue;
So wondrous wild, the whole might seem
The scenery of a fairy dream.

Boat Song

Hail to the chief who in triumph advances!
    Honoured and blessed be the ever-green Pine!
Long may the tree, in his banner that glances,
    Flourish, the shelter and grace of our line!
        Heaven send it happy dew,
        Earth lend it sap anew,
    Gayly to bourgeon and broadly to grow,
        While every Highland glen
        Sends our shout back again,
    Roderigh Vich Alpine dhu, ho! ieroe!

Ours is no sapling, chance-sown by the fountain,
    Blooming at Beltane, in winter to fade;
When the whirlwind has stripped every leaf on the mountain,
    The more shall Clan Alpine exult in her shade.
        Moored in the rifted rock,
        Proof to the tempest's shock,
    Firmer he roots him the ruder it blow;
        Menteith and Breadalbane, then,
        Echo his praise again,
    Roderigh Vich Alpine dhu, ho! ieroe!

Proudly our pibroch has thrilled in Glen Fruin,
    And Bannochar's groans to our slogan replied;
Glen Luss and Ross-dhu, they are smoking in ruin,
    And the best of Loch Lomond lie dead on her side.
        Widow and Saxon maid
        Long shall lament our raid,
    Think of Clan Alpine with fear and with woe;
        Lennox and Leven-glen
        Shake when they hear again,
    Roderigh Vich Alpine dhu, ho! ieroe!

'Row, vassals, row, for the pride of the Highlands!
    Stretch to your oars, for the ever-green Pine!
O! that the rosebud that graces yon islands
    Were wreathed in a garland around him to twine!
        O that some seedling gem,
        Worthy such noble stem,
    Honoured and blessed in their shadow might grow!
        Loud should Clan Alpine then
        Ring from her deepmost glen,
    Roderigh Vich Alpine dhu, ho! ieroe!'

Coronach

He is gone on the mountain,
    He is lost to the forest,
Like a summer-dried fountain,
    When our need was the sorest.
The font, reappearing,
    From the raindrops shall borrow,

But to us comes no cheering,
   To Duncan no morrow!

The hand of the reaper
   Takes the ears that are hoary,
But the voice of the weeper
   Wails manhood in glory.
The autumn winds rushing
   Waft the leaves that are searest,
But our flower was in flushing,
   When blighting was nearest.

Fleet foot on the corrie,
   Sage counsel in cumber,
Red hand in the foray,
   How sound is thy slumber!
Like the dew on the mountain,
   Like the foam on the river,
Like the bubble on the fountain,
   Thou art gone, and for ever!

Lucy Ashton's Song

Look not thou on beauty's charming;
Sit thou still when kings are arming;
Taste not when the wine-cup glistens;
Speak not when the people listens;
Stop thine ear against the singer;
From the red gold keep thy finger;
Vacant heart and hand and eye,
Easy live and quiet die.

'Proud Maisie'

Proud Maisie is in the wood,
   Walking so early;
Sweet Robin sits on the bush,
   Singing so rarely.

'Tell me, thou bonny bird,
　　When shall I marry me?'
'When six braw gentlemen
　　Kirkward shall carry ye.'

'Who makes the bridal bed,
　　Birdie, say truly?'
'The grey-headed sexton
　　That delves the grave duly.

'The glow-worm o'er grave and stone
　　Shall light thee steady;
The owl from the steeple sing
　　Welcome, proud lady!'

WILLIAM SHAKESPEARE (1564–1616)

'Who is Sylvia?'

(from 'Two Gentlemen of Verona', Act 4, Scene 2)

Who is Sylvia? What is she,
　　That all our swains commend her?
Holy, fair, and wise is she;
　　The heaven such grace did lend her
That she might admirèd be.

Is she kind, as she is fair?
　　For beauty lives with kindness.
Love doth to her eyes repair,
　　To help him of his blindness;
And, being helped, inhabits there.

Then to Sylvia let us sing,
　　That Sylvia is excelling;
She excels each mortal thing
　　Upon the dull earth dwelling;
To her let us garlands bring.

'When icicles hang by the wall'

(from 'Love's Labour's Lost', Act 5, Scene 2)

When icicles hang by the wall
    And Dick the shepherd blows his nail,
And Tom bears logs into the hall,
    And milk comes frozen home in pail;
When blood is nipt, and ways be foul,
Then nightly sings the staring owl:
        Tu-whoo!
Tu-whit, Tu-whoo! A merry note!
While greasy Joan doth keel the pot.

When all about the wind doth blow,
    And coughing drowns the parson's saw,
And birds sit brooding in the snow,
    And Marian's nose looks red and raw;
When roasted crabs hiss in the bowl—
Then nightly sings the staring owl:
        Tu-whoo!
Tu-whit, Tu-whoo! A merry note!
While greasy Joan doth keel the pot.

'Now the hungry lion roars'

(from 'A Midsummer Night's Dream' Act 5, Scene 1)

Now the hungry lion roars,
    And the wolf behowls the moon;
Whilst the heavy ploughman snores,
    All with weary task fordone.
Now the wasted brands do glow,
    Whilst the screech owl, screeching loud,
Puts the wretch that lies in woe
    In remembrance of a shroud.
Now it is the time of night
    That the graves, all gaping wide,

Every one lets forth his sprite,
   In the churchway paths to glide:
And we fairies, that do run
   By the triple Hecate's team,
From the presence of the sun,
   Following darkness like a dream,
Now are frolic; not a mouse
Shall disturb this hallowed house:
I am sent with broom before,
To sweep the dust behind the door.

Through the house give glimmering light,
   By the dead and drowsy fire;
Every elf and fairy sprite
   Hop as light as bird from brier;
And this ditty after me
Sing, and dance it, trippingly.
First rehearse your song by rote,
To each word a warbling note:
Hand in hand, with fairy grace,
Will we sing, and bless this place.

'Tell me where is Fancy bred'

(from 'The Merchant of Venice', Act 3, Scene 2)

Tell me where is Fancy bred,
Or in the heart, or in the head?
How begot, how nourishèd?
   Reply, reply.

It is engendered in the eyes;
With gazing fed; and Fancy dies
In the cradle where it lies.
Let us all ring Fancy's knell;
I'll begin it,—Ding-dong, bell.
   —Ding-dong, bell.

'Sigh no more, ladies'

(from 'Much Ado About Nothing', Act 2, Scene 3)

Sigh no more, ladies, sigh no more,
    Men were deceivers ever;
One foot in sea, and one on shore;
    To one thing constant never.
Then sigh not so, but let them go,
    And be you blithe and bonny,
Converting all your sounds of woe
    Into Hey nonny nonny.

Sing no more ditties, sing no more
    Of dumps so dull and heavy;
The fraud of men was ever so,
    Since summer first was leavy.
Then sigh not so, but let them go,
    And be you blithe and bonny,
Converting all your sounds of woe
    Into Hey nonny nonny.

'Under the greenwood tree'

(from 'As You Like It', Act 2, Scene 5)

Under the greenwood tree
    Who loves to lie with me,
    And tune his merry note
    Unto the sweet bird's throat—
Come hither, come hither, come hither!
    Here shall he see
    No enemy
But winter and rough weather.

Who doth ambition shun
And loves to live i' the sun,

Seeking the food he eats
And pleased with what he gets—
Come hither, come hither, come hither!
Here shall he see
No enemy
But winter and rough weather.

'Blow, blow, thou winter wind'
(from 'As You Like It', Act 2, Scene 7)

Blow, blow, thou winter wind,
Thou art not so unkind
As man's ingratitude;
Thy tooth is not so keen
Because thou art not seen,
Although thy breath be rude.
Heigh ho! sing heigh ho! unto the green holly:
Most friendship is feigning, most loving mere folly:
Then, heigh ho! the holly!
This life is most jolly.

Freeze, freeze, thou bitter sky,
Thou dost not bite so nigh
As benefits forgot;
Though thou the waters warp,
Thy sting is not so sharp
As friend remembered not.
Heigh ho! sing heigh ho! unto the green holly:
Most friendship is feigning, most loving mere folly:
Then, heigh ho! the holly!
This life is most jolly.

'It was a lover and his lass'
(from 'As You Like It', Act 5, Scene 3)

It was a lover and his lass
With a hey, and a ho, and a hey nonino,
That o'er the green cornfield did pass
In the spring-time, the only pretty ring-time,

When birds do sing, hey ding a ding, ding;
   Sweet lovers love the spring.

Between the acres of the rye
   With a hey, and a ho, and a hey nonino,
These pretty country folks would lie,
   In the spring-time, the only pretty ring-time,
When birds do sing, hey ding a ding, ding;
   Sweet lovers love the spring.

This carol they began that hour,
   With a hey, and a ho, and a hey nonino,
How that life was but a flower
   In the spring-time, the only pretty ring-time,
When birds do sing, hey ding a ding, ding;
   Sweet lovers love the spring.

And therefore take the present time
   With a hey, and a ho, and a hey nonino,
For love is crownèd with the prime
In the spring-time, the only pretty ring-time,
When birds do sing, hey ding a ding, ding;
   Sweet lovers love the spring.

'O Mistress mine'
(from 'Twelfth Night', Act 2, Scene 3)

O Mistress mine, where are you roaming?
O stay and hear! your true love's coming
   That can sing both high and low;
Trip no further, pretty sweeting,
Journeys end in lovers meeting—
   Every wise man's son doth know.

What is love? 'tis not hereafter;
Present mirth hath present laughter;
   What's to come is still unsure:
In delay there lies no plenty,—
Then come kiss me, Sweet-and-twenty,
   Youth's a stuff will not endure.

Come Away, Death

(from 'Twelfth Night', Act 2, Scene 4)

Come away, come away, Death;
And in sad cypress let me be laid;
Fly away, fly away, breath;
I am slain by a fair cruel maid.
My shroud of white, stuck all with yew,
O prepare it!
My part of death no one so true
Did share it.

Not a flower, not a flower sweet
On my black coffin let there be strown;
Not a friend, not a friend greet
My poor corse, where my bones shall be thrown;
A thousand thousand sighs to save,
Lay me, O where
Sad true lover never find my grave,
To weep there.

'Take, O take those lips away'

(from 'Measure for Measure', Act 4, Scene 1)

Take, O take those lips away
That so sweetly were forsworn,
And those eyes, the break of day,
Lights that do mislead the morn.
But my kisses bring again,
Bring again—
Seals of love, but sealed in vain,
Sealed in vain!

'Fear no more the heat o' the sun'

(from 'Cymbeline', Act 4, Scene 2)

Fear no more the heat o' the sun
    Nor the furious winter's rages;
Thou thy worldly task hast done,
    Home art gone, and ta'en thy wages:
Golden lads and girls all must,
As chimney-sweepers, come to dust.

Fear no more the frown o' the great,
    Thou art past the tyrant's stroke;
Care no more to clothe and eat;
    To thee the reed is as the oak:
The sceptre, learning, physic, must
All follow this, and come to dust.

Fear no more the lightning flash,
    Nor the all-dreaded thunder-stone;
Fear not slander, censure rash;
    Thou hast finished joy and moan:
All lovers young, all lovers must
Consign to thee and come to dust.

'Full fathom five'

(from 'The Tempest', Act 1 Scene 2)

Full fathom five thy father lies:
    Of his bones are coral made;
Those are pearls that were his eyes:
    Nothing of him that doth fade,
But doth suffer a sea-change
Into something rich and strange.
Sea-nymphs hourly ring his knell:
    Hark! now I hear them,—
        Ding-dong, bell.

from 'The Sonnets'

Sonnet 18

Shall I compare thee to a summer's day?
Thou art more lovely and more temperate;
Rough winds do shake the darling buds of May,
And summer's lease hath all too short a date:
Sometime too hot the eye of heaven shines,
And often is his gold complexion dimmed:
And every fair from fair sometime declines,
By chance, or nature's changing course untrimmed:
But thy eternal summer shall not fade
Nor lose possession of that fair thou owest;
Nor shall Death brag thou wanderest in his shade
When in eternal lines to time thou growest.
　　So long as men can breathe, or eyes can see,
　　So long lives this, and this gives life to thee.

Sonnet 29

When in disgrace with fortune and men's eyes
I all alone beweep my outcast state,
And trouble deaf heaven with my bootless cries,
And look upon myself, and curse my fate;
Wishing me like to one more rich in hope,
Featured like him, like him with friends possess'd,
Desiring this man's art, and that man's scope,
With what I most enjoy contented least;
Yet in these thoughts my self almost despising,
Haply I think on thee—and then my state,
Like to the lark at break of day arising
From sullen earth, sings hymns at heaven's gate;
　　For thy sweet love remembered, such wealth brings
　　That then I scorn to change my state with kings.

Sonnet 30

When to the sessions of sweet silent thought
I summon up remembrance of things past,
I sigh the lack of many a thing I sought,

And with old woes new wail my dear time's waste;
Then can I drown an eye, unused to flow,
For precious friends hid in death's dateless night,
And weep afresh love's long-since-cancelled woe,
And moan the expense of many a vanished sight.
Then can I grieve at grievances foregone,
And heavily from woe to woe tell o'er
The sad account of fore-bemoanèd moan,
Which I new pay as if not paid before.
   —But if the while I think on thee, dear friend,
   All losses are restored, and sorrows end.

Sonnet 32

If Thou survive my well-contented day,
When that churl Death my bones with dust shall cover
And shalt by fortune once more re-survey
These poor rude lines of thy deceasèd lover:
Compare them with the bettering of the time,
And though they be outstripped by every pen,
Reserve them for my love, not for their rhyme,
Exceeded by the height of happier men.
O then vouchsafe me but this loving thought—
'Had my friend's muse grown with this growing age,
A dearer birth than this his love had brought,
To march in ranks of better equipage:
   But since he died, and poets better prove,
   Theirs for their style I'll read, his for his love.'

Sonnet 33

Full many a glorious morning have I seen
Flatter the mountain tops with sovereign eye,
Kissing with golden face the meadows green,
Gilding pale streams with heavenly alchemy;
Anon permit the basest clouds to ride
With ugly rack on his celestial face,
And from the forlorn world his visage hide,
Stealing unseen to west with this disgrace:
Even so my sun one early morn did shine
With all-triumphant splendour on my brow;
But out, alack! he was but one hour mine,

The region cloud hath masked him from me now.
    Yet him for this, my love no whit disdaineth;
    Suns of the world may stain, when heaven's sun staineth.

Sonnet 43

When most I wink then do mine eyes best see,
For all the day they view things unrespected,
But when I sleep, in dreams they look on thee,
And darkly bright, are bright in dark directed.
Then thou whose shadow shadows doth make bright
How would thy shadow's form, form happy show,
To the clear day with thy much clearer light,
When to unseeing eyes thy shade shines so!
How would (I say) mine eyes be blessèd made,
By looking on thee in the living day,
When in dead night thy fair imperfect shade,
Through heavy sleep on sightless eyes doth stay!
    All days are nights to see till I see thee,
    And nights bright days when dreams do show thee me.

Sonnet 57

Being your slave, what should I do but tend
Upon the hours and times of your desire?
I have no precious time at all to spend
Nor services to do, till you require:
Nor dare I chide the world-without-end hour
Whilst I, my sovereign, watch the clock for you,
Nor think the bitterness of absence sour
When you have bid your servant once adieu:
Nor dare I question with my jealous thought
Where you may be, or your affairs suppose,
But, like a sad slave, stay and think of nought
Save, where you are, how happy you make those;—
    So true a fool is Love, that in your will
    Though you do anything, he thinks no ill.

Sonnet 60

Like as the waves make towards the pebbled shore,
So do our minutes hasten to their end;
Each changing place with that which goes before,

In sequent toil all forwards do contend.
Nativity, once in the main of light,
Crawls to maturity, wherewith being crowned,
Crooked eclipses 'gainst his glory fight,
And Time that gave, doth now his gift confound.
Time doth transfix the flourish set on youth,
And delves the parallels in beauty's brow;
Feeds on the rarities of nature's truth,
And nothing stands but for his scythe to mow;—
    And yet, to times in hope, my verse shall stand
    Praising thy worth, despite his cruel hand.

Sonnet 64

When I have seen by Time's fell hand defaced
The rich-proud cost of outworn buried age,
When sometime lofty towers I see down-rased,
And brass eternal slave to mortal rage.
When I have seen the hungry ocean gain
Advantage on the kingdom of the shore,
And the firm soil win of the watery main,
Increasing store with loss, and loss with store.
When I have seen such interchange of State,
Or state itself confounded, to decay,
Ruin hath taught me thus to ruminate
That Time will come and take my love away.
    This thought is as a death which cannot choose
    But weep to have, that which it fears to lose.

Sonnet 65

Since brass, nor stone, nor earth, nor boundless sea,
But sad mortality o'ersways their power,
How with this rage shall beauty hold a plea,
Whose action is no stronger than a flower?
O how shall summer's honey breath hold out,
Against the wrackful siege of battering days,
When rocks impregnable are not so stout,
Nor gates of steel so strong but time decays?
O fearful meditation, where alack,
Shall Time's best jewel from Time's chest lie hid?
Or what strong hand can hold his swift foot back,

Or who his spoil of beauty can forbid?
O none, unless this miracle have might,
That in black ink my love may still shine bright.

Sonnet 66

Tired with all these for restful death I cry:
As, to behold desert a beggar born,
And needy nothing trimmed in jollity,
And purest faith unhappily forsworn,
And gilded honour shamefully misplaced,
And maiden virtue rudely strumpeted,
And right perfection wrongfully disgraced,
And strength by limping sway disablèd
And art made tongue-tied by authority,
And folly, doctor-like, controlling skill,
And simple truth miscalled simplicity,
And captive Good attending captain Ill:—
Tired with all these, from these would I be gone,
Save that to die, I leave my love alone.

Sonnet 71

No longer mourn for me when I am dead,
Than you shall hear the surly sullen bell
Give warning to the world that I am fled
From this vile world with vilest worms to dwell:
Nay if you read this line, remember not,
The hand that writ it, for I love you so,
That I in your sweet thoughts would be forgot,
If thinking on me then should make you woe.
O if (I say) you look upon this verse,
When I (perhaps) compounded am with clay,
Do not so much as my poor name rehearse;
But let your love even with my life decay.
Lest the wise world should look into your moan,
And mock you with me after I am gone.

Sonnet 73

That time of year thou may'st in me behold
When yellow leaves, or none, or few, do hang
Upon those boughs which shake against the cold,

Bare ruined choirs, where late the sweet birds sang.
In me thou seest the twilight of such day
As after sunset fadeth in the west,
Which by-and-by black night doth take away,
Death's second self, that seals up all in rest:
In me thou seest the glowing of such fire
That on the ashes of his youth doth lie,
As the death-bed whereon it must expire,
Consumed with that which it was nourished by.
  This thou perceiv'st, which makes thy love more strong,
  To love that well which thou must leave ere long.

Sonnet 87

Farewell! thou art too dear for my possessing,
And like enough thou know'st thy estimate:
The charter of thy worth gives thee releasing;
My bonds in thee are all determinate.
For how do I hold thee but by thy granting?
And for that riches where is my deserving?
The cause of this fair gift in me is wanting,
And so my patent back again is swerving.
Thyself thou gav'st, thy own worth then not knowing,
Or me, to whom thou gav'st it, else mistaking;
So thy great gift, upon misprision growing,
Comes home again, on better judgement making.
  Thus have I had thee as a dream doth flatter,
  In sleep, a king; but waking, no such matter.

Sonnet 94

They that have power to hurt, and will do none,
That do not do the thing they most do show,
Who, moving others, are themselves as stone,
Unmovèd, cold, and to temptation slow—
They rightly do inherit heaven's graces,
And husband nature's riches from expense;
They are the lords and owners of their faces,
Others, but stewards of their excellence.
The summer's flower is to the summer sweet
Though to itself, it only live and die;
But if that flower with base infection meet,

The basest weed outbraves his dignity:
>   For sweetest things turn sourest by their deeds;
>   Lilies that fester, smell far worse than weeds.

Sonnet 104

To me, fair friend, you never can be old,
For as you were when first your eye I eyed,
Such seems your beauty still: three winters cold,
Have from the forests shook three summers' pride,
Three beauteous springs to yellow autumn turned,
In process of the seasons have I seen,
Three April perfumes in three hot Junes burned,
Since first I saw you fresh which yet are green.
Ah, yet doth beauty like a dial hand,
Steal from his figure, and no pace perceived,
So your sweet hue, which methinks still doth stand
Hath motion, and mine eye may be deceived.
>   For fear of which, hear this thou age unbred,
>   Ere you were born was beauty's summer dead.

Sonnet 106

When in the chronicle of wasted time,
I see descriptions of the fairest wights,
And beauty making beautiful old rhyme
In praise of ladies dead, and lovely knights;
Then in the blazon of sweet beauty's best,
Of hand, of foot, of lip, of eye, of brow,
I see their antique pen would have exprest
Ev'n such a beauty as you master now.
So all their praises are but prophecies
Of this our time, all, you prèfiguring;
And for they looked but with divining eyes,
They had not skill enough your worth to sing!
>   For we, which now behold these present days,
>   Have eyes to wonder, but lack tongues to praise.

Sonnet 116

>   Let me not to the marriage of true minds
>   Admit impediments. Love is not love
>   Which alters when it alteration finds,

Or bends with the remover to remove:—
O no! it is an ever-fixèd mark
That looks on tempests, and is never shaken;
It is the star to every wandering bark
Whose worth's unknown, although his height be taken.
Love's not Time's fool, though rosy lips and cheeks
Within his bending sickle's compass come;
Love alters not with his brief hours and weeks,
But bears it out ev'n to the edge of doom:
    If this be error, and upon me proved,
    I never writ, nor no man ever loved.

Sonnet 129

The expense of spirit in a waste of shame
Is lust in action, and till action, lust
Is perjured, murderous, bloody, full of blame,
Savage, extreme, rude, cruel, not to trust;
Enjoyed no sooner but despisèd straight;
Past reason hunted; and no sooner had,
Past reason hated, as a swallowed bait,
On purpose laid to make the taker mad:
Mad in pursuit, and in possession so;
Had, having, and in quest to have, extreme;
A bliss in proof, and proved, a very woe;
Before, a joy proposed; behind, a dream.
    All this the world well knows; yet none knows well
    To shun the heaven that leads men to this hell.

Sonnet 146

Poor Soul, the centre of my sinful earth,
Fooled by those rebel powers that thee array,
Why dost thou pine within, and suffer dearth,
Painting thy outward walls so costly gay?
Why so large cost, having so short a lease,
Dost thou upon thy fading mansion spend?
Shall worms, inheritors of this excess,
Eat up thy charge? is this thy body's end?
Then, Soul, live thou upon thy servant's loss,
And let that pine to aggravate thy store;
Buy terms divine in selling hours of dross;

Within be fed, without be rich no more:—
    So shalt thou feed on Death, that feeds on men,
    And Death once dead, there's no more dying then.

Sonnet 148

O me! what eyes hath love put in my head,
Which have no correspondence with true sight,
Or if they have, where is my judgment fled,
That censures falsely what they see aright?
If that be fair whereon my false eyes dote,
What means the world to say it is not so?
If it be not, then love doth well denote,
Love's eye is not so true as all men's: no,
How can it? O how can love's eye be true,
That is so vexed with watching and with tears?
No marvel then though I mistake my view,
The sun itself sees not, till heaven clears.
    O cunning love, with tears thou keep'st me blind,
    Lest eyes well-seeing thy foul faults should find.

PERCY BYSSHE SHELLEY (1792-1822)

To a Skylark

Hail to thee, blithe Spirit!
    Bird thou never wert,
That from heaven, or near it,
    Pourest thy full heart
In profuse strains of unpremeditated art.

Higher still and higher
    From the earth thou springest
Like a cloud of fire;
    The blue deep thou wingest,
And singing still dost soar, and soaring ever singest.

In the golden lightning
    Of the sunken sun,
O'er which clouds are bright'ning,
    Thou dost float and run,
Like an unbodied joy whose race is just begun.

The pale purple even
    Melts around thy flight;
Like a star of heaven,
    In the broad daylight
Thou art unseen, but yet I hear thy shrill delight:

Keen as are the arrows
    Of that silver sphere,
Whose intense lamp narrows
    In the white dawn clear
Until we hardly see—we feel that it is there.

All the earth and air
    With thy voice is loud,
As, when night is bare,
    From one lonely cloud
The moon rains out her beams, and heaven is overflowed.

What thou art we know not;
    What is most like thee?
From rainbow clouds there flow not
    Drops so bright to see
As from thy presence showers a rain of melody.

Like a poet hidden
    In the light of thought,
Singing hymns unbidden,
    Till the world is wrought
To sympathy with hopes and fears it heeded not:

Like a high-born maiden
    In a palace-tower,
Soothing her love-laden
    Soul in secret hour
With music sweet as love, which overflows her bower:

Like a glow-worm golden
    In a dell of dew,
Scattering unbeholden
    Its aërial hue
Among the flowers and grass, which screen it from the view:

Like a rose embowered
    In its own green leaves,
By warm winds deflowered,
    Till the scent it gives
Makes faint with too much sweet those heavy-wingèd thieves.

Sound of vernal showers
    On the twinkling grass,
Rain-awakened flowers,
    All that ever was
Joyous, and clear, and fresh, thy music doth surpass.

Teach us, sprite or bird,
    What sweet thoughts are thine:
I have never heard
    Praise of love or wine
That panted forth a flood of rapture so divine.

Chorus hymeneal,
    Or triumphal chaunt,
Matched with thine, would be all
    But an empty vaunt—
A thing wherein we feel there is some hidden want.

What objects are the fountains
    Of thy happy strain?
What fields, or waves, or mountains?
    What shapes of sky or plain?
What love of thine own kind? what ignorance of pain?

With thy clear keen joyance
    Languor cannot be:
Shadow of annoyance
    Never came near thee:
Thou lovest, but ne'er knew love's sad satiety.

Waking or asleep,
    Thou of death must deem
Things more true and deep
    Than we mortals dream,
Or how could thy notes flow in such a crystal stream?

We look before and after,
    And pine for what is not:
Our sincerest laughter
    With some pain is fraught;
Our sweetest songs are those that tell of saddest thought.

Yet if we could scorn
    Hate, and pride, and fear;
If we were things born
    Not to shed a tear,
I know not how thy joy we ever should come near.

Better than all measures
    Of delightful sound,
Better than all treasures
    That in books are found,
Thy skill to poet were, thou scorner of the ground!

Teach me half the gladness
    That thy brain must know,
Such harmonious madness
    From my lips would flow
The world should listen then, as I am listening now!

To ———

Music, when soft voices die,
Vibrates in the memory—
Odours, when sweet violets sicken,
Live within the sense they quicken.

Rose leaves, when the rose is dead,
Are heaped for the belovèd's bed;
And so thy thoughts, when thou art gone,
Love itself shall slumber on.

Ozymandias

I met a traveller from an antique land
Who said: Two vast and trunkless legs of stone
Stand in the desert. Near them, on the sand,

Half sunk, a shattered visage lies, whose frown
And wrinkled lip and sneer of cold command,
Tell that its sculptor well those passions read,
Which yet survive stamped on these lifeless things,
The hand that mocked them, and the heart that fed;
And on the pedestal these words appear:
'My name is Ozymandias, King of Kings:
Look on my works, ye Mighty, and despair!'
Nothing beside remains. Round the decay
Of that colossal wreck, boundless and bare
The lone and level sands stretch far away.

The Moon

1

Art thou pale for weariness
Of climbing heaven, and gazing on the earth,
Wandering companionless
Among the stars that have a different birth,—
And ever-changing, like a joyless eye
That finds no object worth its constancy?

2

And like a dying lady, lean and pale,
Who totters forth, wrapped in a gauzy veil,
Out of her chamber, led by the insane
And feeble wanderings of her fading brain,
The moon arose up in the murky East,
A white and shapeless mass—

Ode to the West Wind

1

O Wild West Wind, thou breath of Autumn's being,
Thou from whose unseen presence the leaves dead
Are driven, like ghosts from an enchanter fleeing,

Yellow, and black, and pale, and hectic red,
Pestilence-stricken multitudes! O thou
Who chariotest to their dark wintry bed

The wingèd seeds, where they lie cold and low,
Each like a corpse within its grave, until
Thine azure sister of the Spring shall blow

Her clarion o'er the dreaming earth, and fill
(Driving sweet buds like flocks to feed in air)
With living hues and odours plain and hill:

Wild Spirit, which art moving everywhere;
Destroyer and preserver; hear, oh hear!

2

Thou on whose stream, 'mid the steep sky's commotion,
Loose clouds like earth's decaying leaves are shed,
Shook from the tangled boughs of Heaven and Ocean,

Angels of rain and lightning; there are spread
On the blue surface of thine aery surge,
Like the bright hair uplifted from the head

Of some fierce Maenad, even from the dim verge
Of the horizon to the zenith's height,
The locks of the approaching storm. Thou dirge

Of the dying year, to which this closing night
Will be the dome of a vast sepulchre,
Vaulted with all thy congregated might

Of vapours, from whose solid atmosphere
Black rain, and fire, and hail, will burst: oh hear!

3

Thou who didst waken from his summer dreams
The blue Mediterranean, where he lay,
Lulled by the coil of his crystàlline streams,

Beside a pumice isle in Baiae's bay,
And saw in sleep old palaces and towers
Quivering within the wave's intenser day,

All overgrown with azure moss, and flowers
So sweet, the sense faints picturing them! Thou
For whose path the Atlantic's level powers

Cleave themselves into chasms, while far below
The sea-blooms and the oozy woods which wear
The sapless foliage of the ocean, know

Thy voice, and suddenly grow gray with fear,
And tremble and despoil themselves: oh, hear!

4

If I were a dead leaf thou mightest bear;
If I were a swift cloud to fly with thee;
A wave to pant beneath thy power, and share

The impulse of thy strength, only less free
Than thou, O uncontrollable! If even
I were as in my boyhood, and could be

The comrade of thy wanderings over Heaven,
As then, when to outstrip thy skyey speed
Scarce seemed a vision; I would ne'er have striven

As thus with thee in prayer in my sore need.
Oh, lift me as a wave, a leaf, a cloud!
I fall upon the thorns of life! I bleed!

A heavy weight of hours has chained and bowed
One too like thee: tameless, and swift, and proud.

5

Make me thy lyre, even as the forest is:
What if my leaves are falling like its own!
The tumult of thy mighty harmonies

Will take from both a deep autumnal tone,
Sweet though in sadness. Be thou, Spirit fierce,
My spirit! Be thou me, impetuous one!

Drive my dead thoughts over the universe
Like withered leaves to quicken a new birth!
And, by the incantation of this verse,

Scatter, as from an unextinguished hearth
Ashes and sparks, my words among mankind!
Be through my lips to unawakened earth

The trumpet of a prophecy! O Wind,
If Winter comes, can Spring be far behind?

SIR PHILIP SIDNEY (1554–1586)

Sonnet from 'Astrophel and Stella'

With how sad steps, O moon, thou climb'st the skies;
How silently and with how wan a face.
What! May it be that even in heav'nly place
That busy archer his sharp arrows tries?
Sure, if that long-with-love acquainted eyes
Can judge of love, thou feel'st a lover's case;
I read it in thy looks, thy languished grace,
To me, that feel the like, thy state decries.

Then even of fellowship, O moon, tell me:
Is constant love deemed there but want of wit?
Are beauties there as proud as here they be?
Do they above love to be loved, and yet
Those lovers scorn whom that love doth possess?
Do they call virtue there ungratefulness?

CHRISTOPHER SMART (1722–1771)

from 'Jubilate Agno'

For I will consider my Cat Jeoffry.
For he is the servant of the Living God duly and daily serving him.
For at the first glance of the glory of God in the East he worships in his
way.
For this is done by wreathing his body seven times round with elegant
quickness.
For then he leaps up to catch the musk, which is the blessing of God
upon his prayer.
For he rolls upon prank to work it in.
For having done duty and received blessing he begins to consider
himself.
For this he performs in ten degrees.
For first he looks upon his forepaws to see if they are clean.
For secondly he kicks up behind to clear away there.
For thirdly he works it upon stretch with the forepaws extended.
For fourthly he sharpens his paws by wood.

For fifthly he washes himself.

For sixthly he rolls upon wash.

For seventhly he fleas himself, that he may not be interrupted upon the beat.

For eighthly he rubs himself against a post.

For ninthly he looks up for his instructions.

For tenthly he goes in quest of food.

For having consider'd God and himself he will consider his neighbour.

For if he meets another cat he will kiss her in kindness.

For when he takes his prey he plays with it to give it a chance.

For one mouse in seven escapes by his dallying.

For when his day's work is done his business more properly begins.

For he keeps the Lord's watch in the night against the adversary.

For he counteracts the powers of darkness by his electrical skin and glaring eyes.

For he counteracts the Devil, who is death, by brisking about the life.

For in his morning orisons he loves the sun and the sun loves him.

For he is of the tribe of Tiger.

For the Cherub Cat is a term of the Angel Tiger.

For he has the subtlety and hissing of a serpent, which in goodness he suppresses.

For he will not do destruction if he is well-fed, neither will he spit without provocation.

For he purrs in thankfulness, when God tells him he's a good Cat.

For he is an instrument for the children to learn benevolence upon.

For every house is incomplete without him and a blessing is lacking in the spirit.

For the Lord commanded Moses concerning the cats at the departure of the Children of Israel from Egypt.

For every family had one cat at least in the bag.

For the English Cats are the best in Europe.

For he is the cleanest in the use of his forepaws of any quadruped.

For the dexterity of his defence is an instance of the love of God to him exceedingly.

For he is the quickest to his mark of any creature.

For he is tenacious of his point.

For he is a mixture of gravity and waggery.

For he knows that God is his Saviour.

For there is nothing sweeter than his peace when at rest.

For there is nothing brisker than his life when in motion.

For he is of the Lord's poor and so indeed is he called by benevolence perpetually—Poor Jeoffry! poor Jeoffry! the rat has bit thy throat.

For I bless the name of the Lord Jesus that Jeoffry is better.

For the divine spirit comes about his body to sustain it in complete cat.

For his tongue is exceeding pure so that it has in purity what it wants in music.

For he is docile and can learn certain things.

For he can set up with gravity which is patience upon approbation.

For he can fetch and carry, which is patience in employment.

For he can jump over a stick which is patience upon proof positive.

For he can spraggle upon waggle at the word of command.

For he can jump from an eminence into his master's bosom.

For he can catch the cork and toss it again.

For he is hated by the hypocrite and miser.

For the former is afraid of detection.

For the latter refuses the charge.

For he camels his back to bear the first notion of business.

For he is good to think on, if a man would express himself neatly.

For he made a great figure in Egypt for his signal services.

For he killed the Ichneumon-rat very pernicious by land.

For his ears are so acute that they sting again.

For from this proceeds the passing quickness of his attention.

For by stroking of him I have found out electricity.

For I have perceived God's light about him both wax and fire.

For the Electrical fire is the spiritual substance, which God sends from heaven to sustain the bodies both of man and beast.

For God has blessed him in the variety of his movements.

For, tho he cannot fly, he is an excellent clamberer.

For his motions upon the face of the earth are more than any other quadruped.

For he can tread to all the measures upon the music.

For he can swim for life.

For he can creep.

. . .

For I am under the same accusation with my Saviour
For they said, he is besides himself.
For the officers of the peace are at variance with me
And the watchman smites me with his staff.

For Silly Fellow! Silly Fellow! is against me
And belongeth neither to me nor to my family.
For I am in twelve Hardships,
But he that was born of a virgin shall deliver me out of all.

Stevie Smith (1902–1971)

'What is she writing? Perhaps it will be good'

What is she writing? Perhaps it will be good,
The young girl laughs: 'I am in love.'
But the older girl is serious: 'Not now, perhaps later.'
Still the young girl teases: 'What's the matter?
To lose everything! A waste of time!'
But now the older one is quite silent,
Writing, writing, and perhaps it will be good.
Really neither girl is a fool.

It Filled my Heart with Love

(When I hold in my hand a soft and crushable animal, and feel the fur beat for fear and the soft feather, I cannot feel unhappy.)

In his fur the animal rode, and in his fur he strove,
And oh it filled my heart my heart, it filled my heart with love.

Not Waving but Drowning

Nobody heard him, the dead man,
But still he lay moaning:
I was much further out than you thought
And not waving but drowning.

Poor chap, he always loved larking
And now he's dead
It must have been too cold for him his heart gave way,
They said.

Oh, no no no, it was too cold always
(Still the dead one lay moaning)
I was much too far out all my life
And not waving but drowning.

The Celts

I think of the Celts as rather a whining lady
Who was beautiful once but is not so much so now
She is not very loving, but there is one thing she loves
It is her grievance which she hugs and takes out walking.

The Celtic lady likes fighting very much for freedom
But when she has got it she is a proper tyrant
Nobody likes her much when she is governing.

The Celtic lady is not very widely popular
But the English love her oh they love her very much
Especially when the Celtic lady is Irish they love her
Which is odd as she hates them then more than anyone else,
When she's Welsh the English stupidly associate her chiefly
With national hats, eisteddfods and Old Age Pensions.
(They don't think of her at all when she is Scotch, it is rather a problem.)

Oh the Celtic lady when she's Irish is the one for me
Oh she is so witty and wild, my word witty,
And flashing and spiteful this Celtic lady we love
All the same she is not so beautiful as she was.

CHARLES HAMILTON SORLEY (1895–1915)

The Song of the Ungirt Runners

We swing ungirded hips,
And lightened are our eyes,
The rain is on our lips,
We do not run for prize.
We know not whom we trust
Nor whitherward we fare,
But we run because we must
   Through the great wide air.

The waters of the seas
Are troubled as by storm.
The tempest strips the trees

And does not leave them warm.
Does the tearing tempest pause?
Do the tree-tops ask it why?
So we run without a cause
  'Neath the big bare sky.

The rain is on our lips,
We do not run for prize.
But the storm the water whips
And the wave howls to the skies.
The winds arise and strike it
And scatter it like sand,
And we run because we like it
  Through the broad bright land.

'When you see millions of the mouthless dead'

When you see millions of the mouthless dead
Across your dreams in pale battalions go,
Say not soft things as other men have said,
That you'll remember. For you need not so.
Give them not praise. For, deaf, how should they know
It is not curses heaped on each gashed head?
Nor tears. Their blind eyes see not your tears flow.
Nor honour. It is easy to be dead.
Say only this, 'They are dead.' Then add thereto,
'Yet many a better one has died before.'
Then, scanning all the o'ercrowded mass, should you
Perceive one face that you loved heretofore,
It is a spook. None wears the face you knew
Great death has made all his for evermore.

WILLIAM SOUTAR (1898–1943)

The Halted Moment

Wha hasna turn'd inby a sunny street
And fund alang its length nae folk were there;

And heard his step fa' steadily and clear
Nor wauken ocht but schedows at his feet.[1]
Shuther to shuther in the reemlin heat[2]
The houses seem'd to hearken and to stare;
But a' were doverin whaur they stude and were[3]
Like wa's ayont the echo o' time's beat.
Wha hasna thocht whan atween stanes sae still,
That had been biggit up for busyness,[4]
He has come wanderin into a place
Lost, and forgotten, and unchangeable;
And thocht the far-off traffic sounds to be
The weary waters o' mortality.

The Tryst

O luely, luely cam she in,[5]
    And luely she lay doun:
I kent her be her caller lips[6]
    And her breists sae sma' and roun'.

A' thru the nicht we spak nae word
    Nor sinder'd bane frae bane:[7]
A' thru the nicht I heard her he'rt
    Gang soundin' wi' my ain.

It was about the waukrife hour[8]
    Whan cocks begin to craw
That she smool'd saftly thru the mirk[9]
    Afore the day wud daw.

Sae luely, luely, cam she in,
    Sae luely was she gaen;
And wi' her a' my simmer days
    Like they had never been.

---

[1] wauken ocht = woken anything. [2] shuther = shoulder; reemlin = fearful.
[3] doverin = dozing. [4] biggit = built. [5] luely = quietly. [6] caller = cold.
[7] sinder'd = sundered. [8] waukrife = wakeful. [9] smool'd = slipped away; mirk = darkness.

Who are These Children?

With easy hands upon the rein,
And hounds at their horses' feet,
The ladies and the gentlemen
Ride through the village street.

Brightness of blood upon the coats
And on the women's lips
Brightness of silver at the throats
And on the hunting whips.

Is there a day more calm, more green
Under this morning hour;
A scene more alien than this scene
Within a world at war?

Who are these children gathered here
Out of the fire and smoke
That with remembering faces stare
Upon the foxing folk?

ROBERT SOUTHEY (1774–1843)

After Blenheim

It was a summer evening,
    Old Kaspar's work was done,
And he before his cottage door
    Was sitting in the sun;
And by him sported on the green
His little grandchild Wilhelmine.

She saw her brother Peterkin
    Roll something large and round
Which he beside the rivulet
    In playing there had found;
He came to ask what he had found
That was so large and smooth and round.

Old Kaspar took it from the boy,
    Who stood expectant by;
And then the old man shook his head,
    And with a natural sigh,
''Tis some poor fellow's skull,' said he,
'Who fell in the great victory.

'I find them in the garden,
    For there's many here about;
And often, when I go to plough,
    The ploughshare turns them out;
For many thousand men,' said he,
'Were slain in that great victory.'

'Now tell us what 'twas all about,'
    Young Peterkin he cries;
And little Wilhelmine looks up
    With wonder-waiting eyes;
'Now tell us all about the war,
And what they fought each other for.'

'It was the English,' Kaspar cried,
    'Who put the French to rout;
But what they fought each other for
    I could not well make out.
But everybody said,' quoth he,
'That 'twas a famous victory.

'My father lived at Blenheim then,
    Yon little stream hard by;
They burnt his dwelling to the ground,
    And he was forced to fly:
So with his wife and child he fled,
Nor had he where to rest his head.

'With fire and sword the country round
    Was wasted far and wide,
And many a childing mother then
    And newborn baby died:
But things like that, you know, must be
At every famous victory.

'They say it was a shocking sight
    After the field was won;
For many thousand bodies here
    Lay rotting in the sun;
But things like that, you know, must be
After a famous victory.

'Great praise the Duke of Marlb'ro' won,
    And our good Prince Eugene.'
'Why, 'twas a very wicked thing!'
    Said little Wilhelmine.
'Nay . . . nay . . . my little girl,' quoth he,
'It was a famous victory.

'And everybody praised the Duke
    Who this great fight did win.'
'But what good came of it at last?'
    Quoth little Peterkin.
'Why that I cannot tell,' said he,
'But 'twas a famous victory.'

ROBERT SOUTHWELL (1561–1595)

The Burning Babe

As I in hoary winter's night stood shivering in the snow,
Surprised I was with sudden heat which made my heart to glow;
And lifting up a fearful eye to view what fire was near,
A pretty babe all burning bright did in the air appear;
Who, scorchèd with excessive heat, such floods of tears did shed
As though his floods should quench his flames which with his tears were fed.
'Alas!' quoth he, 'but newly born, in fiery heats I fry,
Yet none approach to warm their hearts or feel my fire but I!
My faultless breast the furnace is; the fuel wounding thorns;
Love is the fire, and sighs the smoke; the ashes shame and scorns;
The fuel justice layeth on, and mercy blows the coals;
The metal in this furnace wrought are men's defilèd souls,
For which, as now on fire I am to work them to their good;
So will I melt into a bath to wash them in my blood.'
With this he vanished out of sight and swiftly shrunk away,—
And straight I called unto mind that it was Christmas Day.

EDMUND SPENSER (1552–1599)

Sonnets from 'Amoretti'

Sonnet 3

The sovereign beauty which I do admire,
Witness the world how worthy to be praised:
The light whereof hath kindled heavenly fire
In my frail spirit, by her from baseness raised;
That being now with her huge brightness dazed,
Base thing I can no more endure to view;
But looking still on her, I stand amazed
At wondrous sight of so celestial hue.
So when my tongue would speak her praises due,
It stopped is with thought's astonishment:
And when my pen would write her titles true,
It ravished is with fancy's wonderment:
 Yet in my heart I then both speak and write
 The wonder that my wit cannot endite.

Sonnet 22

This holy season, fit to fast and pray,
Men to devotion ought to be inclined:
Therefore I likewise on so holy day,
For my sweet saint some service fit will find.
Her temple fair is built within my mind,
In which her glorious image placèd is,
On which my thoughts do day and night attend,
Like sacred priests that never think amiss.
There I to her as th' author of my bliss,
Will build an altar to appease her ire:
And on the same my heart will sacrifice,
Burning in flames of pure and chaste desire:
 The which vouchsafe, O goddess, to accept,
 Amongst thy dearest relics to be kept.

Sonnet 67

 Like as a huntsman after weary chase,
 Seeing the game from him escaped away,

Sits down to rest him in some shady place,
With panting hounds beguilèd of their prey:
So, after long pursuit and vain assay,
When I all weary had the chase forsook,
The gentle deer returned the self-same way,
Thinking to quench her thirst at the next brook.
There she, beholding me with milder look,
Sought not to fly, but fearless still did bide,
Till I in hand her yet half trembling took,
And with her own goodwill her firmly tied.
    Strange thing, me seemed, to see a beast so wild
    So goodly won, with her own will beguiled.

Sonnet 74

Most happy letters, framed by skilful trade,
With which that happy name was first designed:
The which three times thrice happy hath me made,
With gifts of body, fortune, and of mind.
The first my being to me gave by kind,
From mother's womb derived by due descent,
The second is my sovereign Queen most kind,
That honour and large richesse to me lent.
The third my love, my life's last ornament,
By whom my spirit out of dust was raisèd:
To speak her praise and glory excellent,
Of all alive most worthy to be praisèd.
    Ye three Elizabeths for ever live,
    That three such graces did unto me give.

Sonnet 75

One day I wrote her name upon the strand,
But came the waves and washed it away:
Again I wrote it with a second hand,
But came the tide, and made my pains his prey.
'Vain man,' said she, 'that dost in vain assay,
A mortal thing so to immortalise;
For I myself shall like to this decay,
And eke my name be wiped out likewise.'
'Not so,' (quod I) 'let baser things devise
To die in dust, but you shall live by fame:

My verse your virtues rare shall eternise,
And in the heavens write your glorious name:
>   Where, whenas death shall all the world subdue,
>   Our love shall live, and later life renew.'

ROBERT LOUIS STEVENSON (1850–1894)

Requiem

>   Under the wide and starry sky,
>   Dig the grave and let me lie.
>   Glad did I live and Gladly die,
>   And I laid me down with a will.

>   This be the verse you grave for me:
>   *Here he lies where he longed to be;*
>   *Home is the sailor, home from sea,*
>   *And the hunter home from the hill.*

from 'A Child's Garden of Verses'

At the Seaside

>   When I was down beside the sea
>   A wooden spade they gave to me
>   To dig the sandy shore.
>   My holes were empty like a cup.
>   In every hole the sea came up,
>   Till it could come no more.

From a Railway Carriage

Faster than fairies, faster than witches,
Bridges and houses, hedges and ditches;
And charging along like troops in a battle,
All through the meadows the horses and cattle:
All of the sights of the hill and the plain
Fly as thick as driving rain;
And ever again, in the wink of an eye,
Painted stations whistle by.

Here is a child who clambers and scrambles,
All by himself and gathering brambles;
Here is a tramp who stands and gazes;
And here is the green for stringing the daisies!
Here is a cart run away in the road
Lumping along with man and load;
And here is a mill and there is a river:
Each a glimpse and gone for ever!

The Land of Storybooks

At evening when the lamp is lit,
Around the fire my parents sit;
They sit at home and talk and sing,
And do not play at anything.

Now, with my little gun, I crawl
All in the dark along the wall,
And follow round the forest track
Away behind the sofa back.

There, in the night, where none can spy,
All in my hunter's camp I lie,
And play at books that I have read
Till it is time to go to bed.

These are the hills, these are the woods,
These are my starry solitudes;
And there the river by whose brink
The roaring lions come to drink.

I see the others far away
As if in firelit camp they lay,
And I, like to an Indian scout,
Around their party prowled about.

So, when my nurse comes in for me,
Home I return across the sea,
And go to bed with backward looks
At my dear land of Storybooks.

To Any Reader

As from the house your mother sees
You playing round the garden trees,
So you may see, if you will look
Through the windows of this book,
Another child, far, far away,
And in another garden, play.
But do not think you can at all,
By knocking on the window, call
That child to hear you. He intent
Is all on his play-business bent.
He does not hear; he will not look,
Nor yet be lured out of this book.
For, long ago, the truth to say,
He has grown up and gone away,
And it is but a child of air
That lingers in the garden there.

JOHN SUCKLING (1609–1642)

A Constant Lover

Out upon it, I have loved
    Three whole days together!
And am like to love three more,
    If it prove fair weather.

Time shall moult away his wings
    Ere he shall discover
In the whole wide world again
    Such a constant lover.

But the spite on't is, no praise
    Is due at all to me:
Love with me had made no stays,
    Had it any been but she.

Had it any been but she,
    And that very face,
There had been at least ere this
    A dozen dozen in her place.

from 'A Ballad upon a Wedding'

I tell thee, Dick, where I have been,
Where I the rarest things have seen,
   Oh, things beyond compare!
Such sights again cannot be found
In any place on English ground,
   Be it at wake or fair.

At Charing Cross, hard by the way
Where we (thou know'st) do sell our hay,
   There is a house with stairs;
And there did I see coming down
Such folk as are not in our town
   Forty at least, in pairs.

Amongst the rest, one pestilent fine
(His beard no bigger, though, than thine!)
   Walked on before the rest.
Our landlord looks like nothing to him;
The king (God bless him!), 'twould undo him,
   Should he go still so dressed.

. . .

But wot you what? The youth was going
To make an end of all his wooing;
   The Parson for him stayed.
Yet, by his leave, for all his haste,
He did not so much wish all passed,
   Perchance, as did the maid.

The maid (and thereby hangs a tale)
For such a maid no Whitson ale
   Could ever yet produce:
No grape that's kindly ripe could be
So round, so plump, so soft, as she;
   Nor half so full of juice!

Her feet beneath her petticoat,
Like little mice stole in and out,
   As if they feared the light:
But oh! she dances such a way,

No sun upon an Easter-day
 Is half so fine a sight.

Her finger was so small, the ring
Would not stay on, which they did bring,
 It was too wide a peck:
And to say truth, for out it must,
It looked like the great collar, just,
 About our young colt's neck.

. . .

Her cheeks so rare a white was on,
No daisy makes comparison;
 Who sees them is undone;
For streaks of red were mingled there,
Such as are on a Catherine pear,
 The side that's next the sun.

Her lips were red, and one was thin,
Compared to that was next her chin
 (Some bee had stung it newly)
But, Dick, her eyes so guard her face;
I durst no more upon them gaze
 Than on the sun in July.

Her mouth so small, when she does speak,
Thould'st swear her teeth her words did break,
 That they might passage get;
But she so handled still the matter,
They came as good as ours, or better,
 And are not spent a whit!

. . .

Just in the nick, the cook knocked thrice,
And all the waiters, in a trice,
 His summons did obey.
Each serving-man, with dish in hand,
Marched boldly up like our trained band,
 Presented, and away!

The business of the kitchen's great,
For it is fit that men should eat;
 Nor was it there denied.

Passion o' me! how I run on;
There's that that would be thought upon,
   I trow, besides the bride:

When all the meat was on the table
What man of knife or teeth was able
   To stay to be entreated?
And this the very reason was,
Before the parson could say grace
   The company was seated.

Now hats fly off; and youths carouse:
Healths first go round, and then the house.
   The bride's came thick and thick.
And when 'twas named another's health,
Perhaps he made it hers by stealth.
   (And who could help it, Dick?)

O' the' sudden, up they rise and dance:
Then sit again and sigh and glance,
   Then dance again and kiss.
Thus several ways the time did pass;
Whilst every woman wished her place,
   And every man wished his!

JONATHAN SWIFT (1667–1745)

from 'Verses on the Dean Swift, DSPD'

The time is not remote, when I
Must by the course of nature die;
When, I foresee, my special friends
Will try to find their private ends:
Tho' 'tis hardly understood
Which way my death can do them good,
Yet thus, methinks, I hear 'em speak:
   'See, how the Dean begins to break!
Poor gentleman, he droops apace!
You plainly find it in his face.
That old vertigo in his head
Will never leave him till he's dead.
Besides, his memory decays:

He recollects not what he says;
He cannot call his friends to mind,
Forgets the place where last he dined;
Plies you with stories o'er and o'er;
He told them fifty times before.
How does he fancy we can sit
To hear his out-of-fashioned wit?
But he takes up with younger folks,
Who for his wine will bear his jokes.
Faith, he must make his stories shorter,
Or change his comrades once a quarter:
 In half the time he talks them round,
There must another set be found.

    'For poetry he's past his prime;
He takes an hour to find a rhyme;
His fire is out, his wit decayed,
His fancy sunk, his Muse a jade.
I'd have him throw away his pen;—
But there's no talking to some men!'
And then their tenderness appears,
By adding largely to my years:
    'He's older than he would be reckoned
And well remembers Charles the Second.'

ALGERNON SWINBURNE (1837–1909)

The Garden of Proserpine

Here, where the world is quiet;
    Here, where all trouble seems
Dead winds' and spent waves' riot
    In doubtful dreams of dreams;
I watch the green field growing
For reaping folk and sowing,
For harvest-time and mowing,
    A sleepy world of streams.

I am tired of tears and laughter,
    And men that laugh and weep;
Of what may come hereafter
    For men that sow to reap;
I am weary of days and hours,

Blown buds of barren flowers,
Desires and dreams and powers
    And everything but sleep.

Here life has death for neighbour,
    And far from eye or ear
Wan waves and wet winds labour,
    Weak ships and spirits steer;
They drive adrift, and whither
They wot not who make thither;
But no such winds blow hither,
    And no such things grow here.

No growth of moor or coppice,
    No heather-flower or vine,
But bloomless buds of poppies
    Green grapes of Proserpine,
Pale beds of blowing rushes,
Where no leaf blooms or blushes
Save this whereout she crushes
    For dead men deadly wine.

Pale, without name or number,
    In fruitless fields of corn,
They bow themselves and slumber
    All night till light is born;
And like a soul belated,
In hell and heaven unmated,
By cloud and mist abated
    Comes out of darkness morn.

Though one were strong as seven,
    He too with death shall dwell,
Nor wake with wings in heaven,
    Nor weep with pains in hell;
Though one were fair as roses,
His beauty clouds and closes;
And well though love reposes,
    In the end it is not well.

Pale, beyond porch and portal,
    Crowned with calm leaves, she stands

Who gathers all things mortal
  With cold immortal hands;
Her languid lips are sweeter
Than love's who fears to greet her,
To men that mix and meet her
  From many times and lands.

She waits for each and other,
  She waits for all men born;
Forgets the earth her mother,
  The life of fruits and corn;
And spring and seed and swallow
Take wing for her and follow
Where summer song rings hollow
  And flowers are put to scorn.

There go the loves that wither,
  The old loves with wearier wings;
And all dead years draw thither,
  And all disastrous things;
Dead dreams of days forsaken,
Blind buds that snows have shaken,
Wild leaves that winds have taken,
  Red strays of ruined springs.

We are not sure of sorrow;
  And joy was never sure;
Today will die tomorrow;
  Time stoops to no man's lure;
And love, grown faint and fretful,
With lips but half regretful
Sighs, and with eyes forgetful
  Weeps that no loves endure.

From too much love of living,
  From hope and fear set free,
We thank with brief thanksgiving
  Whatever gods may be
That no life lives forever;
That dead men rise up never;
That even the weariest river
  Winds somewhere safe to sea.

Then star nor sun shall waken,
    Nor any change of light:
Nor sound of waters shaken,
    Nor any sound or sight:
Nor wintry leaves or vernal,
Nor days nor things diurnal;
Only the sleep eternal
    In an eternal night.

ALFRED, LORD TENNYSON (1809–1892)

Ulysses

It little profits that an idle king,
By this still hearth, among these barren crags,
Matched with an aged wife, I mete and dole
Unequal laws unto a savage race,
That hoard, and sleep, and feed, and know not me.
I cannot rest from travel: I will drink
Life to the lees: all times I have enjoyed
Greatly, have suffered greatly, both with those
That loved me, and alone; on shore, and when
Thro' scudding drifts the rainy Hyades
Vext the dim sea. I am become a name;
For always roaming with a hungry heart
Much have I seen and known: cities of men
And manners, climates, councils, governments,
Myself not least, but honoured of them all;
And drunk delight of battle with my peers,
Far on the ringing plains of windy Troy.
I am a part of all that I have met;
Yet all experience is an arch wherethro'
Gleams that untravelled world whose margin fades
For ever and for ever when I move.
How dull it is to pause, to make an end,
To rust unburnished, not to shine in use!
As tho' to breathe were life! Life piled on life
Were all too little, and of one to me
Little remains; but every hour is saved
From that eternal silence, something more,
A bringer of new things; and vile it were

For some three suns to store and hoard myself,
And this grey spirit yearning in desire
To follow knowledge, like a sinking star,
Beyond the utmost bound of human thought.

    This is my son, mine own Telemachus,
To whom I leave the sceptre and the isle—
Well-loved of me, discerning to fulfil
This labour, by slow prudence to make mild
A rugged people, and thro' soft degrees
Subdue them to the useful and the good.
Most blameless is he, centred in the sphere
Of common duties, decent not to fail
In offices of tenderness, and pay
Meet adoration to my household gods,
When I am gone. He works his work, I mine.

    There lies the port: the vessel puffs her sail:
There gloom the dark, broad seas. My mariners,
Souls that have toiled, and wrought, and thought with me—
That ever with a frolic welcome took
The thunder and the sunshine, and opposed
Free hearts, free foreheads—you and I are old;
Old age hath yet his honour and his toil;
Death closes all: but something ere the end,
Some work of noble note, may yet be done,
Not unbecoming men that strove with Gods.
The lights begin to twinkle from the rocks:
The long day wanes: the slow moon climbs: the deep
Moans round with many voices. Come, my friends,
'Tis not too late to seek a newer world.
Push off, and sitting well in order smite
The sounding furrows; for my purpose holds
To sail beyond the sunset, and the paths
Of all the western stars, until I die.
It may be that the gulfs will wash us down:
It may be we shall touch the Happy Isles,
And see the great Achilles, whom we knew.
Tho' much is taken, much abides; and tho'
We are not now that strength which in old days
Moved earth and heaven; that which we are, we are;
One equal temper of heroic hearts,
Made weak by time and fate, but strong in will
To strive, to seek, to find, and not to yield.

'Break, break, break'

Break, break, break,
    On thy cold grey stones, O Sea!
And I would that my tongue could utter
    The thoughts that arise in me.

O well for the fisherman's boy,
    That he shouts with his sister at play!
O well for the sailor lad,
    That he sings in his boat on the bay!

And the stately ships go on
    To their haven under the hill;
But O for the touch of a vanished hand,
    And the sound of a voice that is still!

Break, break, break,
    At the foot of thy crags, O Sea!
But the tender grace of a day that is dead
    Will never come back to me.

The Eagle

He claps the crag with hookèd hands:
Close to the sun in lonely lands,
Ringed with the azure world, he stands.

The wrinkled sea beneath him crawls;
He watches from his mountain walls,
And like a thunderbolt he falls.

'Tears, idle tears'

Tears, idle tears, I know not what they mean,
Tears from the depth of some divine despair
Rise in the heart, and gather to the eyes,
In looking on the happy Autumn-fields,
And thinking of the days that are no more.

Fresh as the first beam glittering on a sail,
That brings our friends up from the underworld,
Sad as the last which reddens over one
That sinks with all we love below the verge;
So sad, so fresh, the days that are no more.

Blow, Bugle, Blow
(*Song from 'The Princess'*)

The splendour falls on castle walls
    And snowy summits old in story:
The long light shakes across the lakes
    And the wild cataract leaps in glory.
Blow, bugle, blow, set the wild echoes flying,
Blow, bugle; answer, echoes, dying, dying, dying.

O hark, O hear! how thin and clear,
    And thinner, clearer, farther going!
O sweet and far from cliff and scar
    The horns of Elfland faintly blowing!
Blow, let us hear the purple glens replying:
Blow, bugle; answer, echoes, dying, dying, dying.

O love, they die in yon rich sky,
    They faint on hill or field or river;
Our echoes roll from soul to soul,
    And grow for ever and for ever.
Blow, bugle, blow, set the wild echoes flying,
And answer, echoes, answer, dying, dying, dying.

from 'In Memoriam AHH'

Be near me when my light is low,
    When the blood creeps, and the nerves prick
    And tingle; and the heart is sick,
And all the wheels of Being slow.

Be near me when the sensuous frame
    Is racked with pangs that conquer trust;

And Time, a maniac scattering dust,
And Life, a Fury slinging flame.

Be near me when my faith is dry,
And men the flies of latter spring,
That lay their eggs, and sting and sing
And weave their petty cells and die.

Be near me when I fade away,
To point the term of human strife,
And on the low dark verge of life
The twilight of eternal day.

Charge of the Light Brigade

Half a league, half a league,
Half a league onward,
All in the Valley of Death
Rode the six hundred.
'Forward, the Light Brigade!
Charge for the guns!' he said:
Into the valley of Death
Rode the six hundred.

'Forward, the Light Brigade!'
Was there a man dismayed?
Not tho' the soldier knew
Someone had blundered:
Their's not to make reply,
Their's not to reason why,
Their's but to do and die:
Into the valley of Death
Rode the six hundred.

Cannon to right of them,
Cannon to left of them,
Cannon in front of them
Volleyed and thundered;
Stormed at with shot and shell,
Boldly they rode and well,
Into the jaws of Death,

Into the mouth of Hell
    Rode the six hundred.

Flashed all their sabres bare,
Flashed as they turned in air
Sabring the gunners there,
Charging an army, while
    All the world wondered:
Plunged in the battery-smoke
Right thro' the line they broke;
Cossack and Russian
Reeled from the sabre-stroke
    Shattered and sundered.
Then they rode back, but not
    Not the six hundred.

Cannon to right of them,
Cannon to left of them,
Cannon behind them
    Volleyed and thundered;
Stormed at with shot and shell,
While horse and hero fell,
They that had fought so well
Came thro' the jaws of Death,
Back from the mouth of Hell,
All that was left of them,
    Left of six hundred.

When can their glory fade?
O the wild charge they made!
    All the world wondered.
Honour the charge they made!
Honour the Light Brigade,
    Noble six hundred!

Crossing the Bar

Sunset and evening star,
    And one clear call for me!
And may there be no moaning of the bar,
    When I put out to sea,

But such a tide as moving seems asleep,
    Too full for sound and foam,
When that which drew from out the boundless deep
    Turns again home.

Twilight and evening bell,
    And after that the dark!
And may there be no sadness of farewell,
    When I embark;

For though from out our bourne of Time and Place
    The flood may bear me far,
I hope to see my Pilot face to face
    When I have crossed the bar.

W. M. THACKERAY (1811–1863)

The Sorrows of Werther

Werther had a love for Charlotte
    Such as words could never utter;
Would you know how first he met her?
    She was cutting bread and butter.

Charlotte was a married lady,
    And a moral man was Werther,
And for all the wealth of Indies,
    Would do nothing for to hurt her.

So he sighed and pined and ogled.
    And his passion boiled and bubbled,
Till he blew his silly brains out,
    And no more by it was troubled.

Charlotte, having seen his body
    Borne before her on a shutter,
Like a well-conducted person,
    Went on cutting bread and butter.

Dylan Thomas (1914–1953)

'Do not go gentle into that good night'

Do not go gentle into that good night,
Old age should burn and rave at close of day;
Rage, rage against the dying of the light.

Though wise men at their end know dark is right,
Because their words had forked no lightning they
Do not go gentle into that good night.

Good men, the last wave by, crying how bright
Their frail deeds might have danced in a green bay,
Rage, rage against the dying of the light.

Wild men who caught and sang the sun in flight,
And learn, too late, they grieved it on its way,
Do not go gentle into that good night.

Grave men, near death, who see with blinding sight
Blind eyes could blaze like meteors and be gay,
Rage, rage against the dying of the light.

And you, my father, there on the sad height,
Curse, bless me now with your fierce tears, I pray.
Do not go gentle into that good night.
Rage, rage against the dying of the light.

Edward Thomas (1878–1917)

'And you, Helen'

And you, Helen, what should I give you?
So many things I would give you
Had I an infinite great store
Offered me and I stood before
To choose. I would give you youth,

All kinds of loveliness and truth,
A clear eye as good as mine,
Lands, waters, flowers, wine,
As many children as your heart
Might wish for; a far better art
Than mine can be, all you have lost
Upon the travelling waters tossed,
Or given to me. If I could choose
Freely in that great treasure-house
Anything from any shelf,
I would give you back yourself,
And power to discriminate
What you want and want it not too late,
Many fair days free from care
And heart to enjoy both foul and fair;
And myself too, if I could find
Where it lay hidden and it proved kind.

'If I should ever by chance'

If I should ever by chance grow rich
I'll buy Codham, Cockridden, and Childerditch,
Roses, Pyrgo, and Lapwater,
And let them all to my elder daughter.
The rent I shall ask of her will be only
Each year's first violets, white and lonely,
The first primroses and orchises—
She must find them before I do, that is.
But if she finds a blossom on furze
Without rent they shall all for ever be hers,
Codham, Cockridden, and Childerditch,
Roses, Pyrgo, and Lapwater,—
I shall give them all to my elder daughter.

Adlestrop

Yes, I remember Adlestrop—
The name, because one afternoon
Of heat the express-train drew up there
Unwontedly. It was late June.

The steam hissed. Someone cleared his throat.
No one left and no one came
On the bare platform. What I saw
Was Adlestrop—only the name

And willows, willow-herb, and grass,
And meadowsweet, and haycocks dry,
No whit less still and lonely fair
Than the high cloudlets in the sky.

And for that minute a blackbird sang
Close by, and round him, mistier,
Farther and farther, all the birds
Of Oxfordshire and Gloucestershire.

FRANCIS THOMPSON (1859–1907)

from 'The Hound of Heaven'

I fled Him, down the nights and down the days;
   I fled Him, down the arches of the years;
I fled Him, down the labyrinthine ways
   Of my own mind; and in the mist of tears
I hid from Him, and under running laughter.
     Up vistaed hopes I sped;
     And shot, precipitated,
   Adown Titanic glooms of chasmed fears,
From those strong Feet that followed, followed after.
     But with unhurrying chase,
     And unperturbèd pace,
   Deliberate speed, majestic instancy,
     They beat—and a Voice beat
     More instant than the Feet—
'All things betray thee, who betrayest Me.'

At Lord's

It is little I repair to the matches of the Southron folk,
Though my own red roses there may blow;
It is little I repair to the matches of the Southron folk,
Though the red roses crest the caps I know.

For the field is full of shades as I near the shadowy coast,
And a ghostly batsman plays to the bowling of a ghost,
And I look through my tears on a soundless-clapping host
As the run-stealers flicker to and fro,
To and fro:—
Oh my Hornby and my Barlow long ago!

JAMES THOMSON (1834–1882)

Nightmare
(from 'The City of Dreadful Night')

As I came through the desert thus it was,
As I came through the desert: All was black,
In heaven no single star, on earth no track;
A brooding hush without a stir or note,
The air so thick it clotted in my throat;
And thus for hours; then some enormous things
Swooped past with savage cries and clanking wings:
      But I strode on austere;
      No hope could have no fear.

As I came through the desert thus it was,
As I came through the desert: Eyes of fire
Glared at me throbbing with a starved desire;
The hoarse and heavy and carnivorous breath
Was hot upon me from deep jaws of death;
Sharp claws, swift talons, fleshless fingers cold
Plucked at me from the bushes, tried to hold:
      But I strode on austere;
      No hope could have no fear.

As I came through the desert thus it was,
As I came through the desert: Meteors ran
And crossed their javelins on the black sky-span;
The zenith opened to a gulf of flame,
The dreadful thunderbolts jarred earth's fixed frame:
The ground all heaved in waves of fire that surged
And weltered round me sole there unsubmerged:
      Yet I strode on austere;
      No hope could have no fear. . . .

J. R. R. TOLKIEN (1892–1973)

The Road Goes Ever On

(from 'The Lord of the Rings')

The Road goes ever on and on
　　Down from the door where it began.
Now far ahead the Road has gone,
　　And I must follow, if I can,
Pursuing it with eager feet,
　　Until it joins some larger way
Where many paths and errands meet.
　　And whither then? I cannot say.

THOMAS TRAHERNE (1636?–1674)

Eden

A learnèd and a happy ignorance
　　　　Divided me
　　　From all the vanity,
From all the sloth, care, pain, and sorrow that advance
　　The madness and the misery
Of men. No error, no distraction, I
Saw soil the earth, or overcloud the sky.

I knew not that there was a serpent's sting,
　　　　Whose poison, shed
　　　On men, did overspread
The world; nor did I dream of such a thing
　　As sin, in which mankind lay dead.
They all were brisk and living wights to me,
Yea, pure and full of immortality.

Only what Adam in his first estate,
　　　　Did I behold;
　　　Hard silver and dry gold
As yet lay under ground; my blessed fate
　　Was more acquainted with the old

And innocent delights which he did see
In his original simplicity.

Those things which first his Eden did adorn,
         My infancy
      Did crown: simplicity
Was my protection when I first was born.
   Mine eyes those treasures first did see
Which God first made. The first effects of love
My first enjoyments upon earth did prove,

And were so great, and so divine, so pure;
         So fair and sweet,
      So true; when I did meet
Them here at first, they did my soul allure,
   And drew away my infant feet
Quite from the works of men; that I might see
The glorious wonders of the Deity.

Walking

To walk abroad is, not with eyes,
But thoughts, the fields to see and prize;
      Else may the silent feet,
         Like logs of wood,
Move up and down, and see no good,
      Nor joy nor glory meet.

Even carts and wheels their place do change,
But cannot see; though very strange
      The glory that is by:
         Dead puppets may
Move in the bright and glorious day,
      Yet not behold the sky.

And are not men than they more blind,
Who having eyes yet never find
      The bliss in which they move:
         Like statues dead
They up and down are carried,
      Yet never see nor love.

To walk is by a thought to go;
To move in spirit to and fro;
    To mind the good we see;
    To taste the sweet;
Observing all the things we meet
    How choice and rich they be.

To note the beauty of the day,
And golden fields of corn survey;
    Admire each pretty flower
    With its sweet smell;
To praise their Maker, and to tell
    The marks of his great power.

To fly abroad like active bees,
Among the hedges and the trees,
    To cull the dew that lies
    On every blade,
From every blossom; till we lade
    Our minds, as they their thighs.

Observe those rich and glorious things;
The rivers, meadows, woods, and springs,
    The fructifying sun;
    To note from far
The rising of each twinkling star
    For us his race to run.

A little child these well perceives,
Who, tumbling in green grass and leaves,
    May rich as kings be thought.
    But there's a sight
Which perfect manhood may delight,
    To which we shall be brought.

While in those pleasant paths we talk,
'Tis that towards which at last we walk;
    For we may by degrees
    Wisely proceed
Pleasures of love and praise to heed,
    From viewing herbs and trees.

Measure

All music, sauces, feasts, delights, and pleasures,
Games, dancing, arts, consist in governed measures;
Much more do words and passions of the mind
In temperance their sacred beauty find.

HENRY VAUGHAN (1621-1695)

The World

I saw Eternity the other night,
Like a great ring of pure and endless light,
    All calm, as it was bright;
And round beneath it, Time in hours, days, years,
    Driven by the spheres
Like a vast shadow moved; in which the world
    And all her train were hurled.

The doting lover in his quaintest strain
    Did there complain;
Near him, his lute, his fancy, and his flights,
    Wit's sour delights,
With gloves, and knots, the silly snares of pleasure,
    Yet his dear treasure,
All scattered lay, while he his eyes did pour
    Upon a flower.

The darksome statesman, hung with weights and woe,
Like a thick midnight-fog, moved there so slow,
    He did not stay, nor go;
Condemning thoughts—like sad eclipses—scowl
    Upon his soul,
And clouds of crying witnesses without
    Pursued him with one shout.
Yet digged the mole, and lest his ways be found,
    Worked under ground,
Where he did clutch his prey; (But one did see
    That policy;)
Churches and altars fed him; perjuries
    Were gnats and flies;

It rained about him blood and tears, but he
    Drank them as free.

The fearful miser on a heap of rust
Sate pining all his life there, did scarce trust
    His own hands with the dust,
Yet would not place one piece above, but lives
    In fear of thieves;
Thousands there were as frantic as himself
    And hugged each one his pelf,
The downright epicure placed heaven in sense
    And scorned pretence,
While others, slipped into a wide excess,
    Said little less;
The weaker sort slight, trivial wares enslave,
    Who think them brave;
And poor, despisèd Truth sate counting by
    Their victory.

Yet some, who all this while did weep and sing,
And sing, and weep, soared up into the Ring;
    But most would use no wing.
O fools (said I) thus to prefer dark night
    Before true light!
To live in grots and caves, and hate the day
    Because it shows the way,
The way, which from this dead and dark abode
    Leads up to God,
A way where you might tread the sun, and be
    More bright than he.
But as I did their madness so discuss,
    One whispered thus,
'This Ring the Bridegroom did for none provide,
    But for his bride.'

'They are all gone into the world of light'

They are all gone into the world of light!
    And I alone sit lingering here;
Their very memory is fair and bright,
    And my sad thoughts doth clear.

It glows and glitters in my cloudy breast,
    Like stars upon some gloomy grove,
Or those faint beams in which this hill is drest,
    After the sun's remove.

I see them walking in an air of glory,
    Whose light doth trample on my days:
My days, which are at best but dull and hoary,
    Mere glimmering and decays.

O holy Hope! and high Humility,
    High as the heavens above!
These are your walks, and you have showed them me
    To kindle my cold love.

Dear, beauteous Death! the jewel of the just,
    Shining nowhere, but in the dark;
What mysteries do lie beyond thy dust
    Could man outlook that mark!

He that hath found some fledged bird's nest, may know
    At first sight, if the bird be flown;
But what fair well or grove he sings in now,
    That is to him unknown.

And yet as angels in some brighter dreams
    Call to the soul, when man doth sleep:
So some strange thoughts transcend our wonted themes
    And into glory peep.

If a star were confined into a tomb,
    Her captive flames must needs burn there;
But when the hand that locked her up, gives room,
    She'll shine through all the sphere.

O Father of eternal life, and all
    Created glories under thee!
Resume thy spirit from this world of thrall
    Into true liberty.

Either disperse these mists, which blot and fill
    My perspective still as they pass,
Or else remove me hence unto that hill,
    Where I shall need no glass.

EDMUND WALLER (1606–1687)

'Go, lovely Rose'

Go, lovely Rose!
Tell her, that wastes her time and me,
   That now she knows,
When I resemble her to thee,
How sweet and fair she seems to be.

   Tell her that's young,
And shuns to have her graces spied,
   That hadst thou sprung
In deserts, where no men abide,
Thou must have uncommended died.

   Small is the worth
Of beauty from the light retired.
   Bid her come forth,
Suffer herself to be desired,
And not blush so to be admired.

   Then die, that she,
The common fate of all things rare
   May read in thee;
How small a part of time they share
They are so wondrous sweet and fair!

On a Girdle

That which her slender waist confined
Shall now my joyful temples bind.
No monarch but would give his crown
His arms might do what this has done.

It was my heaven's extremest sphere,
The pale which held that lovely deer;
My joy, my grief, my hope, my love
Did all within this circle move.

A narrow compass! and yet there
Dwelt all that's good, and all that's fair.
Give me but what this riband bound,
Take all the rest the sun goes round.

ISAAC WATTS (1674–1748)

Man Frail and God Eternal

Our God, our Help in Ages past,
Our hope for years to come,
Our shelter from the Stormy Blast,
And our eternal Home.

Under the Shadow of thy Throne
Thy Saints have dwelt secure;
Sufficient is thine Arm alone,
And our Defence is sure.

Before the Hills in order stood,
Or Earth receiv'd her Frame,
From everlasting Thou art God,
To endless years the same.

Thy word commands our Flesh to Dust,
Return, ye sons of men:
All Nations rose from Earth at first,
And turn to Earth again.

A thousand ages in thy Sight
Are like an Evening gone;
Short as the Watch that ends the Night,
Before the rising Sun.

The busy Tribes of Flesh and Blood,
With all their Lives and Cares,
Are carried downwards by thy Flood,
And lost in following Years.

Time like an ever-rolling Stream
Bears all its Sons away;
They fly forgotten as a Dream
Dies at the opening Day.

Like flow'ry Fields the Nations stand
   Pleas'd with the Morning-light;
The Flowers beneath the Mower's Hand
   Ly withering e'er 'tis Night.

Our God, our Help in Ages past,
   Our Hope for Years to come,
Be thou our Guard while Troubles last,
   And our eternal Home.

JOHN WEBSTER (1580?–1625?)

'All the flowers of the spring'
(from 'The Devil's Law-Case', Act 5, Scene 4)

All the flowers of the spring
Meet to perfume our burying;
These have but their growing prime,
And man does flourish but his time.
Survey our progress from our birth—
We are set, we grow, we turn to earth
Courts adieu, and all delights,
All bewitching appetites!
Sweetest breath and clearest eye
Like perfumes go out and die;
And consequently this is done
As shadows wait upon the sun.
Vain the ambitiòn of kings
Who seek by trophies and dead things
To leave a living name behind,
And weave but nets to catch the wind.

'Call for the robin-redbreast'
(from 'The White Devil', Act 5, Scene 4)

Call for the robin-redbreast and the wren,
Since o'er shady groves they hover,
And with leaves and flowers do cover
The friendless bodies of unburied men.
Call unto his funeral dole

The ant, the fieldmouse, and the mole,
To rear him hillocks that shall keep him warm,
And (when gay tombs are robbed) sustain no harm;
But keep the wolf far thence, that's foe to men,
For with his nails he'll dig them up again.

WALT WHITMAN (1819–1892)

from 'Song of Myself'

A child said *What is the grass?* fetching it to me with full hands;
How could I answer the child? I do not know what it is any more than he.

I guess it must be the flag of my disposition, out of hopeful green stuff
    woven.

Or I guess it is the handkerchief of the Lord,
A scented gift and remembrancer designedly dropt,
Bearing the owner's name someway in the corners, that we may see and
    remark, and say *Whose?*

Or I guess the grass is itself a child, the produced babe of the vegetation.

Or I guess it is a uniform hieroglyphic,
And it means, Sprouting alike in broad zones and narrow zones,
Growing among black folks as among white,
Kanuck, Tuckahoe, Congressman, Cuff, I give them the same, I receive
    them the same.

, , ,

I saw the marriage of the trapper in the open air in the far west, the
    bride was a red girl,
Her father and his friends sat near cross-legged and dumbly smoking,
    they had moccasins to their feet and large thick blankets hanging from
    their shoulders,
On a bank lounged the trapper, he was drest mostly in skins, his luxuri-
    ant beard and curls protected his neck, he held his bride by the hand,
She had long eyelashes, her head was bare, her coarse straight locks
    descended upon her voluptuous limbs and reached to her feet.

The runaway slave came to my house and stopt outside,

I heard his motions crackling the twigs of the woodpile,
Through the swung half-door of the kitchen I saw him limpsy and weak,
And went where he sat on a log and led him in and assured him,
And brought water and filled a tub for his sweated body and bruised feet,
And gave him a room that entered from my own, and gave him some
  coarse clean clothes,
And remember perfectly well his revolving eyes and his awkwardness,
And remember putting plasters on the galls of his neck and ankles;
He staid with me a week before he was recuperated and passed north,
I had him sit next me at table, my fire-lock leaned in the corner.
. . .

I believe a leaf of grass is no less than the journey-work of the stars,
And the pismire is equally perfect, and a grain of sand, and the egg of the
  wren,
And the tree-toad is a chef-d'oeuvre for the highest,
And the running blackberry would adorn the parlours of heaven,
And the narrowest hinge in my hand puts to scorn all machinery,
And the cow crunching with depressed head surpasses any statue,
And a mouse is miracle enough to stagger sextillions of infidels.
. . .

I think I could turn and live with animals, they are so placid and self-
  contained,
I stand and look at them long and long.

They do not sweat and whine about their condition,
They do not lie awake in the dark and weep for their sins,
They do not make me sick discussing their duty to God,
Not one is dissatisfied, not one is demented with the mania of owning
  things,
Not one kneels to another, nor to his kind that lived thousands of years
  ago,
Not one is respectable or unhappy over the whole earth.

'O Captain! my Captain!'

O Captain! my Captain! our fearful trip is done,
The ship has weathered every rack, the prize we sought is won,
The port is near, the bells I hear, the people all exulting,
While follow eyes the steady keel, the vessel grim and daring;

But O heart! heart! heart!
   O the bleeding drops of red,
      Where on the deck my Captain lies,
         Fallen cold and dead.

O Captain! my Captain! rise up and hear the bells;
Rise up—for you the flag is flung—for you the bugle trills,
For you bouquets and ribboned wreaths—for you the shores a-crowding,
For you they call, the swaying mass, their eager faces turning;
   Here Captain! dear father!
      This arm beneath your head!
        It is some dream that on the deck,
         You've fallen cold and dead.

My Captain does not answer, his lips are pale and still,
My father does not feel my arm, he has no pulse nor will,
The ship is anchored safe and sound, its voyage closed and done,
From fearful trip the victor ship comes in with object won;
   Exult, O shores, and ring, O bells!
      But I with mournful tread,
        Walk the deck my Captain lies,
         Fallen cold and dead.

OSCAR WILDE (1856–1900)

Requiescat

Tread lightly, she is near
   Under the snow,
Speak gently, she can hear
   The daisies grow.

All her bright golden hair
   Tarnished with rust,
She that was young and fair
   Fallen to dust.

Lily-like, white as snow,
   She hardly knew
She was a woman, so
   Sweetly she grew.

Coffin–board, heavy stone,
    Lie on her breast;
I vex my heart alone,
    She is at rest.

Peace, peace; she cannot hear
    Lyre or sonnet;
All my life's buried here.
    Heap earth upon it.

The Ballad of Reading Gaol

1

He did not wear his scarlet coat,
    For blood and wine are red,
And blood and wine were on his hands
    When they found him with the dead,
The poor dead woman whom he loved,
    And murdered in her bed.

He walked amongst the Trial Men
    In a suit of shabby grey;
A cricket cap was on his head,
    And his step seemed light and gay;
But I never saw a man who looked
    So wistfully at the day.

I never saw a man who looked
    With such a wistful eye
Upon that little tent of blue
    Which prisoners call the sky,
And at every drifting cloud that went
    With sails of silver by.

I walked, with other souls in pain,
    Within another ring,
And was wondering if the man had done
    A great or little thing,
When a voice behind me whispered low,
    'That fellow's got to swing.'

Dear Christ! the very prison walls
    Suddenly seemed to reel,
And the sky above my head became
    Like a casque of scorching steel;
And, though I was a soul in pain,
    My pain I could not feel.

I only knew what hunted thought
    Quickened his step, and why
He looked upon the garish day
    With such a wistful eye;
The man had killed the thing he loved,
    And so he had to die.

★

Yet each man kills the thing he loves,
    By each let this be heard,
Some do it with a bitter look,
    Some with a flattering word,
The coward does it with a kiss,
    The brave man with a sword!

Some kill their love when they are young,
    And some when they are old;
Some strangle with the hands of Lust,
    Some with the hands of Gold:
The kindest use a knife, because
    The dead so soon grow cold.

Some love too little, some too long,
    Some sell, and others buy;
Some do the deed with many tears,
    And some without a sigh:
For each man kills the thing he loves,
    Yet each man does not die.

He does not die a death of shame
    On a day of dark disgrace,
Nor have a noose about his neck,
    Nor a cloth upon his face,
Nor drop feet foremost through the floor
    Into an empty space.

He does not sit with silent men
    Who watch him night and day;
Who watch him when he tries to weep,
    And when he tries to pray;
Who watch him lest himself should rob
    The prison of its prey.

He does not wake at dawn to see
    Dread figures throng his room,
The shivering Chaplain robed in white,
    The Sheriff stern with gloom,
And the Governor all in shiny black,
    With the yellow face of Doom.

He does not rise in piteous haste
    To put on convict-clothes,
While some coarse-mouthed Doctor gloats, and notes
    Each new and nerve-twitched pose,
Fingering a watch whose little ticks
    Are like horrible hammer-blows.

He does not know that sickening thirst
    That sands one's throat, before
The hangman with his gardener's gloves
    Slips through the padded door,
And binds one with three leathern thongs,
    That the throat may thirst no more.

He does not bend his head to hear
    The Burial Office read,
Nor, while the terror of his soul
    Tells him he is not dead,
Cross his own coffin, as he moves
    Into the hideous shed.

He does not stare upon the air
    Through a little roof of glass:
He does not pray with lips of clay
    For his agony to pass;
Nor feel upon his shuddering cheek
    The kiss of Caiaphas.

2

Six weeks our guardsman walked the yard,
    In the suit of shabby grey:
His cricket cap was on his head,
    And his step seemed light and gay,
But I never saw a man who looked
    So wistfully at the day.

I never saw a man who looked
    With such a wistful eye
Upon that little tent of blue
    Which prisoners call the sky,
And at every wandering cloud that trailed
    Its ravelled fleeces by.

He did not wring his hands, as do
    Those witless men who dare
To try to rear the changeling Hope
    In the cave of black Despair:
He only looked upon the sun,
    And drank the morning air.

He did not wring his hands nor weep,
    Nor did he peek or pine,
But he drank the air as though it held
    Some healthful anodyne;
With open mouth he drank the sun
    As though it had been wine!

And I and all the souls in pain,
    Who tramped the other ring,
Forgot if we ourselves had done
    A great or little thing,
And watched with gaze of dull amaze
    The man who had to swing.

And strange it was to see him pass
    With a step so light and gay,
And strange it was to see him look
    So wistfully at the day,
And strange it was to think that he
    Had such a debt to pay.

For oak and elm have pleasant leaves
    That in the springtime shoot:
But grim to see is the gallows-tree,
    With its adder-bitten root,
And, green or dry, a man must die
    Before it bears its fruit!

The loftiest place is that seat of grace
    For which all worldlings try:
But who would stand in hempen band
    Upon a scaffold high,
And through a murderer's collar take
    His last look at the sky?

It is sweet to dance to violins
    When Love and Life are fair:
To dance to flutes, to dance to lutes
    Is delicate and rare:
But it is not sweet with nimble feet
    To dance upon the air!

So with curious eyes and sick surmise
    We watched him day by day,
And wondered if each one of us
    Would end the self-same way,
For none can tell to what red Hell
    His sightless soul may stray.

At last the dead man walked no more
    Amongst the Trial Men,
And I knew that he was standing up
    In the black dock's dreadful pen,
And that never would I see his face
    In God's sweet world again.

Like two doomed ships that pass in storm
    We had crossed each other's way:
But we made no sign, we said no word,
    We had no word to say;
For we did not meet in the holy night,
    But in the shameful day.

A prison wall was round us both,
    Two outcast men we were:
The world had thrust us from its heart,
    And God from out His care:
And the iron gin that waits for Sin
    Had caught us in its snare.

3

In Debtors' Yard the stones are hard,
    And the dripping wall is high,
So it was there he took the air
    Beneath the leaden sky,
And by each side a Warder walked,
    For fear the man might die.

Or else he sat with those who watched
    His anguish night and day;
Who watched him when he rose to weep,
    And when he crouched to pray;
Who watched him lest himself should rob
    Their scaffold of its prey.

The Governor was strong upon
    The Regulations Act:
The Doctor said that Death was but
    A scientific fact:
And twice a day the Chaplain called,
    And left a little tract.

And twice a day he smoked his pipe,
    And drank his quart of beer:
His soul was resolute, and held
    No hiding-place for fear;
He often said that he was glad
    The hangman's hands were near.

But why he said so strange a thing
    No Warder dared to ask:
For he to whom a watcher's doom
    Is given as his task,
Must set a lock upon his lips,
    And make his face a mask.

Or else he might be moved, and try
    To comfort or console:
And what should Human Pity do
    Pent up in Murderers' Hole?
What word of grace in such a place
    Could help a brother's soul?

With slouch and swing around the ring
    We trod the Fools' Parade!
We did not care: we knew we were
    The Devil's Own Brigade:
And shaven head and feet of lead
    Make a merry masquerade.

We tore the tarry rope to shreds
    With blunt and bleeding nails;
We rubbed the doors, and scrubbed the floors,
    And cleaned the shining rails:
And, rank by rank, we soaped the plank,
    And clattered with the pails.

We sewed the sacks, we broke the stones,
    We turned the dusty drill:
We banged the tins, and bawled the hymns,
    And sweated on the mill:
But in the heart of every man
    Terror was lying still.

So still it lay that every day
    Crawled like a weed-clogged wave:
And we forgot the bitter lot
    That waits for fool and knave,
Till once, as we tramped in from work,
    We passed an open grave.

With yawning mouth the yellow hole
    Gaped for a living thing;
The very mud cried out for blood
    To the thirsty asphalte ring:
And we knew that ere one dawn grew fair
    Some prisoner had to swing.

Right in we went, with soul intent
    On Death and Dread and Doom:
The hangman, with his little bag,
    Went shuffling through the gloom:
And each man trembled as he crept
    Into his numbered tomb.

★

That night the empty corridors
    Were full of forms of Fear,
And up and down the iron town
    Stole feet we could not hear,
And through the bars that hide the stars
    White faces seemed to peer.

He lay as one who lies and dreams
    In a pleasant meadow-land,
The watchers watched him as he slept,
    And could not understand
How one could sleep so sweet a sleep
    With a hangman close at hand.

But there is no sleep when men must weep
    Who never yet have wept:
So we—the fool, the fraud, the knave—
    That endless vigil kept,
And through each brain on hands of pain
    Another's terror crept.

Alas! it is a fearful thing
    To feel another's guilt!
For, right within, the Sword of Sin
    Pierced to its poisoned hilt,
And as molten lead were the tears we shed
    For the blood we had not spilt.

The Warders with their shoes of felt
    Crept by each padlocked door,
And peeped and saw, with eyes of awe,
    Grey figures on the floor,
And wondered why men knelt to pray
    Who never prayed before.

All through the night we knelt and prayed,
    Mad mourners of a corse!
The troubled plumes of midnight were
    The plumes upon a hearse:
And bitter wine upon a sponge
    Was the savour of Remorse.

★

The grey cock crew, the red cock crew,
    But never came the day:
And crooked shapes of Terror crouched,
    In the corners where we lay:
And each evil sprite that walks by night
    Before us seemed to play.

They glided past, they glided fast,
    Like travellers through a mist:
They mocked the moon in a rigadoon
    Of delicate turn and twist,
And with formal pace and loathsome grace
    The phantoms kept their tryst.

With mop and mow, we saw them go,
    Slim shadows hand in hand:
About, about, in ghostly rout
    They trod a saraband:
And the damned grotesques made arabesques,
    Like the wind upon the sand!

With the pirouettes of marionettes,
    They tripped on pointed tread:
But with flutes of Fear they filled the ear,
    As their grisly masque they led,
And loud they sang, and long they sang,
    For they sang to wake the dead.

'*Oho!*' they cried, '*The world is wide,
But fettered limbs go lame!
And once, or twice, to throw the dice
    Is a gentlemanly game,
But he does not win who plays with Sin
    In the secret House of Shame.*'

No things of air these antics were,
    That frolicked with such glee:
To men whose lives were held in gyves,
    And whose feet might not go free,
Ah! wounds of Christ! they were living things
    Most terrible to see.

Around, around, they waltzed and wound;
    Some wheeled in smirking pairs;
With the mincing step of a demirep
    Some sidled up the stairs:
And with subtle sneer, and fawning leer,
    Each helped us at our prayers.

The morning wind began to moan,
    But still the night went on:
Through its giant loom the web of gloom
    Crept till each thread was spun:
And, as we prayed, we grew afraid
    Of the Justice of the Sun.

The moaning wind went wandering round
    The weeping prison-wall:
Till like a wheel of turning steel
    We felt the minutes crawl:
O moaning wind! what had we done
    To have such a seneschal?

At last I saw the shadowed bars,
    Like a lattice wrought in lead,
Move right across the whitewashed wall
    That faced my three-plank bed,
And I knew that somewhere in the world
    God's dreadful dawn was red.

At six o'clock we cleaned our cells,
    At seven all was still,
But the sough and swing of a mighty wing
    The prison seemed to fill,
For the Lord of Death with icy breath
    Had entered in to kill.

He did not pass in purple pomp,
　　Nor ride a moon-white steed.
Three yards of cord and a sliding board
　　Are all the gallows' need:
So with rope of shame the Herald came
　　To do the secret deed.

We were as men who through a fen
　　Of filthy darkness grope:
We did not dare to breathe a prayer,
　　Or to give our anguish scope:
Something was dead in each of us,
　　And what was dead was Hope.

For Man's grim Justice goes its way,
　　And will not swerve aside:
It slays the weak, it slays the strong,
　　It has a deadly stride:
With iron heel it slays the strong,
　　The monstrous parricide!

We waited for the stroke of eight:
　　Each tongue was thick with thirst:
For the stroke of eight is the stroke of Fate
　　That makes a man accursed,
And Fate will use a running noose
　　For the best man and the worst.

We had no other thing to do,
　　Save to wait for the sign to come:
So, like things of stone in a valley lone,
　　Quiet we sat and dumb:
But each man's heart beat thick and quick,
　　Like a madman on a drum!

With sudden shock the prison-clock
　　Smote on the shivering air,
And from all the gaol rose up a wail
　　Of impotent despair,
Like the sound that frightened marshes hear
　　From some leper in his lair.

And as one sees most fearful things
    In the crystal of a dream,
We saw the greasy hempen rope
    Hooked to the blackened beam,
And heard the prayer the hangman's snare
    Strangled into a scream.

And all the woe that moved him so
    That he gave that bitter cry,
And the wild regrets, and the bloody sweats,
    None knew so well as I:
For he who lives more lives than one
    More deaths than one must die.

4

There is no chapel on the day
    On which they hang a man:
The Chaplain's heart is far too sick,
    Or his face is far too wan,
Or there is that written in his eyes
    Which none should look upon.

So they kept us close till nigh on noon,
    And then they rang the bell,
And the Warders with their jingling keys
    Opened each listening cell,
And down the iron stair we tramped,
    Each from his separate Hell.

Out into God's sweet air we went,
    But not in wonted way,
For this man's face was white with fear,
    And that man's face was grey,
And I never saw sad men who looked
    So wistfully at the day.

I never saw sad men who looked
    With such a wistful eye
Upon that little tent of blue
    We prisoners called the sky,
And at every careless cloud that passed
    In happy freedom by.

But there were those amongst us all
    Who walked with downcast head,
And knew that, had each got his due,
    They should have died instead:
He had but killed a thing that lived,
    Whilst they had killed the dead.

For he who sins a second time
    Wakes a dead soul to pain,
And draws it from its spotted shroud,
    And makes it bleed again,
And makes it bleed great gouts of blood,
    And makes it bleed in vain!

★

Like ape or clown, in monstrous garb
    With crooked arrows starred,
Silently we went round and round
    The slippery asphalte yard;
Silently we went round and round,
    And no man spoke a word.

Silently we went round and round,
    And through each hollow mind
The Memory of dreadful things
    Rushed like a dreadful wind,
And Horror stalked before each man,
    And Terror crept behind.

The Warders strutted up and down,
    And kept their herd of brutes,
Their uniforms were spick and span,
    And they wore their Sunday suits,
But we knew the work they had been at,
    By the quicklime on their boots.

For where a grave had opened wide,
    There was no grave at all:
Only a stretch of mud and sand
    By the hideous prison-wall,
And a little heap of burning lime,
    That the man should have his pall.

For he has a pall, this wretched man,
    Such as few men can claim:
Deep down below a prison-yard,
    Naked for greater shame,
He lies, with fetters on each foot,
    Wrapt in a sheet of flame!

And all the while the burning lime
    Eats flesh and bone away,
It eats the brittle bone by night,
    And the soft flesh by day,
It eats the flesh and bone by turns,
    But it eats the heart alway.

★

For three long years they will not sow
    Or root or seedling there:
For three long years the unblessed spot
    Will sterile be and bare,
And look upon the wondering sky
    With unreproachful stare.

They think a murderer's heart would taint
    Each simple seed they sow.
It is not true! God's kindly earth
    Is kindlier than men know,
And the red rose would but blow more red,
    The white rose whiter blow.

Out of his mouth a red, red rose!
    Out of his heart a white!
For who can say by what strange way,
    Christ brings His will to light,
Since the barren staff the pilgrim bore
    Bloomed in the great Pope's sight?

But neither milk-white rose nor red
    May bloom in prison-air;
The shard, the pebble, and the flint,
    Are what they give us there:
For flowers have been known to heal
    A common man's despair.

So never will wine-red rose or white,
  Petal by petal, fall
On that stretch of mud and sand that lies
  By the hideous prison-wall,
To tell the men who tramp the yard
  That God's Son died for all.

Yet though the hideous prison-wall
  Still hems him round and round,
And a spirit may not walk by night
  That is with fetters bound,
And a spirit may but weep that lies
  In such unholy ground,

He is at peace—this wretched man—
  At peace, or will be soon:
There is no thing to make him mad,
  Nor does Terror walk at noon,
For the lampless Earth in which he lies
  Has neither Sun nor Moon.

They hanged him as a beast is hanged!
  They did not even toll
A requiem that might have brought
  Rest to his startled soul,
But hurriedly they took him out,
  And hid him in a hole.

They stripped him of his canvas clothes,
  And gave him to the flies:
They mocked the swollen purple throat,
  And the stark and staring eyes:
And with laughter loud they heaped the shroud
  In which their convict lies.

The Chaplain would not kneel to pray
  By his dishonoured grave:
Nor mark it with that blessed Cross
  That Christ for sinners gave,
Because the man was one of those
  Whom Christ came down to save.

Yet all is well; he has but passed
    To Life's appointed bourne:
And alien tears will fill for him
    Pity's long-broken urn,
For his mourners will be outcast men,
    And outcasts always mourn.

5

I know not whether Laws be right,
    Or whether Laws be wrong;
All that we know who lie in gaol
    Is that the wall is strong;
And that each day is like a year,
    A year whose days are long.

But this I know, that every Law
    That men have made for Man,
Since first Man took his brother's life,
    And the sad world began,
But straws the wheat and saves the chaff
    With a most evil fan.

This too I know—and wise it were
    If each could know the same—
That every prison that men build
    Is built with bricks of shame,
And bound with bars lest Christ should see
    How men their brothers maim.

With bars they blur the gracious moon,
    And blind the goodly sun:
And they do well to hide their Hell,
    For in it things are done
That Son of God nor son of Man
    Ever should look upon!

The vilest deeds like poison weeds,
    Bloom well in prison-air;
It is only what is good in Man
    That wastes and withers there:
Pale Anguish keeps the heavy gate,
    And the Warder is Despair.

For they starve the little frightened child
    Till it weeps both night and day:
And they scourge the weak, and flog the fool,
    And gibe the old and grey,
And some grow mad, and all grow bad,
    And none a word may say.

Each narrow cell in which we dwell
    Is a foul and dark latrine,
And the fetid breath of living Death
    Chokes up each grated screen,
And all, but Lust, is turned to dust
    In Humanity's machine.

The brackish water that we drink
    Creeps with a loathsome slime,
And the bitter bread they weigh in scales
    Is full of chalk and lime,
And Sleep will not lie down, but walks
    Wild-eyed, and cries to Time.

★

But though lean Hunger and green Thirst
    Like asp with adder fight,
We have little care of prison fare,
    For what chills and kills outright
Is that every stone one lifts by day
    Becomes one's heart by night.

With midnight always in one's heart,
    And twilight in one's cell,
We turn the crank, or tear the rope,
    Each in his separate Hell,
And the silence is more awful far
    Than the sound of a brazen bell.

And never a human voice comes near
    To speak a gentle word:
And the eye that watches through the door
    Is pitiless and hard:
And by all forgot, we rot and rot,
    With soul and body marred.

And thus we rust Life's iron chain
    Degraded and alone:
And some men curse, and some men weep,
    And some men make no moan:
But God's eternal Laws are kind
    And break the heart of stone.

★

And every human heart that breaks,
    In prison-cell or yard,
Is as that broken box that gave
    Its treasure to the Lord,
And filled the unclean leper's house
    With the scent of costliest nard.

Ah! Happy they whose hearts can break
    And peace of pardon win!
How else may man make straight his plan
    And cleanse his soul from Sin?
How else but through a broken heart
    May Lord Christ enter in?

★

And he of the swollen purple throat,
    And the stark and staring eyes,
Waits for the holy hands that took
    The Thief to Paradise;
And a broken and a contrite heart
    The Lord will not despise.

The man in red who reads the Law
    Gave him three weeks of life,
Three little weeks in which to heal
    His soul of his soul's strife,
And cleanse from every blot of blood
    The hand that held the knife.

And with tears of blood he cleansed the hand,
    The hand that held the steel:
For only blood can wipe out blood,
    And only tears can heal:
And the crimson stain that was of Cain
    Became Christ's snow-white seal.

6

In Reading gaol by Reading town
    There is a pit of shame,
And in it lies a wretched man
    Eaten by teeth of flame,
In a burning winding-sheet he lies,
    And his grave has got no name.

And there, till Christ call forth the dead,
    In silence let him lie:
No need to waste the foolish tear,
    Or heave the windy sigh:
The man had killed the thing he loved,
    And so he had to die.

And all men kill the thing they love,
    By all let this be heard,
Some do it with a bitter look,
    Some with a flattering word,
The coward does it with a kiss,
    The brave man with a sword!

ANNE, COUNTESS OF WINCHELSEA (1661–1720)

A Song

'Tis strange, this heart within my breast,
    Reason opposing, and her pow'rs,
Cannot one gentle moment rest
    Unless it knows what's done in yours.

In vain I ask it of your eyes,
    Which subtly would my fears control:
For art has taught them to disguise
    Which nature made t' explain the soul.

In vain that sound your voice affords,
    Flatters sometimes my easy mind;
But of too vast extent are words
    In them the jewel truth to find.

Then let my fond inquiries cease,
　　And so let all my troubles end:
For sure, that heart shall ne'er know peace
　　Which on another's does depend.

The Soldier's Death

Trail all your pikes, dispirit every drum,
March in a slow procession from afar,
Ye silent, ye dejected men of war!
Be still the hautboys, and the flute be dumb!
Display no more, in vain, the lofty banner.
For see! where on the bier before ye lies
The pale, the fall'n, th' untimely sacrifice
To your mistaken shrine, to your false idol Honour.

CHARLES WOLFE (1791–1823)

The Burial of Sir John Moore at Corunna

Not a drum was heard, nor a funeral note,
　　As his corse to the rampart we hurried;
Not a soldier discharged his farewell shot
　　O'er the grave where our hero we buried.

We buried him darkly at dead of night,
　　The sods with our bayonets turning;
By the struggling moonbeam's misty light
　　And the lantern dimly burning.

No useless coffin enclosed his breast,
　　Nor in sheet nor in shroud we wound him;
But he lay like a warrior taking his rest
　　With his martial cloak around him.

Few and short were the prayers we said,
　　And we spoke not a word of sorrow;
But we steadfastly gazed on the face that was dead,
　　And we bitterly thought of the morrow.

We thought, as we hollowed his narrow bed
　　And smoothed down his lonely pillow,

That the foe and the stranger would tread o'er his head,
    And we far away on the billow!

Lightly they'll talk of the spirit that's gone
    And o'er his cold ashes upbraid him,—
But little he'll reck, if they let him sleep on
    In the grave where a Briton has laid him.

But half of our heavy task was done
    When the clock struck the hour for retiring:
And we heard the distant and random gun
    That the foe was sullenly firing.

Slowly and sadly we laid him down,
    From the field of his fame fresh and gory;
We carved not a line, and we raised not a stone,
    But left him alone with his glory.

HUMBERT WOLFE (1885–1940)

The Grey Squirrel

Like a small grey
coffee-pot,
sits the squirrel.
He is not

all he should be,
kills by dozens
trees, and eats
his red-brown cousins.

The keeper on the
other hand,
who shot him, is
a Christian, and

loves his enemies,
which shows
the squirrel was not
one of those.

The Soldier

1

Down some cold field in a world unspoken
the young men are walking together, slim and tall,
and though they laugh to one another, silence is not broken:
there is no sound however clear they call.

They are speaking together of what they loved in vain here,
but the air is too thin to carry the thing they say.
They were young and golden, but they came on pain here,
and their youth is age now, their gold is grey.

Yet their hearts are not changed, and they cry to one another,
'What have they done with the lives we laid aside?
Are they young with our youth, gold with our gold, my brother?
Do they smile in the face of death, because we died?'

Down some cold field in a world uncharted
the young seek each other with questioning eyes.
They question each other, the young, the golden-hearted,
of the world that they were robbed of in their quiet Paradise.

2

I do not ask God's purpose. He gave me the sword,
and though merely to wield it is itself the lie
against the light, at the bidding of my Lord,
where all the rest bear witness, I'll deny.
And I remember Peter's high reward,
and say of soldiers, when I hear cocks cry,
'As your dear lives ('twas all you might afford)
you laid aside, I lay my sainthood by.'
There are in heaven other archangels,
bright friends of God, who build where Michael destroys,
in music, or in beauty, lute-players.
I wield the sword; and, though I ask naught else
of God, I pray to Him: 'But these were boys,
and died. Be gentle, God, to soldiers.'

'You cannot hope...'

You cannot hope
   to bribe or twist
thank God! the
   British journalist.

But, seeing what
   the man will do
unbribed, there's
   no occasion to.

WILLIAM WORDSWORTH (1770–1850)

The Daffodils

I wandered lonely as a cloud
That floats on high o'er vales and hills,
When all at once I saw a crowd,
A host of golden daffodils,
Beside the lake, beneath the trees,
Fluttering and dancing in the breeze.

Continuous as the stars that shine
And twinkle on the milky way,
They stretched in never-ending line
Along the margin of a bay:
Ten thousand saw I at a glance
Tossing their heads in sprightly dance.

The waves beside them danced, but they
Out-did the sparkling waves in glee:
A poet could not but be gay
In such a jocund company!
I gazed—and gazed—but little thought
What wealth the show to me had brought.

For oft, when on my couch I lie
In vacant or in pensive mood,
They flash upon that inward eye
Which is the bliss of solitude;

And then my heart with pleasure fills,
And dances with the daffodils.

'My heart leaps up'

My heart leaps up when I behold
    A rainbow in the sky:
So was it when my life began;
So is it now I am a man;
So be it when I shall grow old,
    Or let me die!
The Child is father of the Man;
And I could wish my days to be
Bound each to each by natural piety.

from 'The Borderers'

Action is transitory—a step, a blow,
The motion of a muscle,—this way or that—
'Tis done, and in the after-vacancy
We wonder at ourselves like men betrayed:
Suffering is permanent, obscure and dark,
And shares the nature of infinity.

The World is Too Much with Us

The world is too much with us; late and soon,
Getting and spending, we lay waste our powers:
Little we see in Nature that is ours;
We have given our hearts away, a sordid boon!
The sea that bares her bosom to the moon;
The winds that will be howling at all hours
And are up-gathered now like sleeping flowers;
For this, for everything, we are out of tune;
It moves us not.—Great God! I'd rather be
A pagan suckled in a creed outworn.
So might I, standing on this pleasant lea,
Have glimpses that would make me less forlorn;
Have sight of Proteus rising from the sea;
Or hear old Triton blow his wreathèd horn.

Upon Westminster Bridge

Earth has not anything to show more fair:
Dull would he be of soul who could pass by
A sight so touching in its majesty:
This city now doth, like a garment, wear
The beauty of the morning; silent, bare,
Ships, towers, domes, theatres, and temples lie
Open unto the fields, and to the sky:
All bright and glittering in the smokeless air.
Never did sun more beautifully steep
In his first splendour, valley, rock, or hill;
Ne'er saw I, never felt, a calm so deep!
The river glideth at his own sweet will:
Dear God! the very houses seem asleep;
And all that mighty heart is lying still!

London, 1802

O Friend! I know not which way I must look
For comfort, being, as I am, opprest,
To think that now our life is only drest
For show; mean handy-work of craftsman, cook,
Or groom! We must run glittering like a brook
In the open sunshine, or we are unblest:
The wealthiest man among us is the best:
No grandeur now in nature or in book
Delights us. Rapine, avarice, expense,
This is idolatry; and these we adore;
Plain living and high thinking are no more:
The homely beauty of the good old cause
Is gone; our peace, our fearful innocence,
And pure religion breathing household laws.

To Milton

Milton! thou should'st be living at this hour:
England hath need of thee: she is a fen
Of stagnant waters: altar, sword, and pen,
Fireside, the heroic wealth of hall and bower,

Have forfeited their ancient English dower
Of inward happiness. We are selfish men.
Oh! raise us up, return to us again;
And give us manners, virtue, freedom, power.
Thy soul was like a star, and dwelt apart:
Thou hads a voice whose sound was like the sea;
Pure as the naked heavens, majestic, free,
So didst thou travel on life's common way,
In cheerful godliness; and yet thy heart
The lowliest duties on herself did lay.

'It is a beauteous evening'

It is a beauteous evening, calm and free;
The holy time is quiet as a nun
Breathless with adoration; the broad sun
Is sinking down in its tranquillity;
The gentleness of heaven is on the sea:
Listen! the mighty Being is awake,
And doth with his eternal motion make
A sound like thunder—everlastingly.
Dear child! dear girl! that walkest with me here,
If thou appear untouched by solemn thought
Thy nature is not therefore less divine:
Thou licst in Abraham's bosom all the year,
And worshipp'st at the Temple's inner shrine,
God being with thee when we know it not.

Lucy

1

She dwelt among the untrodden ways
    Beside the springs of Dove,
A maid whom there were none to praise
    And very few to love:

A violet by a mossy stone
    Half hidden from the eye!
Fair as a star, when only one
    Is shining in the sky.

She lived unknown, and few could know
    When Lucy ceased to be;
But she is in her grave, and, oh,
    The difference to me!

2

I travelled among unknown men,
    In lands beyond the sea;
Nor, England! did I know till then
    What love I bore to thee.

'Tis past, that melancholy dream!
    Nor will I quit thy shore
A second time; for still I seem
    To love thee more and more.

Among thy mountains did I feel
    The joy of my desire;
And she I cherished turned her wheel
    Beside an English fire.

Thy mornings showed, thy nights concealed
    The bowers where Lucy played;
And thine too is the last green field
    That Lucy's eyes surveyed.

3

A slumber did my spirit seal;
    I had no human fears:
She seemed a thing that could not feel
    The touch of earthly years.

No motion has she now, no force;
    She neither hears nor sees;
Rolled round in earth's diurnal course,
    With rocks, and stones, and trees.

The Solitary Reaper

Behold her, single in the field,
Yon solitary highland lass!
Reaping and singing by herself;
Stop here, or gently pass!
Alone she cuts and binds the grain,
And sings a melancholy strain;
O listen! for the vale profound
Is overflowing with the sound.

No nightingale did ever chaunt
More welcome notes to weary bands
Of travellers in some shady haunt,
Among Arabian sands:
A voice so thrilling ne'er was heard
In springtime from the cuckoo-bird,
Breaking the silence of the seas
Among the farthest Hebrides.

Will no one tell me what she sings?—
Perhaps the plaintive numbers flow
For old, unhappy far-off things,
And battles long ago;
Or is it some more humble lay,
Familiar matter of today?
Some natural sorrow, loss, or pain,
That has been, and may be again?

Whate'er the theme, the maiden sang
As if her song could have no ending;
I saw her singing at her work,
And o'er the sickle bending;—
I listened, motionless and still;
And, as I mounted up the hill
The music in my heart I bore,
Long after it was heard no more.

Ode: Intimations of Immortality

(from 'Recollections of Early Childhood')

> The Child is Father of the Man;
> And I could wish my days to be
> Bound each to each by natural piety.

1

There was a time when meadow, grove, and stream,
    The earth, and every common sight,
        To me did seem
    Apparelled in celestial light,
The glory and the freshness of a dream.
It is not now as it hath been of yore—
    Turn wheresoe'er I may,
        By night or day,
The things which I have seen I now can see no more.

2

    The rainbow comes and goes,
    And lovely is the rose,
    The moon doth with delight
Look round her when the heavens are bare,
        Waters on a starry night
        Are beautiful and fair;
    The sunshine is a glorious birth;
    But yet I know, where'er I go,
That there hath passed away a glory from the earth.

3

Now, while the birds thus sing a joyous song,
    And while the young lambs bound
        As to the tabor's sound,
To me alone there came a thought of grief;
A timely utterance gave that thought relief,
        And I again am strong.
The cataracts blow their trumpets from the steep;
No more shall grief of mine the season wrong;
I hear the echoes through the mountains throng;

The winds come to me from the fields of sleep,
     And all the earth is gay;
        Land and sea
   Give themselves up to jollity,
      And with the heart of May
Doth every Beast keep holiday—
       Thou Child of Joy,
Shout round me, let me hear thy shouts, thou happy Shepherd-boy!

4

Ye blessèd creatures, I have heard the call
   Ye to each other make; I see
The heavens laugh with you in your jubilee;
    My heart is at your festival,
     My head hath its coronal,
The fulness of your bliss, I feel—I feel it all.
     Oh evil day! if I were sullen
     While Earth herself is adorning,
    This sweet May-morning,
    And the Children are culling
     On every side,
In a thousand valleys far and wide,
   Fresh flowers; while the sun shines warm,
And the Babe leaps up on his Mother's arm:—
    I hear, I hear, with joy I hear!
    —But there's a Tree, of many, one,
A single field which I have looked upon,
Both of them speak of something that is gone;
     The Pansy at my feet
    Doth the same tale repeat:
Whither is fled the visionary gleam?
Where is it now, the glory and the dream?

5

Our birth is but a sleep and a forgetting:
The Soul that rises with us, our life's Star,
    Hath had elsewhere its setting,
     And cometh from afar;
    Not in entire forgetfulness,
    And not in utter nakedness,
But trailing clouds of glory do we come
    From God, who is our home.

Heaven lies about us in our infancy!
Shades of the prison-house begin to close
    Upon the growing Boy,
But he beholds the light, and whence it flows.
    He sees it in his joy;
The Youth, who daily farther from the east
    Must travel, still is Nature's priest,
      And by the vision splendid
      Is on his way attended;
At length the man perceives it die away,
And fade into the light of common day.

6

Earth fills her lap with pleasures of her own;
Yearnings she hath in her own natural kind,
And, even with something of a Mother's mind,
    And no unworthy aim,
    The homely Nurse doth all she can
To make her Foster child, her Inmate Man,
    Forget the glories he hath known,
And that imperial palace whence he came.

7

Behold the Child among his newborn blisses,
    A six years' Darling of a pygmy size!
See, where 'mid work of his own hand he lies,
Fretted by sallies of his mother's kisses,
With light upon him from his father's eyes!
See, at his feet, some little plan or chart,
Some fragment from his dream of human life,
Shaped by himself with newly learnèd art;
    A wedding or a festival,
    A mourning or a funeral;
      And this hath now his heart,
    And unto this he frames his song:
      Then will he fit his tongue
To dialogues of business, love, or strife;
    But it will not be long
    Ere this be thrown aside,
    And with new joy and pride
The little Actor cons another part;
Filling from time to time his 'humorous stage'

With all the Persons, down to palsied age,
That Life brings with her in her equipage;
    As if his whole vocation
    Were endless imitation.

8

Thou, whose exterior semblance doth belie
    Thy Soul's immensity;
Thou best Philosopher, who yet dost keep
Thy heritage, thou Eye among the blind,
That, deaf and silent, read'st the eternal deep,
Haunted for ever by the eternal mind,—
    Mighty Prophet! Seer blest!
    On whom those truths do rest,
Which we are toiling all our lives to find,
In darkness lost, the darkness of the grave;
Thou, over whom thy Immortality
Broods like the Day, a Master o'er a Slave,
A Presence which is not to be put by;
Thou little Child, yet glorious in the might
Of heaven-born freedom on thy being's height,
Why with such earnest pains dost thou provoke
The years to bring the inevitable yoke,
Thus blindly with thy blessedness at strife?
Full soon thy Soul shall have her earthly freight,
And custom lie upon thee with a weight,
Heavy as frost, and deep almost as life!

9

    O joy! that in our embers
    Is something that doth live,
    That nature yet remembers
    What was so fugitive!
The thought of our past years in me doth breed
Perpetual benediction: not indeed
For that which is most worthy to be blest—
Delight and liberty, the simple creed
Of Childhood, whether busy or at rest,
With new-fledged hope still fluttering in his breast:—
    Not for these I raise
    The song of thanks and praise;
    But for those obstinate questionings

Of sense and outward things,
Fallings from us, vanishings;
Blank misgivings of a Creature
Moving about in worlds not realized,
High instincts before which our mortal Nature
Did tremble like a guilty Thing surprised:
But for those first affections,
Those shadowy recollections,
Which, be they what they may,
Are yet the fountain light of all our day,
Are yet a master light of all our seeing;
Uphold us, cherish, and have power to make
Our noisy years seem moments in the being
Of the eternal silence: truths that wake,
To perish never;
Which neither listlessness, nor mad endeavour,
Nor Man nor Boy,
Nor all that is at enmity with joy,
Can utterly abolish or destroy!
Hence in a season of calm weather,
Though inland far we be,
Our Souls have sight of that immortal sea
Which brought us hither,
Can in a moment travel thither,
And see the Children sport upon the shore,
And hear the mighty waters rolling evermore.

10

Then sing, ye Birds! sing, sing a joyous song!
And let the young Lambs bound
As to the tabor's sound!
We in thought will join your throng,
Ye that pipe and ye that play,
Ye that through your hearts today
Feel the gladness of the May!
What though the radiance which was once so bright
Be now for ever taken from my sight,
Though nothing can bring back the hour
Of splendour in the grass, of glory in the flower;
We will grieve not, rather find
Strength in what remains behind;
In the primal sympathy

Which having been must ever be;
In the soothing thoughts that spring
Out of human suffering;
In the faith that looks through death,
In years that bring the philosophic mind.

11

And oh, ye Fountains, Meadows, Hills, and Groves,
Forebode not any severing of our loves!
Yet in my heart of hearts I feel your might;
I only have relinquished one delight
To live beneath your more habitual sway.
I love the Brooks which down their channels fret,
Even more than when I tripped lightly as they;
The innocent brightness of a newborn Day
      Is lovely yet;
The Clouds that gather round the setting sun
Do take a sober colouring from an eye
That hath kept watch o'er man's mortality;
Another race hath been, and other palms are won.
Thanks to the human heart by which we live,
Thanks to its tenderness, its joys, and fears,
To me the meanest flower that blows can give
Thoughts that do often lie too deep for tears.

from 'The Prelude'
from Book 1

Dust as we are, the immortal spirit grows
Like harmony in music; there is a dark
Inscrutable workmanship that reconciles
Discordant elements, makes them cling together
In one society.

from Book III

The Evangelist St John my patron was:
Three Gothic courts are his, and in the first
Was my abiding-place, a nook obscure;
Right underneath, the College kitchens made
A humming sound, less tuneable than bees,
But hardly less industrious; with shrill notes

Of sharp command and scolding intermixed.
Near me hung Trinity's loquacious clock,
Who never let the quarters, night or day,
Slip by him unproclaimed, and told the hours
Twice over with a male and female voice.
Her pealing organ was my neighbour too;
And from my pillow, looking forth by light
Of moon or favouring stars, I could behold
The antechapel where the statue stood
Of Newton with his prism and silent face,
The marble index of a mind for ever
Voyaging through strange seas of Thought, alone.

SIR HENRY WOTTON (1568–1639)

Character of a Happy Life

How happy is he born and taught,
That serveth not another's will;
Whose armour is his honest thought
And simple truth his utmost skill!

Whose passions not his masters are,
Whose soul is still prepared for death,
Not tied unto the world with care
Of public fame, or private breath;

Who envies none that chance doth raise,
Or vice; who never understood
The deepest wounds are given by praise;
Nor rules of state, but rules of good:

Who hath his life from rumours freed,
Whose conscience is his strong retreat;
Whose state can neither flatterers feed,
Nor ruin make accusers great;

Who God doth late and early pray
More of his grace than goods to lend;
And entertains the harmless day
With a well-chosen book or friend;

—This man is free from servile bands
Of hope to rise, or fear to fall;

Lord of himself, though not of lands;
And having nothing, yet hath all.

On the Death of Sir Albert Morton's Wife

He first deceased—she, for a little, tried
To live without him, liked it not and died.

SIR THOMAS WYATT (1503-1542)

'They flee from me'

They flee from me that sometime did me seek
With naked foot, stalking in my chamber.
I have seen them gentle, tame, and meek,
That now are wild and do not remember
That sometime they put themself in danger
To take bread at my hand; and now they range,
Busily seeking with a continual change.

Thanked be fortune it hath been otherwise
Twenty times better; but once in special,
In thin array after a pleasant guise,
When her loose gown from her shoulders did fall,
And she me caught in her arms long and small;
Therewithal sweetly did me kiss
And softly said, 'Dear heart, how like you this?'

It was no dream: I lay broad waking.
But all is turned thorough my gentleness
Into a strange fashion of forsaking;
And I have leave to go of her goodness,
And she also, to use newfangleness.
But since that I so kindly am served
I would fain know what she hath deserved.

'I find no peace, and all my war is done'

I find no peace, and all my war is done:
I fear, and hope; I burn, and freeze like ice;
I fly above the wind, yet can I not arise;

And nought I have, and all the world I seize on;
That locketh nor loseth holdeth me in prison,
And holdeth me not, yet can I 'scape nowise:
Nor letteth me live, nor die at my devise,
And yet of death it giveth me occasion.
Without eye I see, and without tongue I 'plain;
I desire to perish, and yet I ask health;
I love another, and thus I hate myself;
I feed me in sorrow, and laugh in all my pain.
Likewise displeaseth me both death and life,
And my delight is causer of this strife.

'My galley'

My galley charged with forgetfulness
Through sharp seas in winter nights doth pass
Tween rock and rock, and eke my foe, alas,
That is my lord, steereth with cruelness.
And every oar, a thought in readiness,
As though that death were light in such a case;
An endless wind doth tear the sail apace
Of forced sighs and trusty fearfulness;
A rain of tears, a cloud of dark distain,
Have done the wearied cords great hindrance;
Wreathed with error and eke with ignorance,
The stars be hid that lead me to this pain.
Drowned is reason that should me consort,
And I remain despairing of the port.

WILLIAM BUTLER YEATS (1865–1939)

The Stolen Child

Where dips the rocky highland
Of Sleuth Wood in the lake,
There lies a leafy island
Where flapping herons wake
The drowsy water-rats;
There we've hid our faery vats,
Full of berries
And of reddest stolen cherries.

Come away, O human child!
To the waters and the wild
With a faery, hand in hand,
For the world's more full of weeping than you can understand.

Where the wave of moonlight glosses
The dim grey sands with light,
Far off by furthest Rosses
We foot it all the night,
Weaving olden dances,
Mingling hands and mingling glances
Till the moon has taken flight;
To and fro we leap
And chase the frothy bubbles,
While the world is full of troubles
And is anxious in its sleep.
Come away, O human child!
To the waters of the wild
With a faery, hand in hand,
For the world's more full of weeping than you can understand.

Where the wandering water gushes
From the hills above Glen-Car,
In pools among the rushes
That scarce could bathe a star,
We seek for slumbering trout
And whispering in their ears
Give them unquiet dreams;
Leaning softly out
From ferns that drop their tears
Over the young streams.
Come away, O human child!
To the waters and the wild
With a faery, hand in hand,
For the world's more full of weeping than you can understand.

Away with us he's going,
The solemn-eyed:
He'll hear no more the lowing
Of the calves on the warm hillside
Or the kettle on the hob
Sing peace into his breast,

Or see the brown mice bob
Round and round the oatmeal-chest.
For he comes, the human child,
To the waters and the wild
With a faery, hand in hand,
From a world more full of weeping than he can understand.

The Lake Isle of Innisfree

I will arise and go now, and go to Innisfree,
And a small cabin build there, of clay and wattles made:
Nine bean-rows will I have there, a hive for the honey-bee,
And live alone in the bee-loud glade.

And I shall have some peace there, for peace comes dropping slow,
Dropping from the veils of the morning to where the cricket sings;
There midnight's all a glimmer, and noon a purple glow,
And evening full of the linnet's wings.

I will arise and go now, for always night and day
I hear lake water lapping with low sounds by the shore;
While I stand on the roadway, or on the pavements grey,
I hear it in the deep heart's core.

BENJAMIN ZEPHANIAH (1958–)

'Dis poetry'

Dis poetry is like a riddim dat drops
De tongue fires a riddim dat shoots like shots
Dis poetry is designed fe rantin
Dance hall style, Big mouth chanting,
Dis poetry nar put yu to sleep
Preaching follow me
Like yu is blind sheep,
Dis poetry is not Party Political
Not designed fe dose who are critical.

Dis poetry is wid me when I gu to me bed
It gets into me Dreadlocks
It lingers around me head

Dis poetry goes wid me as I pedal me bike
I've tried Shakespeare, Respect due dere
But dis is the stuff I like.

Dis poetry is not afraid of going ina book
Still dis poetry needs ears fe hear an eyes fe hav a look
Dis poetry is Verbal Riddim, no big words involved
An if I hav a problem de riddim gets it solved,
I've tried to be more Romantic, it does nu good for me
So I tek a Reggae Riddim an build me poetry,
I could try be more personal
But you've heard it all before,
Pages of written words not needed
Brain has many words in store,
Yu could call dis poetry Dub Ranting
De tongue plays a beat
De body starts skanking,
Dis poetry is quick an childish
Dis poetry is fe de wise an foolish
Anybody can do it fe free,
Dis poetry is fe yu an me,
Don't stretch yu imagination
Dis poetry is fe de good of de Nation,
Chant,
In de morning
I chant
In de night
I chant
In de darkness
An under de spotlight,
I pass thru University
I pass thru Sociology
An den I got a Dread degree
In Dreadful Ghettology.

Dis poetry stays wid me when I run or walk
A when I am talking to meself in poetry I talk,
Dis poetry is wid me,
Below me and above,
Dis poetry's from inside me
It goes to yu
WID LUV.

ACKNOWLEDGMENTS

HarperCollins Publishers gratefully acknowledge permission given by the following people and organisations to reproduce copyright poems in this anthology. We have made every effort to contact all copyright holders, but if any have been missed, the copyright holder should please contact us at: Reference Department, HarperCollins Publishers, Westerhill Road, Bishopbriggs, Glasgow G64 2QT.

Sir Kingsley Amis: 'A Bookshop Idyll' (© 1957 Kingsley Amis), 'L'Invitation au Voyage' (© 1967 Kingsley Amis) and 'The Shrimp in the Rubbish-Bin' (© 1979 Kingsley Amis) are reproduced by kind permission of Jonathan Clowes Ltd on behalf of the Literary Estate of Sir Kingsley Amis.

W. H. Auden: 'Stop all the clocks' and 'Epitaph on a Tyrant' are reproduced by permission of the publishers, Faber and Faber Ltd.

Hilaire Belloc: 'Ha'nacker Mill', 'The World's a Stage' and 'Ballade of Hell and Mrs Roebeck' are reproduced by permission of the Peters Fraser and Dunlop Group Ltd, on behalf of the Estate of Hilaire Belloc.

Sir John Betjeman: 'The Arrest of Oscar Wilde at the Cadogan Hotel' and 'In a Bath Teashop' are reproduced by permission of John Murray Publishers Ltd.

Edmund Blunden: 'Report on Experience' (© Edmund Blunden 1929) is reproduced by permission of PFD on behalf of the Estate of Mrs Claire Blunden.

Roy Campbell: 'The Zulu Girl' is reproduced by permission of Jonathan Ball Publishers (Pty) Ltd.

Wendy Cope: 'Triolet' is reproduced by permission of the publishers, Faber and Faber Ltd.

Walter De La Mare: 'The Listeners', 'Napoleon' and 'An Epitaph' are reproduced by permission of the Literary Trustees of Walter de la Mare, and the Society of Authors as their representative.

T. S. Eliot: 'Preludes' is reproduced by permission of the publishers, Faber and Faber Ltd.

U. A. Fanthorpe: 'BC:AD' (© U.A. Fanthorpe 1982) is reproduced by permission of Peterloo Poets.

Harry Graham: 'Tender-Heartedness', 'The Englishman's Home', and 'Lord Gorbals' are reproduced by permission of Laura Dance.

Robert Graves: 'She tells her love while half asleep' and 'A Slice of Wedding Cake' from *Complete Poems* (1997) are reproduced by permission of the publisher, Carcanet Press Ltd.

Seamus Heaney: 'A Call' is reproduced by permission of the publishers, Faber and Faber Ltd.

Geoffrey Hill: 'September Song', from *King Log* (1968), is reproduced by permission of Penguin Books Ltd.

A. E. Housman: 'Loveliest of Trees', 'On Wenlock Edge', 'Into my heart an air that kills' and 'The Sigh that Heaves the Grasses' are reproduced by permission of the Society of Authors as the Literary Representative of the Estate of A. E. Housman.

Ted Hughes: 'Esther's Tomcat' is reproduced by permission of the publishers, Faber and Faber Ltd.

Rudyard Kipling: 'The Conundrum of the Workshops', 'If', 'The Way Through the Woods', and 'The Rabbi's Song' are reproduced by permission of A. P. Watt Ltd on behalf of the The National Trust for Places of Historical Interest or Natural Beauty.

Philip Larkin: 'Faith Healing' and 'Annus Mirabilis' are reproduced by permission of the publishers, Faber and Faber Ltd.

Alun Lewis: 'All day it has rained' is reproduced by permission of Gweno Lewis.

Norman McCaig: 'Power Dive', from *Collected Poems* by Norman McCaig, published by Chatto & Windus, is reprinted by permission of the Random House Group.

Hugh MacDiarmid: 'Of John Davidson', from *Collected Poems* (1993), is reproduced by permission of Carcanet Press Ltd.

Louis MacNeice: 'Bagpipe Music', from *Collected Poems*, published by Faber and Faber, is reproduced by permission of David Higham Associates.

John Gillespie Magee Jr: 'High Flight' is reproduced by permission of the copyright holder, *This England* magazine.

Leo Marks: 'The Life That I Have', from *Between Silk and Cyanide* by Leo Marks, is reproduced by permission of HarperCollins Publishers.

John Masefield: 'Sea Fever' and 'Cargoes' are reproduced by permission of The Society of Authors as the literary representative of the Estate of John Masefield.

Edna St Vincent Millay: 'Dirge Without Music', from *Collected Poems*,

HarperCollins, copyright © 1928, 1955, is reproduced by permission of Elizabeth Barnett, literary executor.

Sir Henry Newbolt: 'Vitaï Lampada' is reproduced by permission of Peter Newbolt.

George Orwell: 'A Happy Vicar', from *Why I Write*, is reproduced by permission of A. M. Heath & Co. Ltd on behalf of Bill Hamilton as the Literary Executor of the Estate of the Late Sonia Brownell Orwell and Martin Secker & Warburg Ltd.

F. T. Prince: 'Soldiers Bathing' is reproduced by permission of F. T. Prince.

Henry Reed: 'Lessons of the War' is reproduced by permission of the Estate of the late Henry Reed, c/o The Royal Literary Fund.

Siegfried Sassoon: 'The Rearguard' and 'The General' (© Siegfried Sassoon) are reproduced by kind permission of the Barbara Levy Literary Agency on behalf of George Sassoon.

Stevie Smith: 'What is she writing', 'It Filled My Heart With Love', 'Not Waving but Drowning' and 'The Celts' are reproduced by permission of the James McGibbon Estate.

William Soutar: 'The Halted Moment', 'The Tryst' and 'Who are These Children?' are reproduced by permission of the Trustees of the National Library of Scotland.

Dylan Thomas: 'Do not go gentle into that good night', from *Collected Poems*, published by Faber and Faber, is reproduced by permission of David Higham Associates.

J. R. R. Tolkien: 'The Road Goes Ever On', from *The Lord of the Rings*, published by HarperCollins Publishers, is reproduced by permission of The Estate

W. B. Yeats: 'The Stolen Child' and 'The Lake Isle of Innisfree' are reproduced by permission of A. P. Watt Ltd on behalf of Michael B. Yeats.

Benjamin Zephaniah: 'Dis Poetry', from *City Psalms* (1992), is reproduced by permission of Bloodaxe Books.

INDEX OF FIRST LINES

INDEX OF TITLES

INDEX OF AUTHORS

(in Chronological Order)